# Nabokov's Shakespeare

# Nabokov's Shakespeare

Samuel Schuman

With a foreword by Brian Boyd

B L O O M S B U R Y

NEW YORK • LONDON • NEW DELHI • SYDNEY

**Bloomsbury Academic**

An imprint of Bloomsbury Publishing Inc

| | |
|---|---|
| 1385 Broadway | 50 Bedford Square |
| New York | London |
| NY 10018 | WC1B 3DP |
| USA | UK |

**www.bloomsbury.com**

**Bloomsbury is a registered trade mark of Bloomsbury Publishing Plc**

First published 2014

© Samuel Schuman, 2014

**Library of Congress Cataloging-in-Publication Data**
Schuman, Samuel.
Nabokov's Shakespeare / Samuel Schuman.
pages cm
Includes bibliographical references and index.
ISBN 978-1-62892-426-8 (hardback)– ISBN 978-1-62892-271-4 (paperback) 1.
Nabokov, Vladimir Vladimirovich, 1899–1977–Criticism and interpretation.
2. Nabokov, Vladimir Vladimirovich, 1899–1977–Knowledge–Literature.
3. Shakespeare, William, 1564–1616–Influence. 4. Shakespeare, William,
1564–1616–Criticism and interpretation. 5. American fiction–English influences.
I. Title.
PG3476.N3Z8628 2014
813'.54–dc23
2014003389

ISBN: HB: 978-1-6289-2426-8
PB: 978-1-6289-2271-4
ePub: 978-1-6289-2377-3
ePDF: 978-1-6289-2151-9

Typeset by Fakenham Prepress Solutions, Fakenham, Norfolk NR21 8NN
Printed and bound in the United States of America

# Contents

# Foreword

## Brian Boyd

Vladimir Nabokov famously denied that he had been influenced by even the novelists he most admired: Dickens, Tolstoy, Flaubert, Proust, and Joyce. Yet he happily affirmed that "Pushkin's blood runs through the veins of modern Russian literature as inevitably as Shakespeare's through those of English literature."[1] In his most literary novels in each language, *The Gift* (1938) and *Pale Fire* (1962), he has his writer-heroes pay conscious homage to Pushkin and Shakespeare, respectively, even in the very titles of the works they are writing.

In the case of *Pale Fire*, the poet John Shade poses a puzzle for his readers: where in Shakespeare has he gleaned the phrase "pale fire" that he has taken for the title of his poem? In Kinbote's crazy commentary to the poem, Nabokov supplies the answer without Kinbote himself knowing it. Early in the commentary, in another context, Kinbote writes that a variant line in Shade's poem recalls for him a passage from *Timon of Athens*. This happens to be the very passage from which Shade has lifted his title, but Kinbote, working from a mountain cabin, has with him only a Zemblan version of the play, and the retranslation from the Zemblan that he cites makes the key words disappear, along with much else. Kinbote concludes his note with a cross-reference: "For a prudent appraisal of Conmal's translation of Shakespeare's works, see note to line 962." Readers who trust Nabokov's sanity and generosity behind Kinbote's insane egotism can flip ahead to the note to line 962 of Shade's poem. That line begins, after Shade concedes he needs some title for the poem he is writing: "Help me, Will! *Pale Fire*." Kinbote opens his commentary on the line:

> Paraphrased, this evidently means: Let me look in Shakespeare for something I might use for a title. And the find is "pale fire." But in which of the Bard's works did our poet cull it? My readers must make their own research. All I have with me is a tiny vest pocket edition of *Timon of Athens*—in Zemblan! It certainly contains nothing that could be regarded as an equivalent of "pale fire" (if it had, my luck would have been a statistical monster).
>
> English was not taught in Zembla before Mr. Campbell's time. Conmal mastered it all by himself (mainly by learning a lexicon by heart) …

The trusting, responsive and curious reader can zoom straight to *Timon of Athens* and solve the riddle there, and enjoy not only the astonishing speech from which Shade's and Nabokov's title comes but, on returning to *Pale Fire*, the comedy of the Zemblan mistranslation.

But before getting there, or even after, the very good reader of *Pale Fire* and of Shakespeare may wonder at an echo from *Hamlet*—the play, as Sam Schuman notes, that Nabokov refers to most often, a work Nabokov even called "probably the greatest miracle in all literature."[2] The Ghost, speaking to Hamlet, has to vanish when he notices the coming day:

The glowworm shows the matin to be near,
And 'gins to pale his uneffectual fire.
Adieu, adieu, adieu. Remember me.

If indeed we do remember these memorable lines, we may wonder whether they provide the answer to Shade's puzzle—until, or perhaps even after, we find the answer in *Timon of Athens*. Does Nabokov (and perhaps Shade, whose name—a common English word but almost never a surname—can itself mean "ghost") intend us to think *also* of the Ghost's words from *Hamlet*? Readers who know how well Nabokov knows Shakespeare may suspect he could well have recollected "pale his uneffectual fire" as he collected Timon's denunciation of universal thievery, "the moon's an arrant thief, / And *her pale fire* she snatches from the sun." But how would we know that Nabokov intends that glowworm phrase, too, to glow within his "pale fire"? One hauntingly beautiful passage in *Pale Fire* provides the answer: yes, Nabokov did mean the title *Pale Fire* to evoke the parting words of King Hamlet's ghost, along with *Timon of Athens*, and no, he didn't want this to be easy to find out.[3]

The example shows how Nabokov plays with and pays homage to the way Shakespeare pervades English literature at its best. In John Shade's American college town, New Wye, there is even an avenue of all the trees mentioned by Shakespeare (the list of those that Kinbote can recall, poetry in itself, offers a wonderful challenge to our memories or an incitement to future reading). In Onhava, the capital of Zembla, a deposed king—in itself a very Shakespearean role—flees through a theater, in costume, and escapes via Coriolanus Lane and Timon Alley. Shakespeare, for Nabokov, simply saturates and illuminates the world of English literature.

This swift tour through some Shakespearean sites in *Pale Fire* indicates, apart from anything else, just how un-Shakespearean, how uniquely Nabokovian, Nabokov is, as well as how steeped in Shakespeare. No more for Nabokov than for John Shade does Shakespeare's capacity to inspire other writers mean "influence" in a sense anything like imitation.

I began with a list of prose writers Nabokov denied ever having influenced him, and his affirmation nevertheless that Shakespeare and Pushkin flow inevitably through the veins of modern English or Russian literature. Nabokov began his career as a poet but in his early twenties had discovered that prose was his *forte*. Nevertheless he always aspired to impart to his prose every quality of poetry but line, meter and rhyme, and was delighted when his friend, the great Spanish poet Jorge Guillén, inscribed one of his books to him: "*poète en deux langues, en prose et en vers, toujours poète*" ("poet in two languages, in prose and in verse, always a poet").[4] When Nabokov was teaching at Cornell and had begun to become famous in America as he once had been in the Russian emigration, the young writer Steve Katz asked Nabokov for feedback on his unpublished novel. Nabokov wrote on the manuscript: "Nothing ages faster than 'stark realism' … You have to *saturate* yourself with English poetry in order to compose English prose. You must know your tool. You do not. You cannot begin all over again with the *Canterbury Tales*, in comic-strip English … *Suggestion*: Read: Milton, Coleridge, Keats, Wordsworth."[5] Shakespeare hardly needed naming, but Nabokov named poets particularly steeped in their Elizabethan precursor.

Nabokov was harsh on his own early verse. In his autobiography, *Speak, Memory*, whose prose is the most poetic in all his books, he critiques his teenage self:

> The hackneyed order of words (short verb or pronoun—long adjective— short noun) engendered the hackneyed disorder of thought, and some such line as *poeta gorestnïe gryozï*, translatable and accented as "the poet's melancholy daydreams," led fatally to a rhyming line ending in *rozï* (roses) or *beryozï* (birches) or *grozï* (thunderstorms), so that certain emotions were connected with certain surroundings not by a free act of one's will but by the faded ribbon of tradition.[6]

Nabokov, it seems to me, thought that young writers should read poetry not to imitate, not to ride in others' slipstreams, but as a form of resistance training. Instead of exercising language with no resistance, the commonplace conjunctions of everyday speech or the clichés—whether words, images, or rhymes—of conventional verse, writers' imaginations need to be stretched by words at maximum resistance to the norm. No one has ever resisted the norms of his language—the natural words, the set idioms, the expected images, the grammatical grooves—more boldly and incessantly than Shakespeare. Any writer lucky enough to understand Shakespeare in the original should train in his or her mental gym in order to learn to *dare* in every phrase, to write "by a free act of … will" rather than by following "the faded ribbon of tradition."

For Nabokov, Shakespeare is above all a poet, not a dramatist: "The verbal texture of Shakespeare is the greatest the world has known, and is immensely superior to the structure of his plays as plays. With Shakespeare, it is the metaphor that is the thing, not the play."[7] Although he appreciates especially the "dream-plays" *Hamlet* and *King Lear*,[8] this extreme individualist thinks, as Sam Schuman shows, that the collaborative nature of theater makes it inevitably an art of compromise, diluting the uniqueness of genius. For once in keeping with the prejudices of his age, Nabokov also undervalues Shakespeare as a storyteller and a master of dramatic structure.

But he gives full value to Shakespeare as a verbal artist, and to the power of his words, in all their uncompromising boldness, to inspire other imaginations to the full measure of their freedom. That is why for Nabokov translating was so valuable, so demanding, and so rich in ironies. He wanted to translate *Hamlet* himself, and published versions of favorite passages in the early 1930s. He might have continued, had he not had so many new fictional ideas of his own to develop in these particularly fertile years. Had he not managed to flee Russia, he might well have avoided the risk that his originality and independence of mind would have posed in the Soviet Union by devoting himself to translating Shakespeare. After switching to English, he shows in the character of the translator Ember in his novel *Bend Sinister* (1947) just how well he could render into Russian the most demanding and inimitably Shakespearean lines, like this sentence from Hamlet at his most dizzily exuberant, after the play within the play puts Claudius into panic:

> Would not this, sir, and a forest of feathers—if the rest of my fortunes turn Turk with me—with two provincial roses on my razed shoes, get me a fellowship in a cry of players, sir?

No wonder Nabokov thought little of Boris Pasternak's efforts, much acclaimed in the Soviet Union. Interviewing him in the 1960s, Penelope Gilliatt reports Nabokov's spontaneous judgment on Pasternak:

> "As a translator of Shakespeare he is very poor, He is considered great only by people who don't know Russian. An example." His wife helped him to remember a line of a Pasternak translation. "What he has turned it into in Russian is this: 'all covered with grease and keeps wiping the pig-iron.' You see. It is ridiculous. What would be the original?"
> "Greasy Joan doth keel the pot?" [from *Love's Labour's Lost*]
> "Yes. 'Keeps wiping the pig-iron'!"[9]

When Nabokov fled Europe in 1940 for America, he began to translate Pushkin into English, and in an essay on "The Art of Translation" he singles out example after example from both Pushkin and from *Hamlet* that pose difficulties translating into English or Russian.[10] In his most creative phase, between starting *Lolita* and finishing *Pale Fire*, he devoted seven years of his life to translating and annotating Pushkin's masterpiece, *Eugene Onegin*, for an English-speaking audience, sticking ruthlessly to exact sense because he knew no one could match Pushkin's Russian music in another language (and once the translation was published, as Marijeta Bozovic shows, he began to incorporate Pushkin into his late English work as much as he had Shakespeare into his Russian work, now that Pushkin could be accessed as part of the international treasury of literature).[11]

In the midst of his years of library research in translating and annotating *Eugene Onegin*, Nabokov has his hero Pnin, a fine scholar in Russian, with excellent French but insurmountably awkward English, try to place a sudden memory echo. Pnin sits in his college library working on Russian folklore, on pagan games in which

> peasant maidens would make wreaths of buttercups and frog orchises; then, singing snatches of ancient love chants, they hung these garlands on riverside willows; and on Whitsunday the wreaths were shaken down into the river, where, unwinding, they floated like so many serpents while the maidens floated and chanted among them.[12]

He cannot immediately locate the echo—although the good English reader will have the pleasure of doing so already—but succeeds a little later:

> pocketed his index card and, while doing so, recalled without any prompting what he had not been able to recall a while ago:
>
> > ... *plïla i pela, pela i plïla*
> > ... she floated and she sang, she sang and floated ...

Of course! Ophelia's death! *Hamlet!* In good old Andrey Kroneberg's Russian translation, 1844—the joy of Pnin's youth, and of his father's and grandfather's young days! And here, as in the Kostromskoy passage, there is, we recollect, also a willow and also wreaths. But where to check properly? Alas, *"Gamlet" Vil'yama Shekspira* ... was not represented in Waindell College Library, and whenever you were reduced to look up something in the English version, you never found this or that beautiful, noble, sonorous line that you remembered all your life from Kronenberg's text in Vengerov's splendid edition. Sad![13]

In 1931 Nabokov had himself translated Gertrude's speech reporting Ophelia's death, "There is a willow grows aslant the brook," one of his touchstone passages in Shakespeare, but here in *Pnin* (1957) he records both the reach Shakespeare has into audiences beyond English, and the losses those without adequate English will inevitably face in not being able to run their mental fingers over his inimitably rough verbal texture, whatever partial compensations they may find in smoother, prettier translations.

In a 1937 essay in French on Pushkin, on the centenary of the poet's death, Nabokov discusses both the difficulty of translating him for the French reader and the unique relationship the Russian reader has to Pushkin.[14] A good Russian reader has direct access to the words, which become part of his or her very self, but also cannot help trying to conjure up the poet's soul and circumstances: a hopeless task, given the impenetrability of the past, of another person, and especially of genius, yet also an inevitable consequence of the love one feels for a writer whose words beat in one's mind. The same of course applies for readers of Shakespeare, especially for readers who know him in English.

Nabokov found fascinating the irresistible impulse of scholars and readers, himself included, to imagine writers they loved. He found particularly fascinating the special hopelessness of the Shakespearean case, when so few documents survive from his life and when his characters' infinite variety makes it so hard to see any of them as masks or mouthpieces for their author. Just as Nabokov had favorite lines in Shakespeare's work, as Professor Schuman shows, he also had a favorite image from the life and the legends: the story that Shakespeare as an actor played the part of the Ghost of King Hamlet. In the introduction to the first post-*Lolita* translation of one of his Russian novels, *Invitation to a Beheading* (1959), Nabokov writes:

> *Vive le pédant*, and down with the simpletons who think that all is well
> if the 'spirit' is rendered (while the words go away by themselves on a
> naïve and vulgar spree—in the suburbs of Moscow for instance—and
> Shakespeare is again reduced to play the king's ghost).[15]

Asked by an interviewer what scenes he would like to have filmed, he answered at once: "Shakespeare in the part of the King's Ghost."[16]

His Russian poem "Shakespeare" (1924)—written just after he completed his one youthful work actually *imitative* of Shakespeare, his five-act verse play *The Tragedy of Mister Morn* (1924)—focuses especially on the mystery of the man hidden far behind our immediate access to the work. Nabokov toys with the fact that so little is known for sure about Shakespeare's life (true enough, although more documents about him survive than for any other English dramatist of the period except Ben Jonson) that many have proposed others actually wrote the plays signed "Shakespeare." *Pace* Sam Schuman, I do not believe for a moment that Nabokov actually thought Shakespeare's works were written by someone else—he would soon poke pointed and protracted fun at Baconian readings of Shakespeare—but here he seizes on and dramatizes a telling image of how mysterious the *man* remains, for all the unparalleled individuality of the *mind* that we can have such direct access to through so many singular words on so many pages.

Sam Schuman has been eagerly exploring Nabokov's Shakespeare for almost half a century. Let him be your guide along the paths looping from Nabokov's enchanted word garden into Shakespeare's.

Brian Boyd
University of Auckland

# Acknowledgments

A problem with "Acknowledgments" for a work such as this, which has been gestating for years, is that once one begins, it is nearly impossible to stop. Surely if one weighted the few individuals and groups mentioned below, with the hundreds of students, colleagues, friends and family not cited, the contributions of the latter would at least equal those of the former. Still, some particular thanks must be offered.

Below, I note my graduate instructor Samuel Schoenbaum and my supervisor of some fifty years ago, Alfred Appel, Jr for helping to create the two interests that come together in this book. It was at the home of another colleague, Richard Wilson, that I re-encountered *Lolita*. It was in a seminar taught by Gerald Graff that I first heard of *Pale Fire*.

For many years the International Nabokov Society has sponsored a variety of stimulating and helpful events and publications, including a number of international meetings, where some of the ideas in *Nabokov's Shakespeare* were first presented. The Nabokov Museum in St. Petersburg is another valuable incubator of interactive scholarship. *The Nabokovian*, edited since its inception (then called *The Vladimir Nabokov Research Newsletter*) by Stephen Jan Parker (a former student of Nabokov) and *Nabokov Studies* are valuable print periodicals. A growing range of electronic resources has become increasingly important as well. These include the Nabokov Listserv *nabokv.l*, *The Nabokov Online Journal*, and *Zembla* at the University of Pennsylvania, a product of the International Vladimir Nabokov Society.

Among the Nabokovians who have been particularly helpful over the years I should mention Don Barton Johnson, Steve Parker, Brian Boyd, Susan Elizabeth Sweeney, and Zoran Kuzmanovich.

Three institutions have supported research which has contributed to this volume. These include the University of Minnesota, under Presidents Mark Yudof and Robert Bruininks, where I worked at the Morris campus. President Bruininks directly contributed to this work by facilitating a generous research grant. The University of North Carolina Asheville has twice been my academic home, and its current Chancellor Anne Ponder has been a good colleague and steadfast friend. And the University of New Mexico, especially its Honors Program (now Honors College) then led by Dr Rosalie Otero generously gave me time and resources to pursue this work. During the year I had the good fortune to hold UNM's Garrey Carruthers

Distinguished Chair in Honors, the final version of this book began to take shape.

For my work, and for my life, my deepest debt of gratitude is to my family. Especially, I am grateful to my daughter Dr Leah Schuman who has been an emblem of intellectual curiosity and ethical sensitivity, and my son Dr Daniel Schuman, who gave up part of a sabbatical leave to assist me with *Nabokov's Shakespeare*. Every word of this book has carefully perused, sometimes several times, by my kindest and most astute reader, and the love of my life, Nancy G. Schuman.

# Introduction

# Shakespeare, Nabokov, and Me

Early in his career, Vladimir Nabokov was not sure that William Shakespeare of Stratford-upon-Avon was the author of the plays attributed to him. In his poem "Shakespeare" (1924) Nabokov wrote:

*See Welcome in Symposium VN vol I p332-3 for full text*

> Haughty, aloof from theater's alarums,
> you easily, regretlessly relinquished
> the laurels twining into a dry wreath,
> concealing for all time your monstrous genius
> beneath a mask …

> It's true, of course, a usurer had grown
> accustomed, for a sum, to sign your work
> (that Shakespeare—Will—who played the Ghost in *Hamlet*
> who lived in pubs, and died before he could
> digest in full his portion of a boar's head) …

Some two decades after he wrote these lines in Russian, Nabokov would begin his journey towards becoming the greatest English prose stylist of the twentieth century with the first novel in his adopted language, *The Real Life of Sebastian Knight*. In the United States, Nabokov taught at Cornell University, where one of his students was a young man named Alfred Appel, Jr. Appel went on to become an early scholar of Nabokov's writing, teaching at Northwestern University, and he became a confidant and a friend of the author. Sometime in the early 1970s he gave to Nabokov a copy of a book on the strange history of Shakespearean biography, written by a colleague at Northwestern, Samuel Schoenbaum. In that book, *Shakespeare's Lives*, Schoenbaum debunks the anti-Stratfordians, and makes a meticulous case for the Shakespearean authorship of Shakespeare's dramas.[1] Nabokov was convinced, and joined the ranks of scholars who believed in Shakespearean authorship.

Late in the 1960s, when Schoenbaum was finishing his history of Shakespearean biography, I was serving as his graduate assistant at Northwestern as I completed my Ph.D. studies in English Renaissance Drama. He supervised my dissertation on John Webster and the emblem book tradition. At the same time, I also taught several sections of the then-obligatory Freshman English course at Northwestern, where my supervisor was Alfred Appel, Jr. I had, at that time, never read Nabokov, except for a very disappointing and incomplete effort to peruse *Lolita* as a high school student looking for a lurid and sensual tale. After a few dozen pages, I had given up in disgust, convinced that the novel was "literature," which was not what I was seeking at all, and went back to the much more satisfactory *Peyton Place*. But after I completed my doctoral studies, I was hired as an Assistant Professor of English at Cornell College in Mt. Vernon, Iowa, where I was fortunate to receive a small Ford Foundation grant to spend several weeks in England. Staying at the home of another Northwestern colleague in Yorkshire, I stumbled one rainy afternoon upon Alfred Appel's book, *The Annotated Lolita*. Rereading Nabokov, now from the perspective of a teacher of literature rather than that of a lusty adolescent boy, I was enchanted and hooked. I went to the bookstore in our little Yorkshire town and purchased everything by Nabokov I could find, consumed it avidly, and since then my interest has never waned. It is due to these accidents and coincidences in my experiences as a student, teacher, and scholar that I came to focus upon the many and varied links between these two great authors.

Over many years, and during a busy career as a professor and administrator, I have tried to maintain my interest in Nabokov and Shakespeare. I've contributed a number of notes, short articles, and papers at professional meetings on specific ties between the works of these two genius writers. Over those years, my conviction has grown that these short studies could and should lead to a more comprehensive work on Nabokov and Shakespeare. I've been encouraged to undertake this enterprise by the generous suggestions of several fellow Nabokovians. The pages which follow constitute that work. While I have not discussed each and every citation of the Bard in Nabokov's works, I have tried to provide a very broad overview of the ways Nabokov uses Shakespeare in his Russian and all of his English novels, as well as in some short stories, poems, criticism, autobiography, published, and unpublished reviews, and even one handwritten note. My primary focus has been on the fiction, and in this I am only imitating my subject. I have surely not said everything there is to say about Nabokov and Shakespeare, but I've said a lot. Many other scholars have written on this subject, and I have learned much from them. Many of their discoveries and observations are scattered through the following pages, and deepen immensely my own comments. I have tried to acknowledge their work carefully, both in the text and in the Works Consulted section. I really have "consulted" their valuable "works"! Where I have gone awry, of course, I have done it on my own. I am unabashed in declaring this book a labor of love: no authors have moved me so deeply and so often as Vladimir Nabokov and William Shakespeare, and it has been a joy to devote myself to surveying them together.

# "The Sun's a Thief:"
# Nabokov's Shakespeare

Vladimir Vladimirovich Nabokov was *not* born on Shakespeare's birthday. The date of his nativity under the Julian calendar, which was in use in Russia at the time of his birth, was April 10. That day, in Russia, corresponded in 1899, his birth year, to April 22 on the Gregorian calendar used in the West. But with the dawn of the twentieth century, the Julian or Old Style calendar lost another day to the Western version. Thus, his first birthday party, April 10, 1900 in Russia, would have corresponded to April 23—Shakespeare's birthday— in, say Paris or Prague, Montreux or Ithaca, New York (Boyd, *Russian Years*, 37; *Speak, Memory*, 13–14). In the "foreword" to his autobiography, Nabokov mentions this "error" or "problem." He professes his "calculatory ineptitude" leaves him unable to solve it—this from a composer of chess problems! In fact, Nabokov adopts the April 23 option by choice, noting that is also the birthdate of Shakespeare, his nephew Vladimir Sikorski, and Shirley Temple. But, amusingly, the traditional April 23 birthday of Shakespeare is also a day based on the Julian calendar: by the current, Gregorian version, the Bard was born on May 3! So, no matter which calendar one uses, or how cunning the calculation, Nabokov's birthday and Shakespeare's are not the same.

But Nabokov was a creator, a magician, a poet who could "give to airy nothing a local habitation and a name." And one of his prime creations was himself. Given his assertion, in the afterword to *Lolita* that it had taken him "some forty years to invent Russia and Western Europe, and now I was faced with the task of inventing America," the notion that, in some way, he created the persona of novelist Vladimir Nabokov is by no means improbable (*Lolita*, 312). And in that act of self-creation, Nabokov choose to link himself to the English writer he admired the most, from whom he learned the most, and whose works most penetrated his own. Ephim Fogel, Nabokov's colleague at Cornell University in the 1950s, tells us: "He always said that the greatest writer, the one who had the greatest power of expressiveness ever produced on this planet, was Shakespeare" (232).

The title of this chapter comes from an important passage in Shakespeare's *Timon of Athens*, which gives its name to one of Nabokov's finest novels:

I'll example you with thievery:
The sun's a thief, and with his great attraction
Robs the vast sea; the moon's an arrant thief,
And her **pale fire** she snatches from the sun.
The sea's a thief, whose liquid surge resolves
The moon into salt tears. The earth's a thief
That feeds and breeds by a composture stol'n
From gen'ral excrement. Every thing's a thief. (4. 3. 436–43)

It is no accident that Shakespeare's words suggest a cosmos in which even the heavenly bodies borrow some of their luster from each other, and that Nabokov (and his character John Shade) borrow the phrase from Shakespeare.

In a world with no shortage of academic volumes on literary subjects, it makes sense to ask "Why *this* book?" I believe there at least five good reasons for *Nabokov's Shakespeare*:

1. Since Nabokov was so strongly influenced by Shakespeare, and drew so often and in such varied ways from his works, we gain a significantly deeper understanding of his writings by studying the ways he viewed and used the work of the dramatist.
2. In an odd, Nabokovian, twist of time, we can also come to a better, more nuanced understanding of the earlier writer by exploring this connection. In examining Nabokov's Shakespeare, we see how one quirky, brilliant, and sensitive non-academic intellect perceived Shakespeare and his works. This is especially interesting in that Nabokov's native language was not English, so we can discover how Shakespeare's words influenced a Russian consciousness. (Nabokov, however, read English before Russian, and his initial exposure to Shakespeare was in Shakespeare's native tongue, not his own.)
3. Curiously, a number of contemporary authors who have been deeply influenced by Nabokov (e.g., Michael Chabon, Benjamin Hale, David Mitchell) show a kind of second generation of literary relationships. So, for example, Hale's *The Evolution of Bruno Littlemore* is deeply indebted to *Lolita*, and it shares *Lolita*'s connections to *The Tempest*.
4. An examination of Nabokov's use of Shakespeare and Shakespeare's works offers an insight into the nature and varieties of literary influence. T. S. Eliot suggested that modern authors know more than Shakespeare knew: they know Shakespeare. Here, we have the opportunity to observe

and analyze one author influencing another, across more than three centuries, and much of the globe.

5. Finally, the study of Shakespeare and Nabokov offers the unalloyed joy of wallowing in the words and works both of the greatest stylist the English language has yet produced, and of arguably finest wordsmith in our tongue of the twentieth century. These two authors teach us as well or better than any how much our language can do.

In *Lolita*, Humbert Humbert and Dolores Haze journey across Nabokov's invented America. One of the actual places through which they travel without ever pausing for long is the ghost town of Shakespeare, New Mexico.[1] Dolly and Humbert just go right past Shakespeare, but their creator, their sole begetter, Vladimir Nabokov, lingered!

## Nabokov, English, and English literature

How did a Russian writer become so deeply linked to a Renaissance British dramatist? Surely, some part of this linkage derives from an inexplicable synchrony between the creative consciousnesses of two geniuses. But, on a far more pedestrian level, we can review the mechanisms which enabled such a strong connection to develop. Although it is not a new story, it is worth retelling the circumstances which brought Nabokov together with the English language, English literature, and, hence, its greatest author. That story involves the culture and history of pre-revolutionary Russian intellectual aristocracy, and the account of their post-revolutionary diaspora. More specifically, it revolves around the particularities of the Nabokov family at the end of the nineteenth century and the first decades of the twentieth.

For many contemporary Americans, myself among them, our first image of pre-revolutionary Russia involved a kind of comic-book stereotype vision of two monolithic social classes. On the one hand, there was an oppressed peasantry of serfs and proletarians, living in abject and medieval rural poverty or Dickensian urban squalor. On the other side were the oppressors: opulent, self-indulging, cruelly exploitive fat cats. For those of us of a certain age, the character of Victor Komarovsky as depicted by Rod Steiger in David Lean's 1965 film *Doctor Zhivago* typified our vision of the Russian ruling class at the turn of the twentieth century. Like most simple stereotypes, this one is seriously flawed. Some of those agricultural peasants had become prosperous agriculturalists; many had not. Russia's cities supported merchants (large and small) and professionals (prosperous or struggling) like Pasternak's Zhivago. And, importantly for the Nabokov saga, there were on the other side of the socio-economic divide progressive, intellectual aristocrats, such as those who were among the many Russians from many backgrounds who founded the Kadet (Constitutional Democratic) party in 1905. A leader among that group was our author's father, Vladimir Dmitrievich Nabokov (b. 1870). V. D. Nabokov himself descended from a line of liberal, courageous, and highly educated aristocrats. He was, among other accomplishments, an uncompromising opponent of the virulent and often-violent Russian anti-Semitism which sparked murderous pogroms into the early years of the twentieth century. He was an opponent of capital punishment, a distinguished jurist, and a leader in the Provisional Government which attempted to build a constitutional model of politics in the brief period between the overthrow of the Czar and the triumph of the Communists.[2]

In such progressive families, as Vladimir Nabokov points out in the early pages of his autobiography, Anglophilism was rampant:

> The kind of Russian family to which I belonged—a kind now extinct—had, among other virtues, a traditional leaning toward the comfortable products of Anglo-Saxon civilization. Pears soap ... the English collapsible tub ... "We could not improve the cream, so we improved the tube," said the English toothpaste ... Golden Syrup imported from London... All sorts of snug, mellow things came in a steady procession from the English Shop on Nevski Avenue: fruitcakes, smelling salts, playing cards, picture puzzles, striped blazers, talcum-white tennis balls. (*Speak, Memory*, 79)

Much more to the point of Nabokov's development as a literary artist was his early exposure not just to English soap and syrup, but to the English language:

> I learned to read English before I could read Russian. My first English friends were four simple souls in my grammar—Ben, Dan, Sam and Ned ... On later pages longer words appeared; and at the very end of the brown, inkstained volume, a real, sensible story unfolded its adult sentences ... the little reader's ultimate triumph and reward. I was thrilled by the thought that someday I might attain such proficiency. The magic has endured and whenever a grammar book comes my way, I instantly turn to the last page to enjoy a forbidden glimpse of the laborious student's future, of that promised land where, at last, words are meant to mean what they mean. (*Speak, Memory*, 79–81)

His first exposure to more literary tales was also in English:

> In the drawing room of our country house, before going to bed, I would often be read to in English by my mother ... There were tales about

knights whose terrific but wonderfully aseptic wounds were bathed by damsels in grottoes. From a windswept clifftop, a medieval maiden with flying hair and a youth in hose gazed at the round Isles of the Blessed ... I particularly liked the blue-coated, red-trousered, coal-black Golliwogg [*sic*], with underclothes buttons for eyes, and his meager harem of five wooden dolls. (*Speak, Memory*, 81–2)

If his mother introduced young Vladimir to the Golliwogs, it was his father who probably first acquainted him with Shakespeare. According to Nabokov's biographer, V. D. Nabokov's favorite authors were Pushkin, Flaubert, and Shakespeare, and Vladimir Nabokov himself reports that by the age of fifteen he had read "*all* of Shakespeare in English" (italics mine) (Boyd, *Russian Years*, 91). It is difficult to imagine that many American or British school children, then or now, could make such a claim!

In the Russian Revolution, the constitutional and democratic aspirations of enlightened liberals such as V. D. Nabokov and the Kadets (the Constitutional Democratic Party) were crushed as surely as the monarchial traditions of czardom. The Nabokovs, like many other similar families, were forced to flee, first to the Crimea from 1917 to 1919 and then to Western Europe. In October of 1919, young Vladimir, just at the dawn of his third decade of life, was admitted to Trinity College, Cambridge University in England. Although Nabokov focused much of his creative energy on writing Russian poetry at this time, he also read extensively in English and composed some English poetry, including one poem which was published.[3] Before he graduated at the age of 23, he had published at least one other poem in English, as well as translations of verse from English to Russian.

It would be nearly two decades until Nabokov, now married to Vera Slonim and with a young son, Dmitri Vladimirovich Nabokov, fled a second totalitarian regime, as the Nazi empire spread across Western Europe. The Nabokovs settled in the United States, and Vladimir became an English-language novelist. But surely his childhood, youth, and young adulthood had given him a substantial grounding in the language and the works of Shakespeare.

## Theme

I am thinking of aurochs and angels, the secret of durable pigments, prophetic sonnets, the refuge of art. And this is the only immortality you and I may share, my Lolita.

Vladimir Nabokov, the conclusion of *Lolita*

But thy eternal summer shall not fade,
Nor lose possession of that fair thou ow'st,
Nor shall death brag thou wander'st in his shade,
When in eternal lines to time thou grow'st;
So long as men can breathe, or eyes can see,
So long lives this, and this gives life to thee.

Shakespeare, the final sestet of Sonnet 18

In many of their works, Shakespeare and Nabokov express a shared thematic vision. These themes are by no means exclusive to these two authors. But it is significant that Nabokov's view of the place of humankind in the cosmos, our mortal, temporal, and consciousness limitations, and the potential to escape those bounds is congruent with Shakespeare's.

Both authors often begin with the motif of exile. Of course, in the case of Nabokov, this theme has a biographical root. In 1919 he left Russia, never again to see the country of his birth, and never again to live in a home he himself owned. For the rest of his life, in poverty and in wealth, in transition and in security, Nabokov, and later his wife and son, lived in rental housing, transients, and exiles. He spent his last years in a splendid suite at the lavish Montreux Palace Hotel overlooking Lake Geneva (or, more poetically, Lac Léman) in Switzerland. Shakespeare, of course, is an entirely different case. Unsupported speculation aside, we have no evidence that he ever strayed very far from the Stratford/London axis, a distance of about 100 miles.

Nabokov's protagonists are almost always strangers living in strange lands. His very first novel, *Mary*, written in 1925, was advertised as "a novel of émigré life," according to Boyd, "a portrait of exile" (Boyd, *Russian Years*, 244). Its hero, Ganin, is a Russian émigré, living in Germany. The last novel published during his lifetime, almost exactly a half-century after *Mary*, is *Look at the Harlequins!*. Similarly, it centers on Vadim, a Russian exile living first in Western Europe and then America. Many of Nabokov's greatest works focus upon exiled characters. Humbert Humbert in *Lolita* is a European living in America; *Pale Fire*'s Charles Kinbote wants his readers to believe he is the exiled king of mythic Zembla. Timofey Pnin is a comic yet heroic Russian professor trying to reinvent himself in the United States, while clinging to his lost language and culture.

A surprising number of Shakespeare's plays also feature central characters who are, at least temporarily, exiles. Perhaps most notably among the tragedies is *Othello*, the hero of which is, of course, a Moor in Venice, then Cyprus. King Lear spends most of his tragic time on stage wandering, homeless, across the kingdom he once ruled. Macduff flees from Macbeth to England, to which Hamlet, too, is banished. The comedies, as well, often involve leaving home. The core of the action of *A Midsummer Night's Dream* takes place as the lovers have fled to the woods. In *The Taming of the Shrew*, Petruchio has to leave home to come to Padua to woo and wed Katherina. The two gentlemen of Verona leave Verona for Milan; *As You Like It*'s characters have fled to the forest. In an interesting twist, it is the female characters in *Love's Labour's Lost* who have left the court of France, and are encamped outside the precincts of the court of Navarre. *The Tempest* (as we shall see, one of Nabokov's favorite Shakespearean sources) centers upon the theme of exile. And, importantly for Nabokov and *Pale Fire*, Shakespeare's *Timon of Athens* leaves Athens to live and ultimately die in a cave in the wilderness.

The physical isolation of exile is, clearly, rich in philosophical possibilities. Literary characters who have had to leave their homes and homelands and live permanently or temporarily alone, surrounded by strangers, can be powerful emblems of human psychological solitary confinement, and what Nabokov calls in his autobiography the prison of time, which "is spherical and without exits" (*Speak, Memory*, 20). Physical exile is an obvious but potent metaphor for spiritual and/or temporal isolation. The human being trapped within his—or her—solitary consciousness and limited to one "brief crack of light" (*Speak, Memory*, 18) is an important thematic corollary to physical exile in both Nabokov and Shakespeare. In a rather serious comment in one of his lightest comedies, Shakespeare observes:

> Brief as lightning in the collied night
> That in a spleen, unfolds both heaven and earth
> And ere a man hath power to say "behold"
> The jaws of darkness do devour it up
> So quick bright things come to confusion.
> Lysander, *A Midsummer Night's Dream* (1. 1. 145–9)

Indeed, one way of understanding the Shakespearean dramatic monologue is to see it arising from a character who can only speak to himself (and an eavesdropping audience) but who cannot escape the prison of selfhood sufficiently to speak of important matters with others, in dialog. Shakespearean characters from Hamlet to Timon seem victims of such psycho/spiritual exile. And certainly many of Nabokov's most memorable characters— Humbert Humbert, Timofey Pnin, Charles Kinbote—suffer from a similar affliction. Authors such as these two who wish to study the essential nature of humankind, that "poor, bare, forked" human animal, can perhaps do so best when they create individuals who are removed from the physical and interpersonal comforts of home and companionship.

While both Nabokov and Shakespeare frequently depict humans and humankind as isolated, in exile, alone in time, consciousness and/or space, neither believes such solitary confinement is a life sentence. For both, there is an exit. That way out of the prison of individual consciousness is found in the conjunction of art and love. In Sonnet 18, cited above, Shakespeare affirms that it is poetry, specifically the very poetry of Sonnet 18, which will unshackle his love and his loved one from the bonds of time, and make her (or him) live forever. Indeed, the ability of art to transcend the barriers of time's trap is a recurring theme of the Sonnets.[4] Similarly, at the conclusion of his most famous novel, Nabokov's narrator Humbert Humbert addresses "my Lolita." Presumably this is the novel's pedophilic protagonist speaking of his child love. And at the same time, it is the novelist speaking of his book. And those two merge: Lolita the girl has disappeared into *Lolita* the book, just as in a later novel, *Ada*, the work's central lovers "die, as it were, into the finished book … into the prose of the book or the poetry of its blurb" (587).

Nabokov's characters, and Shakespeare's, are liberated from loneliness by love. Humbert Humbert discovers at the end of *Lolita* that he actually loves Dolores Haze, not any longer his safely solipsized Lolita; Van has Ada; even Charles Kinbote "may turn up yet, on another campus, as an old, happy, healthy, heterosexual Russian." Prospero has his daughter, and so does Lear. Those exiles wandering in the woods in *A Midsummer Night's Dream* and *As You Like It* find love and come back home. Indeed, in the latter comedy, four couples are wed in the play's finale.

Through art, and through love, Shakespeare's and Nabokov's characters find an escape from the imprisonment of exile, self-reflexivity, and the trap of time. Love and art can open the doorway to immortality. It is in prophetic sonnets (presumably Shakespeare's) and the refuge of art that Humbert and Lolita and Nabokov and *Lolita* can share immortality. And Shakespeare boldly claims that as long as humans breathe and human eyes can see, for just that long his poem will live, and as long as his poem lives, so long will the object of his love be alive.

## A taxonomy of Nabokov's Shakespeareanisms

*How* does Vladimir Nabokov use Shakespeare? It proves to be the case that there are quite a number of ways in which one author may use another as a source or an inspiration. Indeed, it is instructive to observe what a wide variety of kinds of connections to a source an author such as Nabokov can conjure up. It is useful to review this range of literary adaptations, and illustrate each.

Clearest are direct explicit references to specific Shakespeare works.

- First, sometimes Nabokov names the **titles** of the works. So, for example, the protagonist Fyodor in *The Gift*, thinking of his just-cremated friend, thinks of "the braked line from 'King Lear', consisting entirely of five 'nevers.'" (See below for a parodic reference to this same line, which seems to be a particular favorite of Nabokov's.) A character in *Look at the Harlequins!* observes that "throughout adolescence I read, in pairs, and both with the same thrill, *Othello* and *Onegin* …"
- Second are references to Shakespearean **characters**, such as the wonderful names in the Ramsdale class list in *Lolita*, including Anthony and Miranda from *The Tempest* and Viola from *Twelfth Night*. Similarly, a lead character in *The Real Life of Sebastian Knight*, but one we never actually see in the narrative present time of the novel, is named Sebastian. The Clements' maid in *Pnin* is Desdemona, who speaks directly to God.
- Third are direct **quotations** from the works. In *Look at the Harlequins!* Nabokov quotes from Othello when he says "I too can speak of 'deserts idle, rough quarries, rocks.'" (This is from the scene where Othello explains how his descriptions of his early adventures won the heart of Desdemona.) Exactly the same citation also appears in *Glory*: "he imagined how, after many adventures, he would arrive in Berlin, look up Sonia, and like Othello, begin to tell a story of his hair breadth escapes, of most disastrous chances."
- Fourth is the particular reference in a Nabokov work to a particular **action**, **place**, or **era** in a Shakespearean one. So, for example, in *Pale Fire*, Charles Kinbote describes himself as retreating to his "Timonian" cave, as did Shakespeare's misanthropic protagonist in the play which gave the novel its title. In *Ada*, Van says "we are lost 'in another part of the forest,'" a stage direction from *A Midsummer Night's Dream* and *As You Like It*.

Of course, some of the more exhaustively Shakespearean sections of Nabokov's works combine several or all of these sorts of citations. The discussion of *Hamlet* in *Bend Sinister* and the pervasive allusions to *Timon of Athens* in *Pale Fire* are examples of such multiple and concatenated references.

A second, surprisingly common, set of references are not to specific works of Shakespeare's but invoke William Shakespeare in more general ways.

- These can be **biographical** comments. As we shall discover, there are a large number of references in Nabokov to Shakespeare's life. As one example, in *Transparent Things*, we read: "Going back a number of seasons (not as far, though, as Shakespeare's birth year when pencil lead was discovered)." In *Ada*, we find a calendar reference: "ever since Shakespeare's birthday on a green rainy day."

- There are also a cluster of comments which concern Shakespeare's **works** generally. Thus, a list of literary masterpieces in "The Art of Translation" includes "Shakespeare, Flaubert, Tyutchev, Dante, Cervantes and Kafka." Wordsmith College in *Pale Fire* is home to "the famous avenue of all the trees mentioned by Shakespeare."
- Finally, sometimes Nabokov's citations of Shakespearean works, characters, lines, and actions drift into the realm of parody. Thus, in *Ada*, we learn that "genius is not all gingerbread even for Billionaire Bill with his pointed beardlet and stylized bald dome," or Margot's bigoted description in *Laughter in the Dark* of "that play we saw, with the nigger and the pillow, and I'm just as innocent as she was." I'm particularly fond of Ada's translation of mad Lear's fivefold "never": "Ce beau jardin fleurit en mai, Mais en hiver, jamais, jamais, jamais, jamais, jamais, n'est vert, n'est vert, n'est vert, n'est vert, n'est vert" ("… never, never, never, never, never, it is not green [sounds like 'never']', it is not green, it is not green, it is not green, it is not green.").

There is also a group of what might be called "shadow" Shakespeareanisms. Here, of course, is where the quasi-scientific quantitative (see the Appendix) method gets a bit more subjective. Here are just two examples from *Ada*: in the midst of a rather torrid scene, Van says to Ada "Squeeze, you goose, can't you see I'm dying." Boyd notes that the Kyoto Reading Circle observed: "In light of the Egyptian theme, Van's words have a certain echo from Antony's famous cry, 'I am dying, Egypt, dying' from Shakespeare's *"Antony and Cleopatra."* This attribution seems possible, perhaps even likely, but not certain. Similarly, Ada says "this cannot be taken away, can it" and Van injects "it will, it was." Is this an echo of *I Henry IV*: "FALSTAFF: banish plump Jack, and banish all the world! PRINCE HAL: I do, I will."? I think it is; I think I can make a plausible case for the connection. In both cases, speakers are lamenting the loss of a youthful idyllic time of carefree frolicking. But I am not sure I could, in any scientific sense, "prove" that this is a citation of Shakespeare. Often, Nabokov's Shakespeareanisms are conspicuously front and center, but sometimes we can only sense their spectral presence, or see them from the corners of our eyes.

# Preview

The organization of the pages that follow is straightforward. I first turn in Chapter 2 to some of Vladimir Nabokov's early Russian-language works. These writings draw less heavily upon Shakespeare, but the presence of the Bard, particularly in some of Nabokov's early dramatic works, is certainly evident. I examine briefly Nabokov's play *The Tragedy of Mr. Morn*, recognized by virtually all scholars and critics to be heavily dependent upon Shakespearean drama in language, plot, characters, and theme. Then, I discuss the poem *Shakespeare*, translated by Dmitri Nabokov, in which Vladimir expresses doubt regarding Shakespeare's authorship of his works, an opinion he subsequently changed or at least modified. Still working as a Russian writer, Nabokov did some translations of passages from Shakespeare. He had planned a complete translation of *Hamlet*, but never completed that task. Finally, I turn to some early, Russian-language, prose: a short story, *The Wood Sprite*; three novels which make some use of Shakespearean sources, but in which those citations are not of core importance, *Glory*, *The Gift*, and *Invitation to a Beheading*; and two significant early novels, *Laughter in the Dark* and *Despair*. (Because they are relatively barren of Shakespearean materials, I do not discuss at any length the Russian novels *Mary*, *King, Queen, Knave*, *The Defense*, and *The Eye*.)

The next several chapters discuss Nabokov's greatest work—his English-language novels—in chronological order. These novels span a period of about a third of a century, from 1941 to 1974. Nabokov's first American novel, *The Real Life of Sebastian Knight*, derives the names of some of its major characters as well as some key motifs from *Twelfth Night* and *The Tempest*. *Bend Sinister* has the most extended discussion of a Shakespearean work within the Nabokov corpus, as its protagonist and an old friend and colleague of his muse on various productions of, and issues within, *Hamlet*. The novel as a whole, as well, seems to cite thematic material from that play. The most important novel in Nabokov's career, and what many readers consider to be his best (and one of the greatest of the twentieth century), was *Lolita*, in which there are many Shakespeareanisms. I pay particular attention to references to *The Tempest*, Shakespeare's late play of a magician, a monster, a naïve and innocent girl, an enchanted island, and the sorcery of art. *Pnin*, Nabokov's most accessible and gentle novel, followed *Lolita*. It has relatively few references to Shakespeare and his works, but some of those it has are amusing, while others point to more disturbing themes in the novel. Shakespeare's late, dark play *Timon of Athens* gives Nabokov's *Pale Fire* its title. The novel makes constant reference to the play. Indeed, one of the complex puzzles which give *Pale Fire* its dense texture involves tracing the pathway from Shakespeare's play to the novel's title. *Pale Fire's* narrator, the wildly unreliable Charles Kinbote, sees himself as "Timon in his cave." Nabokov's longest and perhaps his most convoluted novel is *Ada*. This massive work is encyclopedic in its citations of English and Russian literature and culture, and Shakespeare plays a substantial role in that comprehensive character. Here, once again, *Hamlet* is the dominant Shakespearean element in the novel. I argue that its hero, Van Veen, has much in common with the melancholy Dane; the Ophelia theme is of substantial importance in *Ada*; the uncomfortable topic of incest is at the core of both these works. Finally, I turn to Nabokov's two final complete works, *Transparent Things* and *Look at the Harlequins!* While neither of these novels approaches the level of Nabokov's masterpieces, both make interesting use of Shakespearean materials. *Transparent Things* has a number of allusions, mostly parodic, to *Romeo and Juliet*. It is, in some ways, a deliberate and polar opposite of that sad tale of tragic, young, innocent love. *Look at the Harlequins!* has, for a relatively short novel, quite a range of Shakespeareanisms, with a particular emphasis on Shakespeare's late, bitter, comedy, *Troilus and Cressida*.

Chapter 9 focuses upon four non-novelistic works from Nabokov's English-language period. His short story *That in Aleppo Once*, like *Pale Fire*, derives its title from Shakespeare. Not just the story's name, but much of its theme, owe a great deal to *Othello*. Nabokov's massive scholarly edition of Pushkin's *Eugene Onegin* has several Shakespeareanisms. These are of particular interest, since Pushkin and Shakespeare are the twin luminaries, one Russian, one English, in Nabokov's very small pantheon of great writers. The autobiography *Speak, Memory* has relatively few references to Shakespeare, but those are quite revealing. Shakespeare seems to appear at several points of particularly poignant moments of recollection here. Finally, Nabokov wrote three reviews, one published, two unpublished, of books of about Shakespeare. Those articles, and some unpublished notes from the Nabokov archive, reveal much about Nabokov's attitude regarding the theatrical production of Shakespeare's plays, in contrast to their status as written literary documents. He was not particularly fond of the process of translating Shakespeare from page to stage.

*Nabokov's Shakespeare* ends with some concluding thoughts about the nature of the twentieth-century novelist's debt to the Elizabethan playwright. I review the broad panoply of Shakespeareanisms in Nabokov's works, his particular interests in Shakespeare's plays (and his particular disinterests in others), and some of the themes which these two great authors share.

In an Appendix, I present a quantifiable approach to this literary relationship, comparing the frequency of Shakespearean references in Nabokov's various works, and at various periods of his creative life, and looking as well at the numbers which indicate the choice he makes of which Shakespearean works to cite. This seemingly dry exercise reveals some interesting developments in Nabokov's Shakespeareanisms, and clarifies both his general taste in Shakespearean materials and his sense of which most appropriately connect to, and illuminate, his novels.

# The Russian Works

For about two and a half decades, from the mid-teens of the twentieth century until the 1930s, Vladimir Nabokov was a Russian writer, albeit for most of that time one who did not live in Russia (the Nabokov family left Sevastopol in 1919, never to see Russia again). His works were published under the pseudonym "Sirin" (a mythological bird), while he lived the life of an exile, an émigré, in Germany, England, the former Czechoslovakia, and France. For most non-Russian readers, Nabokov's masterpieces are not his early Russian writings, but his English novels—*Lolita*, *Pale Fire*, and *Ada*, especially. And in his English language works, there is, not surprisingly, a deeper kind of tie to Shakespearean sources than when he wrote in Russian. There are, however, several important milestones in Nabokov's early (Slavic) literary career in which Shakespeare and his works are key. Among these, are the play *The Tragedy of Mr. Morn*, some translations of Shakespearean materials, the short story *The Wood Sprite*, and the poem *Shakespeare*. There are, as well, some noteworthy Shakespearean moments in a few of his early novels, including *Despair* and *Laughter in the Dark*.

## *The Tragedy of Mr. Morn*

*The Tragedy of Mr. Morn* (*Tragediia Gospodina Morna*) was written, Nabokov's biographer tells us, during a rather uncomfortable stay in Prague during the winter of 1923–4, when Nabokov was 24 years old.[1] To several Nabokovians, *Morn* seems Nabokov's first mature, even "major" work. Boyd, for example, declares it "by far the most significant work Nabokov had yet written in any medium" and adds that it "still remains in some ways the best of all his plays" (*Russian Years*, 222). Benjamin Taylor declares it "Nabokov's first major work," and the "Introduction" to the 2013 English translation of the play by Thomas Karshan reiterates "*The Tragedy of Mister Morn* was Vladimir Nabokov's first major work" (vii). The play is in some ways the most conspicuously "Shakespearean" work Nabokov wrote. That is, it is overtly and thoroughly written under the shade of Shakespeare's influence, and is clearly an imitation of Shakespeare in plot, character, language, structure, and theme. Taylor, like most readers of *Morn* is unequivocal: "The play looks to Shakespeare in its metre and metaphorical imagery."

The drama was given a few readings in Germany shortly after it was written and virtually ignored for the next 85 years. Since its recent translation, it has received more critical attention, and was given a staged reading at Pushkin House in London in June 2012, and another in 2013 in the US.

*Morn* takes place in an unnamed country, presumably European, at an unspecified but more or less modern time. Its plot is, to put it mildly, complex and convoluted. For a few years, that country has been ruled by a mysterious and anonymous king, who has brought peace and prosperity, and reduced civil conflict. The anonymous king is, in fact, Mr. Morn, an energetic and optimistic leader. He is in love with Midia, who is married to a former revolutionary named Ganus, who has been imprisoned during Morn's reign, but who has, at the play's start, escaped. Ganus no longer considers himself a rebel and admires the changes the new monarch has brought about. Disguised as an actor playing Othello, he attends a ball, where he discovers his wife's infidelity. He does not know that it is the king with whom his wife is enamored. At the same time, his former co-conspirator, Tremens, remains determined to sow destruction across the land. Tremens has a daughter, Ella, who is in love with a court poet, Klian, but she becomes taken with Ganus. Ganus challenges Morn to a contest of honor. They will each draw a card, and the loser must kill himself. Morn loses, but reneges and runs away with Midia. Morn grows depressed by his cowardice, and Midia leaves him, now infatuated with Morn's ally, Edmin. Ganus finds Morn and shoots him, wounding him but not ending his life. Meanwhile, Tremens has stirred up revolution and counter-revolution, the capitol is in flames, blood runs freely. The revolution is suppressed, and Morn prepares to resume his kingship. But, ashamed of his dishonorable behavior, he kills himself at the play's conclusion.

As this brief plot outline makes clear, the drama's story is one in which the fate of a kingdom is entwined with the personal tale of a flawed monarch's private life. Such a narrative is common in Shakespeare's history plays and, indeed, in Shakespearean dramas as diverse as *Midsummer Night's Dream* or *Romeo and Juliet*. Michiko Kakutani comments in *The New York Times* upon the Shakespearean flavor of this attention to "kingship and the relationship between personality and politics" (C1). Similarly, Leslie Chamberlain, writing in *The Times Literary Supplement* (*TLS*), characterizes the play as "this early imitation of Shakespeare."

*The Tragedy of Mr. Morn*'s characterization also shows a heavy influence of Shakespeare. Perhaps most obvious is Ganus's disguise as Othello. When

Ganus seeks to attend Midia's party as Othello, Ella suggests that he attend as "an actor, an acquaintance of mine, / and haven't taken off your make-up— / because it was so good … You shall be Othello— / the curly-haired, old, dark-skinned Moor" (14). Of course, this is not a random choice of Shakespeare disguises, as Ganus embodies the theme of sexual jealousy in *Morn*. Not surprisingly, Ella, who came up with the Othello disguise for Ganus, quotes Desdemona in act I, scene 1:

> ELLA: Really, Othello, I am pleased with you …
>  [declaims]
> "But yet I fear you; for you are fatal then
> When your eyes roll so: why should I fear I know not,
> Since guiltiness I know not; but yet I feel fear …" (1. 1. 298–301)

Nabokov is citing the exact lines from *Othello*, in the scene in which the Moor kills Desdemona:

> DESDEMONA: And yet I fear you; for you're fatal then
> When your eyes roll so. Why I should fear I know not,
> Since guiltiness I know not; but yet I feel fear. (5. 2. 36–8)

Another echo of Shakespearean characters is certainly Edmin, the king's (semi-) loyal retainer. The name itself has a Shakespearean sound: not only is there an Edmund in *King Lear* but Edmund Shakespeare was the youngest son of John Shakespeare and Mary Arden, and thus William's young brother. And the character of a king's counselor, whose good advice is not taken as the play descends toward tragedy, is a stock figure in the Bard's works (e.g. John of Gaunt in *Richard II*). Similarly, Dandilio, an old courtier, is characterized by a "florid sagacity" (Boyd, *Russian*, 224), which is very reminiscent of *Hamlet*'s Polonius.

A very minor character in *Morn* called simply "Old Man" makes one appearance, for 12 lines, at the very end of Act III, scene 1. He mumbles to himself, straightens out some of the items left on stage, and ends the act:

> Old age isn't some ugly mug daubed on
> a fence, you can't just paint over it …
> [*And, muttering, he exits.*] (3. 1, 225–37 s.d.)

This walk-on character is, surely, the first cousin of the gravedigger in *Hamlet* or the porter in *Macbeth*!

The play's title character has also seemed to some readers to have a Shakespearean flavor. For Kakutani, Morn, the king who "behind his mask is an ordinary man," seems "Prospero-like" (C1). Karshan, too, sees a "kinship between Prospero and Morn, both of them magician-kings" (xiv). Certainly, his ability to work miraculous public good while finally revealing himself a mere mortal recalls *The Tempest*. Karshan notes the way in which Morn's attitude toward the crown parallels that of

> Shakespeare's history plays, such as Henry IV, Part 2, towards the end of which Prince Henry stares uneasily at the crown lying on his dying father's pillow, "so troublesome a bedfellow," which, he says, "dost pinch thy bearer" and "dost sit / Like a rich armour worn in the heat of day, / That scalds with safety." (xiii)

Similarly, in *Morn* too, the crown is "fiery" and "the knight's body is dark and sweaty, locked in its fairy tale armour" (5. 2. 124–6).

Another conspicuously Shakespearean aspect of *The Tragedy of Mr. Morn* is "its three thousand lines of blank verse" (Boyd 222), divided into a traditional five-act structure. Karshan notes that in *Morn* Nabokov emulates Shakespeare's verbal rhythm: "The simplest expression of this is that Morn is written in the iambic pentameter of Shakespearean tragedy" (xv). In addition to prosody, Karshan finds the language of the play "densely metaphorical and highly compressed in the manner of late Shakespeare." Boyd even suggests that at times the language of the play is "reminiscent of Hamlet's and Claudio's great speeches" (225). Of course, *Morn* was written in Russian, not English, so its blank verse has a Slavic character. The play has only recently been translated into English by Karshan and Anastasia Tolstoy, who declare that they have tried "to retain the shimmering pale fire of Shakespeare's language which is often glimpsed in Nabokov's original Russian" (xxi). The translators note that, as in Shakespearean texts, when Nabokov's characters slip out of the "high heroic mode," the language shifts as well, between "prosody and prose" (xxiv).

Some of the themes of *The Tragedy of Mr. Morn* have already been touched upon. Nabokov like Shakespeare is interested in the intersection of the private and the public; the amorous adventures and personal relationships of a monarch and the fate of the state. Morn's adulterous love affair with Midia takes place at that intersection: Their liaison undermines the political wellbeing that Morn has brought to his country and leads to public chaos. The depiction of the chaos of revolution is another thematic thread linking *Morn* and Shakespeare's political works. Both authors, social conservatives as they are, depict the terrors of a society which descends into what they see as the anarchy of revolutionary bloodshed. Nabokov's Tremens, like Shakespeare's Richard III, seems an emblem of the darkest of impulses which come to the fore when the social order is broken:

> Hang on, hang on! Did you really think
> that I worked with such determination

for the good of an imaginary "people"?
So that every manure-filled soul, some
drunken goldsmith or another, some gnarled
stable-boy could polish his dainty nails
up to a mirror sheen, and bend his little
finger back in affectation, when shaking
off his snot? ...
Everything, Ganus, everything is destruction. And
the faster it is, the sweeter, the sweeter ... (1. 1, 245 ff.)

Perhaps the most Nabokovian theme of *The Tragedy of Mr. Morn* is what
Kakutani calls the "mirror game played out between reality and art, the
actual and the imagined" (C1). This theme is embodied in an enigmatic
character called "The Foreigner." This character is obviously a visitor to
the play from another reality—one rather like our own, it turns out. He
first appears at a party scene in 2. 2, and begins by asking who the others
attending the ball are. He then speaks to Dandilio, in a short and curious
dialog:

FOREIGNER [*approaching*]:
    I often heard your voice
in my childhood dreams ...
DANDILIO:
        Really, I never
can remember who has dreamt me. But
your smile I do remember. I meant to ask you
courteous traveler, where have you come from?
FOREIGNER:
I have come from the Twentieth Century, from
a northern country called ...                    *Russie*
    [*Whispers.*]
MIDIA:                    Which one is it?
I don't know that one ...
DANDILIO:
                How can you say that!
Don't you remember, from children's fairy tales?
Visions ... bombs ... churches ... golden princes ...
revolutionaries in raincoats ... blizzards.
MIDIA:
But I thought it didn't exist?
FOREIGNER:
        Perhaps. I

> entered a dream, but are you sure that I
> have left that dream? ... So be it, I'll believe
> in your city. Tomorrow I shall call it
> A dream ..."
> MIDIA:                      Our city is beautiful ...
> [*She moves away.*]
> FOREIGNER:        I find
> in it a ghostly resemblance to the distant
> city of my birth—that likeness which exists
> between truth and high fantasy ... (1. 2. 43–60)

The Foreigner's city is surely Nabokov's St. Petersburg; his era is explicitly the time of the play's writing. He appears to be a kind of emissary between the "high fantasy" of the play and the "truth" of Nabokov's world of 1923. This reading is strongly reinforced later in the same scene, when the character reappears, and declares:

> I won't
> forget my stay in your bewitching city:
> the closer a fairy tale is to reality,
> the more magical it is. (318–21)

The Foreigner makes his next and final appearance in the fifth act, very near the end of the play, when he affirms, multiple times, "I'm simply asleep ... I'm pleased: I dreamt you up well ... All this is a dream ... That's it ... an elaborate dream ... But you know, I was glad to wake up ... When I wake up, I will tell them what a magnificent king I dreamt of ... I'll try to wake up ..." And he disappears!

Are we to understand that the Foreigner has dreamt up *The Tragedy of Mr. Morn* wholly in his own imagination? This would certainly be a device Nabokov uses later in his fiction, for example in the conclusion to *Bend Sinister* when the author steps forward and reveals himself in the act of concluding his novel, or the end of *Ada*, when the fictional world dissolves into the blurb of the book itself. Or is this character simply a thematic reminder of the "likeness which exists between truth and high fantasy"? Kakutani describes the Foreigner as "a mysterious character ... who hails from a place very much like Russia suffering from the throes of revolution, and who seems to have created the king (or the idea of the king) as a kind of fantasy—as a fairy-tale antidote to what happened in his homeland" (C1). Since the Foreigner's homeland seems to coincide with Nabokov's, and it was Nabokov who actually created the king, it would not be unreasonable to equate the Foreigner with Nabokov himself.

The concept of a character in a play who serves as an ambassador between the fictional world of the play and the "real" world of the audience is certainly familiar to students of Shakespeare as well as Nabokov. Examples might include the Chorus of *Henry V*, who tells the audience how to enlarge in their imaginations what they are seeing on stage; the epilogues of *A Midsummer Night's Dream* and *The Tempest*, where actors step partially out of their roles to comment upon the drama which is concluding; or the prologue to *The Taming of the Shrew*, which establishes a frame for the ensuing drama, and then disappears.

Amusingly, more than a decade later, when Nabokov returned to writing drama shortly before he immigrated to the United States, Shakespeare was still ingrained in his consciousness. In *The Waltz Invention* we find a brief but unmistakable reference to *Richard III's* plea for "a horse, a horse, my kingdom for a horse" (V. iv. 7) when a character named Bump exclaims: "What mountain? Where is the mountain? A kingdom for a pair of glasses!" (21).

## "Shakespeare"

As *The Tragedy of Mr. Morn* shows, Nabokov drawing heavily upon the forms and conventions of Shakespearean tragedy in his early dramatic writings, the poem "Shakespeare," written in Russian at the same time, shows the ways in which Nabokov's interpretation of Shakespeare's life harmonized with emerging major themes in his fiction:

Shakespeare

Amid grandees of times Elizabethan
you shimmered too, you followed sumptuous customs;
the circle of ruff, the silv'ry satin that
encased your thigh, the wedgelike beard—in all of this
you were like other men ... Thus was enfolded
your godlike thunder in a succinct cape.

Haughty, aloof from theater's alarums,
you easily, regretlessly relinquished
the laurels twining into a dry wreath,
concealing for all time your monstrous genius
beneath a mask; and yet, your phantasms' echoes
still vibrate for us: your Venetian Moor,
his anguish; Falstaff's visage, like an udder
with pasted-on mustache; the raging Lear ...

You are among us, you're alive; your name, though,
your image, too—deceiving, thus, the world—
you have submerged in your beloved Lethe.
It's true, of course, a usurer had grown
accustomed, for a sum, to sign your work
(that Shakespeare—Will—who played the Ghost in *Hamlet*
who lived in pubs, and died before he could
digest in full his portion of a boar's head) ...

The frigate breathed, your country you were leaving.
to Italy you went. A female voice
called singsong through the iron's pattern,
called to her balcony the tall *inglese*,
grown languid from the lemon-tinted moon
amid Verona's streets. My inclination
is to imagine, possibly, the droll
and kind creator of *Don Quixote*
exchanging with you a few casual words
while waiting for fresh horses—and the evening
was surely blue.[2] The well behind the tavern
contained a pail's pure tinkling sound ... Reply—whom did you love?
Reveal yourself—whose memoirs
refer to you in passing? Look what numbers
of lowly, worthless souls have left their trace,
what countless names Brantome[3] has for the asking!
Reveal yourself, god of iambic thunder,
you hundred-mouthed, unthinkably great bard!

No! At the destined hour, when you felt banished
by God from your existence, you recalled
those secret manuscripts, fully aware
that your supremacy would rest unblemished
by public rumor's unashamed brand
that ever, midst the shifting dust of ages,
faceless you'd stay, like immortality
itself—then, in the distance, smiling, vanished.

The two manuscripts of "Shakespeare" (entitled in Russian "Posle chteniia Shekspira"—"After Reading Shakespeare") date from February 1924. Dmitri Nabokov's translation appeared in *The Nabokovian* (Spring 1988, pp. 15–16).[4]

The poem's opening stanza observes that Shakespeare's divine thunder was housed within the body of a normal Elizabethan man, indeed, one who seems to have been a bit of a dandy, following "sumptuous customs" in style. In stanza two, Nabokov introduces a vein of anti-Stratfordianism which has been the subject of considerable discussion: the "real" author of Shakespeare's works is hidden behind a mask; what remains are his eternal characters (Othello, Falstaff, Lear). Shakespeare the author is alive and among us; Shakespeare the man—his name and image—have been forgotten. Instead, a usurper has been credited with the Bard's works; an actor and carouser. Clearly, at this early point in his own literary career, Nabokov was entertaining the notion that someone other than William Shakespeare, the son of a Stratford glover, wrote the plays. In a 1998 contribution to the Nabokov Listserv, Brian Boyd reports that Nabokov was impressed with Samuel Schoenbaum's history of Shakespearean biography, *Shakespeare's Lives*, which debunks the anti-Stratfordians. Alfred Appel Jr, a colleague of Schoenbaum at Northwestern University, had given Nabokov a copy of the book, and Nabokov found it an exemplary scholarly work.[5] A quarter century later, in Nabokov's novel *Bend Sinister*, Krug and Ember have a cheerful good time demolishing the folly of the anti-Stratfordian position:

> Krug suggested tampering with Hamlet's name too. Take "Telemachos" he says, which means "fighting from afar"—which again was Hamlet's idea of warfare. Prune it, remove the unnecessary letters, all of them secondary additions, and you get the ancient "Telmah." Now read it backwards. Thus does a fanciful pen elope with a lewd idea and Hamlet in reverse gear becomes the son of Ulysses slaying his mother's lovers. (115)

In a short note, Michael Seidel suggests Nabokov "amused himself considerably with just such an off-beat theory of Shakespearean composition" (359). Today, it is generally understood by serious Shakespeareans that Shakespeare probably did not write every word of every play included among his "complete works," and that not every word he ever wrote is included therein, either. Patterns of collaboration and adaptation in Renaissance England make such sole authorship unlikely. But likewise, it is also the overwhelming consensus that Shakespeare was Shakespeare: the man from Stratford who wrote *Hamlet* and *King Lear*, all the other tragedies, comedies and histories. They were not the work of some disguised nobleman, falsely attributed to some Elizabethan theatrical lout. It is ironic that Sigmund Freud, for whom Nabokov famously had no respect, was inclined to an anti-Stratfordian theory of Shakespearean authorship.

In the second stanza, as well, Nabokov suggests that theatrical production was not important to the dramatist: "aloof afrom the theater's alarums." This is a recurrent theme in Nabokov's writing about the drama, which I discuss at greater length below in the context of Nabokov's reviews of several scholarly books about Shakespeare in the 1940s.

In the penultimate stanza of "Shakespeare," Nabokov imagines Shakespeare (or, more accurately, the author of Shakespeare's works) sailing to Italy, where, in Verona, he seems to have some Romeo-esque amorous adventures, and to have a chat with "the droll and kind creator of *Don Quixote*." This encounter is, as the poem itself makes clear, purely imaginary. Indeed, the notion that Shakespeare ever left England, although it has been attractive to romantic biographers for centuries, is wholly unsupported by any evidence.

In the poem's final lines, Nabokov envisions his subject, whose true identity is hidden forever from public rumor, thinking of the supremacy and immortality of his manuscripts, smiling, and then vanishing (exactly the same word used to describe the disappearance of the Foreigner in *The Tragedy of Mr. Morn*).

There are some clear links between "Shakespeare" and *The Tragedy of Mr. Morn*. Interestingly, in both, "Othello" seems particularly important. Perhaps more important, however, is the shared theme of hidden identity. The poem focuses upon the mystery of the true author of the Bard's dramas; the play's central character hides his identity.[6]

In this poem Nabokov develops, through his mulling of Shakespearean biography, two of his perennial, and related, themes. Exploiting the mythic, and probably spurious, issue of the true identity of the authorship of the plays, Nabokov evokes the illusory nature of human life, the often dreamlike and fantastic quality of the true identity of each individual human being. We are reminded of all his wildly unreliable narrators, the puppets of *Invitation to a Beheading*, the ghosts of *Transparent Things*, and the puzzle of who and what is "real" in *Pale Fire*. But set against the often-dreamlike illusion of individual existence is the reality and durability of literary art. "Dead is the mandible, alive the song," says *Pale Fire*'s John Shade (l. 244). The narrator(s) of *Ada* die, as it were, into the book. Likewise, we will never know Shakespeare the man, the poem asserts, but we will never forget the Shakespeare canon. Shakespeare is more alive in the poetry of *Othello* than he ever was on the streets of Elizabethan London. As Samuel Schoenbaum has noted throughout his definitive *Shakespeare's Lives*, studies of Shakespeare's life have often been a mirror of the preoccupations of the biographers. Certainly, Nabokov's poetic interpretation justifies this conclusion. The emphasis on the primacy, the "reality," and eternality of art, and the transitory, illusive quality of human existence is pure Nabokov.

# Translations

A continuing early fascination with Shakespeare is demonstrated by Nabokov's never-completed project to translate *Hamlet* into Russian. In 1930–1 he published three excerpts from this projected translation—two in the Russian émigré newspaper *Rul* and one in *Les Mois*. It was perhaps this effort which made Nabokov so sensitive to what he judged the woeful inadequacies of Pasternak's 1941 translation, which he termed in private correspondence "vulgar and illiterate" (*Selected Letters*, 470). Pasternak was rather like *Pale Fire*'s inept Shakespearean translator Conmal when it came to the relationship between Shakespearean text and translation. Eleanor Rowe recounts the story that when Pasternak was once charged with a string of inaccuracies in his text, he shrugged off criticism by affirming "What difference does it make? Shakespeare and I—we're both geniuses, aren't we?" (158). One recalls Conmal's "extraordinary sonnet composed directly in colorful, if not quite correct, English beginning:

> I am not slave! Let be my critic slave.
> I cannot be. And Shakespeare would not want thus.
> Let drawing students copy the acanthus
> I work with Master on the architrave! (202)

The three translated passages Nabokov published were Hamlet's "To be or not to be" soliloquy (a speech to which Nabokov made very frequent reference in later works such as *Bend Sinister* and *Pale Fire*), Gertrude's speech in Act 4, scene 7, narrating the watery death of Ophelia (another very important scene for Nabokov, for example with strong echoes in the death of Aqua Veen in *Ada* and in *Pnin*), and the section of Act 5, scene 1, in which Laertes and Hamlet tussle on Ophelia's grave.

In the Nabokov archives formerly kept in the Montreux Palace Hotel in Switzerland (now, for the most part, transferred to the Berg Collection in the New York Public Library), a somewhat greater portion of the translation of *Hamlet* is recorded on 25 sides of Nabokovian note cards.[7] These selections also include some material from the play-within-the-play, Hamlet's mousetrap to trap the conscience of the king, a section of the work one would assume would intrigue as self-conscious an artificer as Nabokov. Another card, presumably from this same period, contains some additional material on Gertrude: on side one are some lines (in English) of Nabokov-imagined speculation by Hamlet about his mother ("My good mother? Well, she had one remarkable capacity—to forget") and on side two are what appear to be some more direct notes and comments by Nabokov ("She bridges life and eternity by means of a comfortable platitude, and with a pout of mature petulance makes a coquettish trochee of 'Wittenberg.'") One regrets that the speculations never evolved into one of the "Lectures on Literature" and the complete translation never hatched.

# Early prose

## *The Wood Sprite*

*The Wood Sprite*, a short story, was published in Russian (as *Nezhit*) in *Rul* in 1921. It was the first story Nabokov published, and according to its translator, his son Dmitri, one of the very first he ever wrote (640). It is a curious blending of the nostalgic and the grotesque. A melancholy émigré is visited by a real or imagined sprite, rather gargoylesque in appearance:

> His right eye was still in the shadows, the left peered at me timorously, elongated, smoky green. The pupil glowed like a point of rust … That mossy-gray tuft on his temple, the pale-silver, scarcely noticeable eyebrow, the comical wrinkle near his whiskerless mouth … those cranberry lips, those pointy ears, that amusing Adam's apple. (3)

The sprite laments the despoliation of his and the narrator's and the author's lost Slavic homeland, then disappears. At four pages, the story is very short, and its handling of the theme of exile and loss may seem a bit self-indulgent. But with its conclusion leaving a lingering "subtle scent in the room, of birch, of humid moss …," *The Wood Sprite* is a rather haunting and more-than-competent youthful work by an author still at the start of his twenties.

The four pages of the story contain two allusions to Shakespeare's works, both of which, unsurprisingly, are to sprite-like, magical creatures. In the first reference, the Wood Sprite mentions a co-creature, a "kindred spirit, a Water-Sprite" (5). Of this watery elvish colleague we learn that:

> In olden times, he had his fun, used to lure people down (a hospitable one, he was!), and in recompense how he petted and pampered them on the gold river bottom, with what songs he bewitched them! (5)

The vision of rich, glittering drowning, coupled with bewitching songs, reminds us of Ariel in *The Tempest*:

> Ariel *sings*:
> Full fathom five thy father lies;
> Of his bones are coral made:
> These are pearls that were his eyes:

Nothing of him that doth fade,
But doth suffer a sea-change
Into something rich and strange
Sea nymphs hourly ring his knell. (1. 2. 394–400)

(Wagnerians might find a familiar ring, too, in this subaquatic gold.)

A second, even clearer, Shakespeare reference comes during the Wood Sprite's description of himself in conversation with the narrator. Recounting their jolly Russian days together, he reminisces:

In the old days, I'd frolic from dawn to dusk, whistle furiously, clap my hands, frighten passersby. You remember yourself—you lost your way once in a dark nook of my wood, you and some little white dress, and I kept tying the paths up in knots, spinning the tree trunks, twinkling through the foliage. Spent the whole night playing tricks. But I was only fooling around, it was all in jest. (4)

This certainly echoes that "shrewd and knavish sprite / Called Robin Goodfellow ... that frights the maidens of the villager" (*A Midsummer Night's Dream*, 2. 1. 32–3). Indeed, Puck, like Nabokov's sprite, is known to "mislead night-wanderers, laughing at their harm" especially couples ("you and some little white dress," as Nabokov's character says). Of course, at the center of *A Midsummer Night's Dream*, Puck does just that, keeping the lovers in the woods all night, bewildering them, causing them to lose their ways, tying their paths in knots:

Up and down, up and down:
I will lead them up and down
I am fear'd in field and town
Goblin, lead them up and down
...
Yet but three? Come one more
Two of both kinds make up four. (3. 2. 396–9, 437–8)

Puck and Ariel are surely Shakespearean creations close to Nabokov's mischievous, somewhat melancholy, funny, and just slightly spooky Wood Sprite. Some of their Elizabethan antics seem to be translated into the young émigré Nabokov's nostalgic lament. In his very first published story, what Nabokov has already found in Shakespeare—as he was to find for the rest of his rich career—is magic.

\*\*\*

Three of Nabokov's Russian novels of the 1930s, *Glory* (in Russian *Podvig*), *The Gift* (*Dar*), and *Invitation to a Beheading* (*Priglashenie na kazn*), have a handful of references to Shakespeare and his works, but in no case do those citations link in a serious fashion to the main themes, plot, or characters of the novels. They are, however, worth a quick look to see how Nabokov could casually cite Shakespeare with no particular deep implications.

## *Glory*

*Glory* was written in 1930–2, published in Paris in 1932, and translated by Dmitri Nabokov and his father in 1971. It follows the story of the early life of Martin Edelweiss, born in St. Petersburg, in exile in Western Europe, as a student at Cambridge, and his final projected adventure of sneaking back into the Soviet Union from Switzerland. The novel ends with Martin's disappearance. Has he returned to his homeland? It is not clear.

As a student at Cambridge, Martin considers studying "the grief of old Lear, uttering the mannered names of his daughter's whippets that barked at him (62)." He does not, however, settle upon Shakespeare for his primary studies.

Martin is attracted to a young woman named Sonia, who at one point remarks "they used to play football in Shakespeare's time, too" (67). And, in a reference to one of Nabokov's favorite passages from *Othello*, Martin:

> imagined how, after many adventures he would arrive in Berlin, look up Sonia, and, like Othello, begin to tell a story of hair breadth escapes, of most disastrous chances. (119) [Othello wins the love of Desdemona by speaking of "most disastrous chances" and "hairbreadth scapes"—1. 3. 133, 135.]

Martin becomes a kind of protégé of a teacher of Russian, Archibald Moon, who, we learn,

> Would occasionally be seen in the street in the company of a beautifully chubby youth with abundant blond hair who impersonated girls in the university productions of Shakespeare's plays. (98)

There are, as well, a few more tenuous possible echoes of Shakespearean themes. For example, Martin has a fantasy "of a desolate, stormy sea, after a shipwreck … cast up onto the same uninhabited island …" (18). This passage could remind us of *The Tempest*, but that association is hardly unassailable.

Shakespeare's works are part of the texture of *Glory*, one element in the background of the novel, but they do not ever come to the fore.

## *The Gift*

*The Gift* was translated by Michael Scammell with Nabokov, and published in 1970. It first appeared serially in 1937–8. At that time, the fourth of its five chapters, a biography of the Russian author Chernyshevsky, was not printed. *The Gift* is Nabokov's final Russian novel, seen by many as his greatest achievement as a Russian novelist. It is a dense, richly textured work which tells the story of Fyodor, a Russian exile living in Germany. Fyodor is an aspiring writer (who, perhaps, grows up to write *The Gift*). We learn of his daily life, his thoughts, his love affair with Zina, and, especially, the loss of his respected father, an explorer, scientist, and writer who disappeared on an expedition to the Far East. Throughout the novel are scattered several Shakespearean references:

> Fyodor ekes out a living teaching English to Berlin businessmen: "In the late afternoon he would give a lesson—to a business man … Fyodor unconcernedly read him Shakespeare …." (72)

> Nabokov writes that Fyodor returns in his mind "to that world which was as natural to him as snow to the white hare or water to Ophelia." (37)

Later in the work, we find a description of a night in the theater:

*Suhoshchokov*

> Instead of treating him to a new Russian comedy we showed him *Othello* with the famous black tragedian Aldridge. At first our American planter seemed to be highly amused by the appearance of a genuine Negro on stage. But he remained indifferent to the marvelous power of his acting and was more taken up with examining the audience, especially our St. Petersburg ladies (one of whom he soon afterwards married), who were devoured at that moment with envy for Desdemona … I looked at those harsh wrinkles, that broad nose, those large ears … shivers ran down my back, and not all of Othello's jealousy was able to drag me away. (112–13)

An early reference to Nabokov's distrust of staging Shakespeare's works is the remark "as if somebody parodying an actor's slovenly reading of Shakespeare had been carried away, had started a theater in earnest, but had accidently garbled a line" (351). This theme recurs in much greater depth in Nabokov's later works.

Chernyschevsky (Lenin's favorite author) proclaims that "the juxtaposition of Gogol's name with those of Homer and Shakespeare offends both decency and common sense" (266). And Fyodor notes his "last, hopeless attempts to shout down the silence (a feat even more difficult than Lear's attempt to shout down the storm) (307). A bit of Shakespearean playfulness appears when an Arctic explorer is said to have sat "on an empty soapbox and thought gloomily: the pole or not the pole?" (327).

Finally, Nabokov cites the speech from *King Lear* which appears over and over again in his subsequent works. Fyodor's friend has just been cremated, and Fyodor mulls "the braked line from *King Lear*, consisting entirely of five 'nevers'—that was all he could think of" (325).

## Invitation to a Beheading

*Invitation to a Beheading* was first published in 1938 and appeared in an English translation by Vladimir and Dmitri Nabokov in 1959. It is the story of a political prisoner, one Cincinnatus C., and his surreal time in prison leading up to his execution. His crime is "gnostical turpitude," that is to say he is not, like all those around him, transparent. In jail, he receives a procession of visitors, all of whom are (in the words of the novel) "specters, werewolves, parodies" (40). At the book's conclusion, as Cincinnatus is about to be beheaded, he realizes that he is real, and is surrounded by shadows. He gets up, walks away from the platform where he is to be executed, and "made his way in that direction where, to judge by the voices, stood beings akin to him" (223).

As with *The Gift* and *Glory*, there are few references to Shakespeare in *Invitation to a Beheading*. Those that can be found are not central to the novel's theme, plot, or characters. In his introduction to the novel, Nabokov expresses his contempt for translators who seek to capture the "spirit" of a work, and ignore the words. He uses a Shakespearean image:

> down with the simpletons who think all is well if the "spirit" is rendered (while the words go away by themselves on a naïve and vulgar spree—in the suburbs of Moscow for instance—and Shakespeare is again reduced to play the king's ghost). (7)

To catch the spirit and ignore the words is the equivalent of a poetic genius reduced to playing a minor role.

In the novel itself, there are a number of Shakespearean hints: not clear references, but suggestions that may evoke Shakespearean echoes. So, for example, at one point when the prison director leaves Cincinnatus' cell, he is said to "exit, backing out like a courtier" (130). This seems reminiscent of the foppish Osric taking his excessive leave of Hamlet in Act 5. Similarly, when Cincinnatus's executioner-to-be says to the prison director Rodrig Ivanovich "Let's away, Rodrigo" (154), there is, perhaps, an echo of *Othello's* Iago and his henchman Rodrigo. Finally, some discussion of "drugged potions" (153) may recall the most famous such medications in English literature, those of

*Romeo and Juliet*. And surely, when the prisoner and his executioner attend a grotesque banquet in their honor "identically clad in Elsinore jackets" (182) we see some connection between the unreal world of the novel and the corrupt Danish court of Claudius in *Hamlet*.

As Nabokov's career as a Russian author moved towards its conclusion, we can see that Shakespeare had a small but significant role in his tessellated literary consciousness. When he became an English author, that role became conspicuously larger and moved to the forefront in the rich mosaic of his worlds of fiction. Two Russian novels, *Laughter in the Dark* and *Despair*, foreshadow the increasing presence and importance of Shakespeare and his works in Nabokov's literary imagination.

## *Laughter in the Dark*

At the same time he was working on the Shakespearean translations (c. 1931), Nabokov was also creating the novel which was entitled *Kamera obskura* in Russian, *Camera Obscura* in its first English-language edition, and subsequently *Laughter in the Dark*. This novel affords a revealing illustration of the ways in which Nabokov utilized Shakespearean materials to heighten the themes and enrich the texture of his prose works. Just after the hero of *Laughter in the Dark*, Albinus, discovers that his girlfriend Margot has been cheating on him with the diabolic artist Axel Rex, Margot exclaims to Albinus: "'Please, shoot me, do,' she said. 'It will be just like that play we saw, with the nigger and the pillow, and I'm just as innocent as she was'" (226). It would be over-reading the novel to find in it a consistent pattern of parody of *Othello*, but it would be under-reading to ignore Nabokov's awareness of the ways in which this work is a grotesque reflection of Shakespeare's play. Margot's comparison of herself to Desdemona and of Albinus to Othello is ironically inapt, to say the least. Where Shakespeare's hero is a black man, Nabokov's has a name which suggests a kind of insipid whiteness (Axel Rex, too, is exceptionally pallid, "dull white as if coated with a thin layer of powder"—32).

The plot of *Laughter in the Dark*, like that of *Othello*, focuses upon two men and one woman, ensnared together in a web of sexual misunderstanding, treachery, and jealousy. But where Shakespeare's play involves the false suspicion of sexual deception, Nabokov's novel is based upon an exactly opposite twist: Albinus believes Margot is true to him (even after his initial doubts) and is blind (figuratively and then literally) to her relationship with Rex. Where Iago torments Othello with untrue accusations of infidelity, Rex torments Albinus with equally false assurances of Margot's sexual faithfulness. A final ironic contrast between these two works involves their conclusion. Shakespeare ends *Othello* with the Moor's murder of his wife, followed by his own suicide. Albinus tries to imitate Shakespeare's conclusion, but he can't pull it off. Blinded, he attempts to shoot the unfaithful Margot, but she shoots him instead.

*Laughter in the Dark* is, as its title suggests, one of Nabokov's more sardonic works. The hint of a parodic literary relationship with Shakespeare's tragedy of misguided nobility adds another layer of ironic self-consciousness to the novel.

## *Despair*

Nabokov's novel *Despair* offers a fascinating example of the extent to which Shakespearean materials permeated Nabokov's consciousness and early prose. The novel (in Russian *Otchayanie*) first appeared in serial format in the journal *Sovremennye zapiski* in 1934, then was published (in Russian) as a book in 1936. The following year, Nabokov translated the novel into English, but most of that edition was lost in World War II. He retranslated it in 1965 and it was published in English in 1966. The plot concerns Hermann Karlovich, a Russian émigré who believes (ludicrously and tragically incorrectly) that he has discovered his double and hatches a plot to kill his doppelganger and collect on his own life insurance. Not surprisingly, the plot fails. In a paragraph which seems remarkably Shakespearean, Hermann speaks in justification of his own skepticism about things supernatural:

> Now tell me, please, what guarantee do you possess that those beloved ghosts are genuine; that it is really your dear dead mother and not some pretty demon mystifying you, masked as your mother and impersonating her with consummate art and naturalness? There is the rub, there is the horror; the more so as the acting will go on and on, endlessly; never, never, never, never, never will your soul in that other world be quite sure that the sweet gentle spirits crowding about it are not fiends in disguise, and forever, and forever, and forever shall your soul remain in doubt, expecting every moment some awful change, some diabolical sneer to disfigure the dear face bending over you. (112–13)

Among the Shakespeare references, parodies, and quotations in this passage are these:

- The idea that what one perceives as the ghost of a dear, dead parent might in fact be an impersonating demon is certainly familiar from

*Hamlet.* In Shakespeare's work, of course, it is the spirit of Hamlet's father; in Nabokov's novel it is a mother. The melancholy Dane wonders if the ghost he encounters on the battlements of Elsinore Castle is "a spirit of health, or goblin damned" (1. 4. 40). Later, he observes that:

The spirit that I have seen
May be a devil, and the devil hath power
T' assume a pleasing shape, yea, and perhaps
Out of my weakness and my melancholy,
As he is very potent with such spirits,
Abuses me to damn me. (2. 2. 605–10)

There are, of course, a handful of ghosts in Shakespeare, and more than a handful in Nabokov's works, including in at least two cases ghostly shades serving as narrators ("The Vane Sisters," *Transparent Things*).

- Lest the readers of *Despair* miss this rather obvious reference to *Hamlet* Nabokov cites the famed "To be or not to be" soliloquy: Hamlet says "There's the rub" (3. 1. 65); Hermann says "There is the rub." Of course, this soliloquy is Hamlet's, and Shakespeare's, best-known meditation on the matter of life after death.
- Another echo of Shakespeare's tragedies follows at once in the five-times-repeated "never," exactly duplicating King Lear's quintuple negation in Act 5 in his very last utterance. Lear is also meditating upon the question of the permanence of death:

Why should a dog, a horse, a rat, have life,
And thou no breath at all? Thou'lt come no more,
Never, never, never, never, never.
Pray you, undo this button. Thank you, sir.
Do you see this? Look on her. Look, her lips,
Look there, look there. *He dies.* (5. 3. 308–13)

This line seems to have made a particularly strong impression on Nabokov. It appears multiple times throughout his works, as, for example, in *The Gift*, where Fyodor, thinking of his just-cremated friend, mulls on "the braked line from *King Lear*, consisting entirely of five 'nevers'—that was all he could think of" (325).

- The other repetition in Hermann's monologue, "forever, and forever, and forever," recalls Macbeth's triple "tomorrow and tomorrow and tomorrow" where, once again, a Shakespearean tragic hero contemplates "the way to dusty death" (5. 5. 19, 23). It, too, may be a shadow of the quintuple "never" of *King Lear*.

It is a mark of Nabokov's style, and Shakespeare's, that mental dysfunction is sometimes indicated by linguistic compulsiveness. Certainly Hermann's thoughts on death and the afterlife demonstrate, in their obsession with the language and imagery of Shakespeare's tragic heroes, a narrator more disturbed than he would like to have us believe.

There are several other Shakespearean references in *Despair*. For example, Hermann proudly affirms that he:

> Had a way of my own with Russian and foreign classics: thus, for example, when rendering "in my own words" the plot of *Othello* (which was, mind you, perfectly familiar to me) I made the Moor skeptical and Desdemona unfaithful. (56)

Elsewhere, he cites the Shakespearean stage direction "in another part of the country" (151) and refers to Othello's final soliloquy: "stage asides." The eloquent hiss: "soft now!" (64) (Othello's speech begins "Soft you, a word or two before you go" (5. 2. 337).

In his early Russian-language writings, we see the young Nabokov, who as an adolescent had devoured the complete works of Shakespeare, incorporating Shakespearean materials in a wide range of ways and in a wide range of works. In his Russian plays, poems, translations, short stories, and novels, Nabokov's consciousness and his literary output is colored by his familiarity with Shakespeare. Sometimes, as in *The Tragedy of Mr. Morn*, his work seems saturated with a Shakespearean influence; in other writing, such as *Laughter in the Dark*, that influence is less pervasive, but never is it absent. As Nabokov evolved from his identity as a Russian author into an English language literary artist, he had before him always the life and works of William Shakespeare, the greatest writer in the history of the English language.

# "Which is Sebastian?" What's in a (Shakespearean and Nabokovian) Name?

My brother he is in Elysium (*Twelfth Night*, 1. 2. 4)

I remember you did supplant your brother ... (*The Tempest*, 2.1. 273–4)

*The Real Life of Sebastian Knight* was Nabokov's first English-language novel, published in 1941, not long after his arrival in the New World in May, 1940. Still somewhat tentative about his mastery of literary English, he sought the assistance of Professor Agnes Perkins of Wellesley College as he read the final proofs (Boyd, *American Years* 39). He need not have bothered: in plot, character, theme, and language, the novel is clearly the work of a master. *The Real Life of Sebastian Knight* offers a rewarding and tantalizing first taste of the English language and Nabokov's links to Shakespeare, once both authors were writing in the same tongue.

In his very clever note "See Under Sebastian," Gennady Barabtarlo speaks for many readers of Nabokov and of *The Real Life of Sebastian Knight* when he observes "Something in the name of Sebastian Knight has often made me pause and wonder" (24). He observes that the name is most uncommon in the Russian social circle into which Sebastian was born, and partly for that reason, there "seems to be something deliberate about Sebastian" (25). Barabtarlo suggests that "Sebastian Knight" is a near-perfect anagram of "Knight is absent," with only a single "a" left out. This seems a perceptive and persuasive reading; I propose a Shakespearean alternative below.

The plot of the novel involves the search of the living narrator, known only as "V," to find his dying half-brother Sebastian, both physically and biographically. "V" recounts his desperate rush to reach the bedside of Sebastian, only to fall victim to a grotesque case of mistaken identity which results in his watching over the final moments of the wrong man, and his discovery that Sebastian has already died and disappeared. Sebastian is, as Barabtarlo points out, "absent." The novel also revolves around "V's" trying to reconstruct the biography of Sebastian, an effort which ultimately seems as frustrating as the rush to the death bed. At the end of the work, in a phrase which foreshadows the Humbert Humbert–Claire Quilty tussle in

*Lolita* ("he rolled over me, I rolled over him. We rolled over me. They rolled over him. We rolled over us ..." [299]), "V" proclaims, "I am Sebastian, or Sebastian is I, or perhaps we both are someone whom neither of us knows" (205). I would not dispute Barabtarlo's anagrammatic explanation for the name "Sebastian." But I do propose an alternative, or supplemental reading. There are two characters with that name in Shakespeare's works, and in both cases they function in the dramas primarily in their role as *brothers* of other more central characters, just as Nabokov's Sebastian. In one case, *Twelfth Night*, Shakespeare's Sebastian is the brother of a "V"—Viola. Andrew Field in his controversial *Nabokov: His Life in Art* noticed "the Shakespearean echoes in the characters' given names."[1]

In *The Tempest*, Sebastian is the caustic and malevolent brother of Alonso, King of Naples. Early in the play, Antonio, who has usurped *his* brother Prospero's position as Duke of Milan, tempts Sebastian to emulate him, slay Alonso, and take over the throne of Naples.

> ANTONIO:          Say this were death
> That now hath seized them, why, they were no worse
> Than they are now. There be that can rule Naples
> As well as he that sleeps ... O, that you bore
> The mind that I do! What a sleep were this
> For your advancement! Do you understand me?
> SEBASTIAN: Methinks I do ... I remember
> You did supplant your brother Prospero.
> ANTONIO: And look how well my garments sit upon me ...
> SEBASTIAN:          Thy case, dear friend,
> Shall be my precedent. As thou got'st Milan
> I'll come by Naples. Draw thy sword. (2. 1. 264–96)

Sebastian embraces the plot, but it is foiled when Ariel wakes the sleeping shipwrecked nobles.

In the play's final scene, in which Prospero reveals himself to Alonso and his party, including Antonio and Sebastian, many readers of *The Tempest* have noted that Antonio says not a word to Prospero, who has forgiven him: no apology, no recognition of his malfeasance. Sebastian, however, offers a couple of comments during this scene. His words do not clearly convey either regret or continued culpability: he remarks on the drunkenness of Stephano, then teases him, then accuses Caliban, Stephano, and Trinculo of robbing the "luggage"—stolen apparel—in which they appear. Without violating Shakespeare's words, a theatrical director of *The Tempest* could easily present Sebastian at play's end as an unrepentant fratricidal plotter, or as relieved and pleased by Prospero's restoration and the generally just and

happy conclusion of the action (Alonso's son Ferdinand will wed Prospero's
daughter, Miranda, and they will become the rulers of Naples).[2]

Clearly, Sebastian is in *The Tempest* in order to be a *brother*, set in parallel
with Antonio, the evil brother of Prospero: Sebastian and Alonso echo
and reinforce the fraternal relationship between Prospero and Antonio. It
is also almost exclusively in the part of *brother* that we see Shakespeare's
other Sebastian, in *Twelfth Night*. (Of course, "Knight" and "night" are
homophones.)

Twins Viola and Sebastian are separated in a shipwreck, and Viola,
the play's protagonist, believes Sebastian perished. Disguising herself as
a boy, she enters the service of the Duke of Illyria, wooing, on his behalf,
Lady Olivia. Olivia, believing the gender-altering disguise, falls in love
with Viola, who calls herself Cesario. After much comic mischief in the
subplot, Sebastian appears, and Olivia promptly asks *him* to marry her,
not understanding that she is speaking to the twin brother rather than the
sister disguised as a male. All is, of course, finally cleared up when Viola and
Sebastian finally appear together, to the amazement of all:

> DUKE: One face, one voice, one habit, and two persons—
> A natural perspective that is and is not ....
> ANTONIO: [a sea captain, friend of Sebastian]: How have you made
> division of yourself?
> An apple cleft in two is not more twin
> Than these two creatures. Which is Sebastian? (5. 1. 215–23)

The play concludes with Olivia paired with Sebastian, the Duke with Viola.

A. M. Lyuksemburg, who annotated the translation of *The Real Life
of Sebastian Knight* into Russian (Symposium, 1997), suggests that the
reference to "a packet of sugared violets" in Nabokov's work "introduces the
Shakespearean motifs."[3] "Viola," of course, is the scientific name of the family
of plants commonly called "violet." Thus, this reading suggests, *Twelfth
Night*'s Viola becomes *The Real Life of Sebastian Knight*'s many violets. Are
violets a kind of "key" to the *Twelfth Night* motif in *The Real Life of Sebastian
Knight*?

There are several references to violets in Nabokov's novel, including these
three:

1. When Sebastian's mother comes to pay him a visit (the only time she
   does so), "she thrust into Sebastian's hand a small parcel of sugar-coated
   violets" (10).

2. Later, as a boy, "V" discovers the key to a drawer Sebastian keeps
   locked, opens the drawer, and finds "a small muslin bag of violet

sweets" (17). This could well be the same violet sweets his mother gave Sebastian earlier.

3. Still later, when "V" goes through Sebastian's belongings after his death, he finds in his brother's bathroom "The glass shelf, bare save for an empty talc-powder tin with violets figured between its shoulders, standing there alone, reflected in the mirror like a coloured advertisement" (37). It does not seem to me to be over-reading to suggest that what is being "advertised" here is the paired violets—the tin and its reflection; as Viola and Sebastian are, as twins, "reflected in the mirror."

Yet another link between Shakespeare's comedy and Nabokov's novel comes when Viola, in the play's final scene, proves her identity to her twin Sebastian by noting that her father died when she was thirteen (5. 1. 244). Of course, her twin Sebastian was exactly her age. The very first sentence of Nabokov's work, tells us that "Sebastian Knight was born on the thirty-first of December, 1899 ..." (5). Later, we learn that Sebastian's father died early in 1913 (6–7), when Nabokov's Sebastian would have been 13, just as Shakespeare's Sebastian when he lost his father.

A curious connection between "knight" and "knight's move," Russian literature, and Shakespeare can be found in the writings of the Russian writer Viktor Shklovsky. His works began appearing in English in the 1970s; he wrote extensively on Shakespeare; and he is the author of a series of formalist essays entitled *The Knight's Move*. Elsewhere, he writes:

> Therefore, to the question of Tolstoi: "Why does Lear not recognize Kent and Kent, Edgar?" one may answer: because this is necessary for the creation of the drama and the unreality disturbed Shakespeare no more than the question "Why cannot a Knight move straight?" disturbs a chess player.

This is an inviting triangular connection which might be worth exploring further by scholars more familiar than I with Shklovsky's writings.[4]

Shakespeare figures elsewhere in *The Real Life of Sebastian Knight*, the play *Hamlet* most prominently. Sebastian declares that one of the things he most likes about England and English is "a purple passage in Hamlet" (68). (Priscilla Meyer believes that "purple passage" is Queen Gertrude's citation of purple, "violet" flowers when speaking of Ophelia's death.) When "V" catalogs a list of books he finds on Sebastian's bookshelf, the list begins with *Hamlet* and ends with *King Lear*. And, amusingly, "V" describes Sebastian's pulling the leg of his secretary, Mr. Goodman: "Sebastian speaking of his very first novel (unpublished and destroyed) explained that it was about a fat young student who travels home to find his mother married to his uncle; this uncle, an ear-specialist, had murdered the student's father. Mr. Goodman misses the joke" (64).

To return to *The Tempest* and *Twelfth Night*, there are other obvious and subtle thematic links between Nabokov's novel and the two Shakespeare plays. Clearly, *Twelfth Night*, with the confusion between Viola and Sebastian (as well as the gender confusion between Viola and Cesario, her male disguise) parallels the Sebastian—"V" theme of *The Real Life of Sebastian Knight*. In both works, characters mistake the identity of other characters, and, more originally, key characters seem to mistake their own identities. A similar theme, in a more minor key, operates in *The Tempest*. Here, too, characters do not really know each other: Ferdinand does not know until the last scene that Miranda is the daughter of a former Duke of Milan; Caliban does not realize that Stephano and Trinculo are comic incompetents; Alonso and Sebastian do not recognize that their actions are being overseen by Prospero. The theme of identity is tantalizingly raised at the end of the First Folio edition of *The Tempest*, where the setting is described, tellingly and mysteriously, as "The Scene, an un-inhabited island." What does this mean? That "no one" lives there? What about Prospero and Miranda? What about Caliban and Ariel and the spirits?

These queries lead us from the issue of "identity" to the metadramatic level of both plays. Prospero's moving soliloquy in Act IV recognizes that *The Tempest* is a play, set in a theater:

> Our revels now are ended. These our actors,
> As I foretold you, were all spirits and
> Are melted into air, into thin air;
> And, like the baseless fabric of this vision,
> The cloud-capped towers, the gorgeous palaces,
> The solemn temples, the great globe itself,
> Yea, all which it inherit, shall dissolve,
> And, like this insubstantial pageant faded,
> Leave not a rack behind. We are such stuff
> As dreams are made on, and our little life
> Is rounded with a sleep. (4. 1, 148–58)

*The Tempest* was long seen, understandably but probably incorrectly, as representing Shakespeare's farewell to the stage in Prospero's farewell to his own magic art. Most modern students of the play would not wholly subscribe to the autobiographical reading. But seeing the parallels between Prospero's art and that of his creator is inescapable.

Similarly, *Twelfth Night* is shot through with self-referential images of the theater. Thus, when Olivia asks Viola in the disguise of Cesario if she/he is a "comedian" (actor), Viola's response, noted by Anne Richter in *Shakespeare and the Idea of the Play*, is "I am not that I play" (1. 5. 180–1) (130–6). When Feste, the Clown, taunts Malvolio in 4. 2, he compares himself to the traditional character in the Morality plays:

> I'll be with you again
> In a trice
> Like to the old Vice. (124–6)

And, of course, the play ends with the same character proclaiming:

> But that's all one, our play is done,
> And we'll strive to please you every day. (5. 1. 408–9)

Self-reflexivity—writing fiction about writing fiction—is a frequent feature of Nabokov's work, and *The Real Life of Sebastian Knight* is certainly no exception. As Stephen Jan Parker has pointed out, the novel is a work of art which is an exploration of "the nature of art" (128). Discussing the narrator "V's" explanation of Sebastian's aesthetics, Vladimir E. Alexandrov notes how close Sebastian's literary philosophy and practice are to Nabokov's own "metaliterary themes and praxis" (143). He cites "V"'s description of a painter who paints "not the painting of a landscape, but the painting of different ways of painting a certain landscape." (In *Pnin*, Victor, the titular character's son, paints a picture of the sky … as reflected in the complex curve of an automobile fender.) In describing Knight's book *The Prismatic Bezel*, "V" observes that the work "can be thoroughly enjoyed once it is understood that the heroes of the book are what can be loosely called 'methods of composition'" (95). Priscilla Meyer hypothesizes that not only is *The Real Life of Sebastian Knight* a book about doubles—it has itself a "double," the novel *Despair*. Nabokov, then, like Shakespeare, creates a work of art about the workings of art.

Finally, in Shakespeare's *Twelfth Night* and *The Tempest*, and Nabokov's *The Real Life of Sebastian Knight*, the shared "Sebastian" names lead us to what may be the deepest theme of both authors, that magical place where the motifs of identity and of self-reflexive art come together. "I am Sebastian, or Sebastian is I, or perhaps we both are someone whom neither of us knows" (205), says "V." If "V" is in some sense "Viola," seeking her lost brother, "V" is also "Vladimir," whose literary works are very much like those of Sebastian Knight. "V" and Sebastian are both someone neither of them knows: they are simultaneously their creator and they are the creations of their creator. Is Shakespeare's Viola actually Viola, or is she Cesario, her male counterpart, or is she the male actor playing both Viola and Cesario, or is she, ultimately, the words Shakespeare found to create Viola, Sebastian, Cesario, and *Twelfth*

*Night?* "A great while ago the world begun, / Hey, ho, the wind and the rain; / But that's all one, our play is done, / And we'll strive to please you every day" (5. 1. 406–9). If *Twelfth Night* is really a play of mistaken identity, the biggest identity mistake of all would be to forget that Viola and Sebastian are figments of Shakespeare's imagination. At the end of *The Tempest*, too, Shakespeare reminds the audience members that they *are* an audience, that what they have been watching are "actors," who "were all spirits and are melted into air, into thin air." In the play's epilogue, the actor playing Prospero continues to play Prospero, and also simultaneously plays the actor playing Prospero:

> Now my charms are all o'erthrown,
> And what strength I have's mine own,
> Which is most faint. Now 'tis true
> I must here be confined by you,
> Or sent to Naples. Let me not,
> Since I have my dukedom got
> And pardoned the deceiver, dwell
> In this bare island by your spell
> But release me from my bands,
> With the help of your good hands.
> Gentle breath of yours my sails
> Must fill, or else my project fails,
> Which was to please. (Epilogue, 1–13)

The real *Real Life of Sebastian Knight* is a novel, a fiction, in which the titular character owes his name, at least in part, and his reality, which is the reality of art, to two other fictional persons invented by Shakespeare.

# 4

# No Left Turn, or Something Rotten in the State: *Bend Sinister* and *Hamlet*

*Bend Sinister*, written between 1941 and 1946 and published in 1947, was Nabokov's second novel in English, following *The Real Life of Sebastian Knight*. It was reprinted in 1964, with a new Introduction by the author, as part of the *Time* Magazine Reading Program.[1]

The novel tells the story of Adam Krug, a philosopher of impressive physical and intellectual strength. Just before the action of the book begins, Krug's wife has died, and his country has been overwhelmed by a revolution not unlike that depicted in *The Tragedy of Mr. Morn* ... that is, a kind of grotesque parody of the Russian Revolution. The new, dictatorial, government is headed by a lout named Paduk, nicknamed "The Toad," who is an old schooldays acquaintance and playground victim of Krug's bullying. Paduk's regime attempts to glorify the "common man"—indeed, his party is called the "Party of the Average Man" (67). The links to the Russian Communist revolution, party, and government are inescapable (although Nabokov steadfastly sought to escape them). Paduk and his party's political philosophy is based upon the work of one Skotoma, namely:

> At every given level of world-time there was, he said, a certain computable amount of human consciousness distributed throughout the population of the world. This distribution was uneven and therein lay the root of all our woes. Human beings, he said, were so many vessels containing unequal portions of this essentially uniform consciousness. It was, however, quite possible, he maintained, to regulate the capacity of human vessels ... He introduced the idea of balance as a basis for universal bliss and called his theory "Ekwilism" ... He died soon after his treatise appeared and so was spared the discomfort of seeing his vague and benevolent Ekwilism transformed (while retaining its name) into a violent and virulent political doctrine, a doctrine that proposed to enforce spiritual uniformity upon his native land through the medium of the most standardized section of the inhabitants, namely the army, under the supervision of a bloated and dangerously divine State. (67)[2]

Trying to win the endorsement of Adam Krug, Paduk and his thugs destroy most of his family and friends. Still, Krug refuses to believe in the seriousness of the threat to him until it is too late. His beloved son is abducted, then grotesquely and brutally tortured to death.

Just as the whole weight of this intolerable news is about to crush the protagonist, his creator, the narrator/author of *Bend Sinister*, decides to be merciful to his own fictional hero:

> It was at that moment, just after Krug had fallen through the bottom of a confused dream and sat up on the straw with a gasp—and just before his reality, his remembered hideous misfortune could pounce upon him—it was then that I felt a pang of pity for Adam and slid towards him along an inclined beam of pale light—causing instantaneous madness, but at least saving him from the senseless agony of his logical fate. With a smile of infinite relief on his tear-stained face, Krug lay back on the straw. (233)

> The novel ends with the totally insane, but mercifully happy, Adam Krug shot by Paduk's guards and an abrupt transition back to the narrator's study as he puts the late-night finishing touches on his book. Moths bump into his screen, and he declares it a "good night for mothing." (241)

*Bend Sinister* is permeated by a complex network of Shakespearean references, ranging from vague allusions to lengthy, overt discussions.

An example of the most casual and questionable of such allusions might be the "faint hint of Shakespearean yokels in the first set of guards" in the novel's opening scene, as noted by Hyde (142), or the fact that Krug's wife's sister has the Shakespearean name we have already encountered in *The Real Life of Sebastian Knight*—Viola.

Here is a quick catalog of some other passing references in the novel. To begin with, Nabokov alludes directly to many of Shakespeare's works:

> "No, no," said Yanovski, "not Me Nisters [*sic*]. He all alone. Like King Lear." (39)

> "I doubt," said Krug as he went through his pockets, "whether these fancies which have bred maggot-like from ancient taboos could be really transformed into acts ..." [*The Merchant of Venice*, 3. 2. 63, "Tell me where is fancy bred ..."] (6)

Quite a bit less casual or passing is the fact that the novel's villain Paduk or The Toad almost certainly gets his name from Act 3, scene 5 of *Hamlet*, in which the Prince, speaking to Gertrude, says, describing his uncle Claudius, that work's villain:

'T'were good you let him know,
For who that's but a queen, fair, sober, wise,
Would from a paddock [an Elizabethan word meaning "toad"], from a
    bat, a gib [tomcat]
Such dear concerning hide? (192)

Perhaps the most interesting pseudo-Shakespeareanism in all of Nabokov's
work is this passage from a non-existent play:

The unfinished translation of his favorite lines in Shakespeare's greatest
play—
    Follow the pertaunt jaucing 'neath the rack
    With her pale skein-mate.
Crept up tentatively but it would not scan because in his native tongue
"rack" was anapestic. (28)

Of this passage, Nabokov writes in his Introduction:

In this crazy-mirror of terror and art a pseudo quotation made up of
obscure Shakespeareanisms (Chapter III) somehow produces, despite
its lack of literal meaning, the blurred diminutive image of the acrobatic
performance that so gloriously supplies the bravura ending for the next
chapter. (xvi)

The novel also contains a number of references to Shakespeare the man—
biographical comparisons, images, and the like:

Nature had once produced an Englishman whose domed head had
been a hive of words; a man who had only to breathe on any particle
of his stupendous vocabulary to have that particle live and expand and
throw out tremulous tentacles until it became a complex image with a
pulsing brain and correlated limbs. Three centuries later, another man,
in another country, was trying to render those rhythms and metaphors
in a different tongue. (107)

One day Ember and he had happened to discuss the possibility of their
having invented *in toto* the works of William Shakespeare, spending
millions and millions on the hoax, smothering with hush money
countless publishers, librarians, the Stratford-on-Avon people, since
in order to be responsible for all references to the poet during three
centuries of civilization, these references had to be assumed to be
spurious interpolations injected by the inventors into actual works
they had re-edited. (73–4). [Note: a cogent argument contra the anti-
Stratfordian thesis.][3]

… imagine the patronizing smile of the *ci-devant* William Shakespeare on seeing a former scribbler of hopelessly bad plays blossom anew as the Poet Laureate of heaven. (67)

The majority of shorter Shakespearean citations, however, focus upon *Hamlet*, for example:

It bristled with farcical anachronisms; it was suffused with a sense of gross maturity (as in *Hamlet* the churchyard scene); its somewhat meager setting was patched up with odds and ends from other (later) plays. (55)

(Why? Ah, "that is the question," as Monsieur Homais once remarked, quoting *le journal d'hier*; a question which is answered in a wooden voice by the Portrait on the title page of the First Folio.) (93)

"He was a great man, a brilliant brain, a gentle heart, but he had had the misfortune of jokingly referring to my young sister as 'cet petite Phyrne que se croit Ophelie.' You see, the romantic little thing had attempted to drown herself in his swimming pool." (162)

[Krug's deceased wife is described, Ophelia-like as] following in willowed shade. (27)

Olga and the boy taking part in some silly theatricals, she getting drowned, he losing his life … (213)

A full-scale discussion of *Hamlet*, the most amplified such passage in any of Nabokov's novels, takes place in Chapter 7, where from pages 94 to 110 we find a review from 1947 by Nathan Rothman in *Saturday Review*, "a conscious tribute to the master … where Nabokov stops his narrative cold, to insert a long and fanciful dialog on Shakespeare and *Hamlet*, as Joyce did in *Ulysses*" (33). In this section, a straightforward and attractive character named Ember, an academic colleague of Krug, is trying to distract his friend from brooding upon the death of his wife. Like *Pale Fire*'s Conmal, but with considerably greater competence, Ember is working as a Shakespearean translator. His discussion with Krug focuses first upon some difficulties of a production of *Hamlet* with which he is currently involved. The two actors capable of playing the role of the protagonist have wisely fled the country. Ember and Krug are amused by the clumsy politicized version of the play currently in favor, based upon "the late Professor Hamm's extraordinary work 'The Real Plot of Hamlet'" (95). Hamm's ham-handed *Hamlet* is a "tragedy of the masses" in which the real hero is Fortinbras, "this fine Nordic youth," who assumes control over the "decadent democracy [of] miserable Denmark which had been so criminally misruled by degenerate King Hamlet and Judeo-Latin Claudius" (96).[4] Krug, in turn, tells Ember of another deformed *Hamlet*, an American filmed version:

> We might be shown, he said ... R. following young L. [*sic*—That is, of course, Laertes and Reynaldo] through the Quartier Latin, Polonius in his youth acting Caesar at the University Playhouse, the skull in Hamlet's gloved hands developing the features of a live jester (with the censor's permission), perhaps even lusty old King Hamlet smiting with a poleaxe the Polacks skidding and sprawling on the ice ... And then there was Ophelia's death. To the sounds of Liszt's *Les Funerailles* she would be shown wrestling—or as another rivermaid's father would have said "wrustling"—with a willow. A lass, a salix. He recommended a side shot of the glassy water. To feature a phloating leaph. Then back to her little white hand, holding a wreath trying to reach, trying to wreathe a phallacious sliver. (100–1)

As is evident in this passage, both scholars enjoy some rather erudite word-play concerning Hamlet. Clearly Nabokov is enjoying it himself: in oral conversation, of course, those "ph" substitutions for "f" [phloating leaph] would not be audible. There follows the passage cited earlier, concerning over-complexifying authorial mysteries, which "proves" Homer wrote Shakespeare's works.

Finally, there is some additional play with translational possibilities for the "To be or not to be" soliloquy (remembering always that Nabokov himself had attempted to translate the play including this speech into Russian):[5]

> But enough of this, let us hear Ember's rendering of some famous lines:
> Ubit'il ne ubit'? Vot est'oprosen.
>
> Vto bude edler: v rasume tzerpieren
> Ognepraschchi I strely zlovo roka –
> (Or as a Frenchman might have it:)
> L' engorgerai-je ou non? Voci le vrai problem.
> Est-il plus noble en sol de supporter quand meme
> Et les dards et le feu d'un accablant destin— (105)

What must be clear from this anthology of quotations is that Hamlet is of considerably more than tangential importance in *Bend Sinister*. There are important and illuminating links between the drama and the novel in character development and in such thematic areas as social criticism, literary gamesmanship, and artistic self-consciousness.

***

There are several revealing and important ways in which Nabokov's Adam Krug resembles Shakespeare's Hamlet. Both, to begin with, are essentially thinkers. One is a teacher, the other a student. Both are thrust against their will and against their nature into intensely dangerous and physically threatening socio/political situations. "The time is out of joint," as Hamlet observes, and concludes even more accurately, "O cursed spite, / That ever I was born to set it right" (1. 5. 188–9). Among Krug's first words in *Bend Sinister*, when he is cautioned not to venture out into the night without a proper pass, are "I am not interested in politics ... and I have only the river to cross" (5). Later, the President of the university where he teaches chides him,

> My dear friend, you know well my esteem for you. But you are a dreamer, a thinker. You do not realize the circumstances. You say impossible, unmentionable things. Whatever we think of—of that person, we must keep it to ourselves. We are in deathly danger. You are jeopardizing the—everything ..." (46)

In both of the works, the authors go out of their ways to stress the "noble minds" the heroes possessed before the tumultuous events described in novel and play began. Ophelia, of course, praises the Hamlet of the past.

> O what a noble mind is here o'erthrown!
> The courtier's, soldier's, scholar's, eye, tongue, sword,
> Th' expectancy and rose of the fair state
> The glass of fashion, and the mold of form
> Th' observed of all observers ... (3. 1. 151–5)

Nabokov offers a similarly impressive description of Krug:

> Professor Adam Krug, the philosopher, was seated somewhat apart from the rest, deep in a cretonned armchair, with his hairy hands on its arms. He was a big heavy man in his early forties, with untidy, dusty, or faintly grizzled locks and a roughly hewn face suggestive of the uncouth chess master or of the morose composer, but more intelligent. The strong compact dusky forehead had that particular hermetic aspect (a bank safe? A prison wall?) which the brows of thinkers possess. (141)

Indeed, both Krug and Hamlet are thinkers of the same sort: they are not scientists, pragmatists, or problem-solvers, but speculative philosophers. Hamlet, obviously, thinks deeply on the issues of life, death, and dying throughout the play and especially in the most famous soliloquy in Western literature. Krug, too, broods, especially after the death of his wife, on the same eschatological issues as Hamlet. Shakespeare's hero thinks about "the undiscover'd country, from whose bourn / No traveler returns" (except, of course, for ghosts). He probes what it means "to be" dead, as contrasted with the instantaneous moment of dying. Krug ruminates:

> Are not these problems so hard to solve because my own mind is not made up yet in regard to your death? My intelligence does not accept the transformation of physical discontinuity into the permanent continuity of a non-physical element escaping the obvious law, nor can it accept the inanity of accumulating incalculable treasures of thought and sensation, and thought-behind-thought and sensation-behind-sensation, to lose them all at once and forever in a fit of black nausea followed by infinite nothingness. (87–8).

The habit of deep thought leads both men to patterns of behavior, or more accurately, patterns of the lack of behavior, which are indecisive and dangerous. Hamlet's lack of action throughout most of *Hamlet* is of course a critical truism. Certainly the figure of the brooding, passive Prince of Denmark is no longer our sole image of Hamlet. But it remains true that his inaction throughout most of the drama is an important ingredient of his tragedy. Of course, he himself calls our attention forcefully to this element of his character:

> Yet I,
> A dull and muddy-mettled rascal, peak
> Like John-a-dreams, unpregnant of my cause,
> And can say nothing. No, not for a king,
> Upon whose property and most dear life
> A damned defeat was made. (2. 2. 572–7)

Likewise, Krug is inactive in the face of a situation which demands quick action. He refused to flee Paduk's despotism when such flight was still possible; he fails either to support or oppose the new regime; most catastrophically, he does not protect himself or his family.

Tragically, Krug is just like Hamlet in that the indecision and inaction springing from his speculative and philosophical temper is, in no small part, responsible for the deaths of his loved ones and finally himself. Krug's habit of precise and careful reasoning, like Hamlet's, leaves him incapable of comprehending and responding to the irrational but very real horror in the political world around him. Krug and Hamlet are both first seen mourning the recent loss of a close family member—Krug's wife and Hamlet's father. Before *Hamlet* and *Bend Sinister* are over, the two will see the deaths of others about whom they care deeply—sweetheart and son. Both works conclude with the death of the hero, a demise which has been growing more and more inevitable as the action progresses. Clearly, in neither work is reason or deep thought any kind of "tragic flaw" in the characters' natures. Shakespeare and Nabokov both admire the minds of their protagonists. But that quality in both characters becomes fatal and tragic as a consequence of flaws in the societies around them, and in their failure to react to those external exigencies. Hamlet would have been a good student and prince, Krug a good philosopher and family man, in an ordered and sane state. Put another way, the "tragedy" in *Hamlet* and *Bend Sinister* (and perhaps in most tragedies) occurs in the explosive combination of an admirable if somewhat over-developed character trait, and a defective context.

***

These similarities between Nabokov's and Shakespeare's protagonists in *Hamlet* and *Bend Sinister* lead us deeper into the thematic cores of both works. We have seen how both Krug and Hamlet engage in considerable eschatological speculation. In a larger way, though, the novel and the play also brood on questions centered on dying and death.

Both *Hamlet* and *Bend Sinister* view death from a dual perspective. On the one hand, death looms over the entire action and assumes a gigantic aspect. It defines life, and is the prime source of raising ultimate questions about the meaning of life, the nature of humankind, and the existence of the supernatural. Both works begin with mourning (Krug's wife; Hamlet's father) and end with slaughter. And yet, for both Nabokov and Shakespeare, death, no matter how huge and overwhelming, also contains an accidental, casual, almost coincidental element. Thus, for example, Hamlet slays Polonius "by accident," thinking he is Claudius hiding behind the arras. Adam Krug's son is also killed "accidentally":

> This ought never to have happened. We are terribly sorry … You will certainly appreciate … the effort we make to atone for the worst blunder that could have been committed under the circumstances. We are ready to condone many things, including murder, but there is one crime which can never, never be forgiven; and that is carelessness in the performance of one's official duty. (204–5)

These events seem to be random and accidental to those participating in, and suffering through, them, and to us at first. But they are not. Both works make clear, finally, that there is a shaping consciousness directing these "accidents."

Adam Krug, tormented throughout *Bend Sinister* by the diabolical social forces which are reshaping his world, is finally rescued, as I noted earlier, by the mercy of his creator. The deity/author feels "a pang of pity for Adam and slid towards him along an inclined beam of pale light—causing instantaneous madness" (232). (It is interesting that the author of *Pale Fire* sees himself moving along a shaft of "pale light."). Krug smiles in relief, lies down "amazed and happy" (233). Throughout the novel's remaining few pages, he is repeatedly described as "playful," "cheerful," and "happy." In the Introduction to the 1964 reprinting of *Bend Sinister*, Nabokov comments upon Krug's revelation and his happy ending. Nabokov insists that an important character is:

> An anthropomorphic deity impersonated by me. In the last chapter of the book this deity experiences a pang of pity for his creature and hastens to take over. Krug, in a sudden moonburst of madness, understands that he is in good hands: nothing on earth really matters, there is nothing to fear, and death is but a question of style, a mere literary device, a musical resolution. And as Olga's rosy soul, emblematized already in an earlier chapter (Nine), bombinates in the damp dark at the bright window of my room, [the moth cited earlier] comfortably Krug returns unto the bosom of his maker. (xviii)

One fairly standard definition of "madness" or "insanity" suggests that it is the condition of an individual totally unable to function cognitively within his or her world. This is certainly a valid description of Krug's state at the conclusion of *Bend Sinister*. (It could also be argued that it is a valid description of his state throughout the novel!) Nabokov, in the passage cited above, asserts that Krug is "insane" because Adam realizes—correctly—that his world is without meaning, because it is not real. And, of course, he is right: it isn't. It is a fiction created by Vladimir Nabokov. Krug receives a kind of literary/religious revelation, a visit from his Creator, assuring him that he is but a character in a novel. The knowledge that he is nothing more than the creature of the "anthropomorphic deity" impersonated by Nabokov enables Krug to ignore the pain and suffering of his world, and to meet his "death" with confidence and good cheer. He is, after all, comfortably returned to the bosom of his maker as the novel ends. None of us could ask for more …

Nabokov's seemingly unique resolution of this novel is, when stripped of some touches of meta-literary gamesmanship, strikingly parallel to the resolution of *Hamlet*. Like Adam Krug, Shakespeare's protagonist comes to the resolution of the tortuous problems which beset him during the action of the drama when he realizes he is but a "creature" of a maker who is controlling his world. Hamlet spends much of the play lashing himself because *he* cannot put right the wrongs he so clearly sees in his surroundings—his father's death and his mother's remarriage. It is only when he realizes that he does not to have to take sole, or even primary, responsibility for those corrections that he is free to act. Hamlet begins to learn that his life is being directed by a

Creator when he uncovers Claudius' plot to have him killed in England, and escapes to return to Denmark. Describing that revelation, he says,

> Sir, in my heart there was a kind of fighting
> That would not let me sleep. Methought I lay
> Worse than the mutines in the bilboes. Rashly
> (And praised be rashness for it) let us know
> Our indiscretion sometime serves us well
> When our deep plots do pall, and that should learn us
> There's a divinity that shapes our ends,
> Rough-hew them how we will. (5. 2. 6–13)

Later in the same scene, Hamlet reaffirms that because there is a controlling force shaping his life and destiny, he too has "nothing to fear, and death is but a question of style":

> Not a whit, we defy augury. There is special providence in the fall of a sparrow. If it be now, 'tis not to come; if it be not to come, it will be now; if be not now, yet it will come. The readiness is all. Since no man of aught he leaves knows, what is't to leave betimes? Let be. (221–6) [Hamlet here is citing the Bible: Matthew 10:29.]

Like Krug, Hamlet meets his end calmly and with an enlarged understanding of the limits of human volition and the infinite scope of providential care. His new-found peace is not identical to Adam Krug's lunatic cheerfulness, but it is close kin to it. Both are finally able to escape the agony of their shattered lives and achieve a kind of serenity in the face of death, through their new-found understanding that they are the creations of a "special providence," a "deity" who watches over them closely and guides their fates with mercy.

***

Nabokov's use of Shakespearean materials in *Bend Sinister* affords an irresistible and unresisted opportunity for some literary games and parody, but even in this more lighthearted area, serious thematic implications are never far from the surface. The grotesque parodies of *Hamlet*, described and mocked by Krug and Ember in Chapter 7, are, of course, humorous. But at the same time, they are also a chilling mirror of the distortions which have been forced upon the societies which spawned them. It is sobering to note that one of these parody versions of the play is a new version prepared specifically for the new government of Krug and Ember's homeland (never specifically named, but obviously of a Soviet flavor); the other is the scheme of an American film maker. Because Nabokov values and even venerates Shakespeare, it is clear that he has nothing but contempt for the impulse to degrade *Hamlet* into a piece of cheap, topical, social propaganda, or a backdrop for silly cinematic stunts. And he reveals here, once again, his distrust of actual theatrical productions of Shakespeare's dramas, which he is inclined to regard as unmatched literary achievements, but not as "scripts" for the stage. As G. M. Hyde observed, there is an important and revealing contrast between the "civilized literary consciousness represented by these two men [Krug and Ember]" and the "vulgar materialistic assaults on Shakespeare" they discuss (144). Nabokov takes the enterprise of artistic creation and literary understanding very seriously. He is suggesting here that grotesque literary criticism and revision is more than poor playing of an intellectual game: it is a reflection of a deformed, deforming, inhuman, vision of the world. Both *Bend Sinister* and *Hamlet* are works about men of intellectual power and moral tenderness trapped in vicious, "rotten" states, with which they have no effective power to contend. Nabokov always affirmed his total lack of interest in social satire and criticism, just as Shakespeare and his fellow Elizabethan authors were always under severe constraints when it came to contemporary political commentary. Nevertheless, it is clear that both write strongly and directly about the fate of individual consciousness when ensnared by a despotic social order. For Nabokov, a most successful emblem of that corrupted society is its distortion of art, particularly its distortion of *Hamlet*.

*Bend Sinister*'s strong sense of the importance of the literary imagination is linked to the motif of "translation." Ember is a translator of Shakespeare; the word games he and Krug play are based on translations, retranslations, and mistranslations of Shakespearean materials. The parody versions of *Hamlet* in Chapter 7 are translations. The issue of Shakespeare translation figures very importantly later in Nabokov's canon, of course, in *Pale Fire*. The larger general issue of translation, as such, explodes in Nabokov's monumental and controversial version of *Eugene Onegin*. For an author as sensitized to the precisions of language as Nabokov, perhaps there can be no possibility of true, successful translation. Instead, as Frank Kermode suggested in his review of *Bend Sinister* in *Encounter*, Ember's sincere attempts to translate Shakespeare are analogous to the crude handwriting traceries of the invented "Padukgraph" described in the novel: both are mechanical and lifeless mimicry, which miss all that is of value in the original (81–6).

A corollary of the theme of art in opposition to the despotic consciousness is the heightened meta-literary self-consciousness of both *Bend Sinister* and *Hamlet*. While hardly unique, both works call attention to themselves as art and artifice in a much more direct manner than is usual.

Shakespeare chose to embed in the midst of *Hamlet* another play which shadowed the plot within which it occurs. Whatever other effects the play-within-the-play has, it certainly reminds the audience of the drama that they are witnessing a theatrical production, just as the characters they are watching. Further, as countless commentators have noted, this device enables Shakespeare to make a number of telling observations on the art of the theater. Most notable of these are Hamlet's advice to the players ("the purpose of playing whose end, both at the first and now, was and is, to hold, as 'twere, the mirror up to nature ..." [3. 2. 20–2]) and his remarks on the state and nature of the theater:

> Good my lord, will you see the players well bestowed? Do you hear? Let them be well used, for they are the abstract and brief chronicles of the time. After your death you were better have a bad epitaph than their ill report while you live. (2. 2. 529–33)

It is revealing to observe that the two dramas in which Shakespeare seems to make the most sustained and direct commentary upon his own art of the theater are *Hamlet* and *The Tempest*, a pair of works which were among the most influential for Nabokov (as noted earlier, *Hamlet* is the most cited Shakespearean play in Nabokov's works, *The Tempest* is the third most common, after *Othello*).

Certainly *Bend Sinister* is a novel acutely aware of itself as literary artifice. Frequently Nabokov interrupts the narrative line of the work to remind the reader that the plot is just that, a *plot*, and that there is an author behind it.

> Which, of course, terminated the interview. Thus? Or perhaps in some other way? Did Krug really glance at the prepared speech? And if he did, was it really as silly as all that? He did; it was. The seedy tyrant, or the president of the State, or the dictator, or whoever he was—the man Paduk in a word, the Toad in another—did hand my favorite character a mysterious batch of neatly typed pages. The actor playing the recipient should be taught not to look at his hand while he takes the papers ... (135)

Most dramatic, of course, is the novel's conclusion. As Krug flings himself at Paduk and is shot down, the pretense of novelistic verisimilitude vanishes wholly, and the author himself appears:

> Krug ran towards him, and just a fraction of an instant before another and better bullet hit him, he shouted again: You, you—and the wall vanished, like a rapidly withdrawn slide, and I stretched myself and got up from among the chaos of written and rewritten pages, to investigate the sudden twang that something had made in striking the wire netting of my window. (241)

G. M. Hyde observes, correctly I believe, that *Bend Sinister*'s use of *Hamlet* is based upon a vision of Shakespeare's "faith in the power of language to renew thought and feeling by means of metaphor: the quintessential artistic function of language, as Nabokov sees it" (141). In the novel's self-consciousness, that "faith" proclaims itself overtly. In a passage like that cited just above from the end of the book, Nabokov seems to be saying: "here is what I can do; watch, now I'm doing it."

Nabokov has linked *Bend Sinister* to *Hamlet* through similarities in plot, character, and theme. He emphasizes that bond through extensive  Shakespearean quotation, generally, and from *Hamlet* in particular, and especially through the extended discussion of the play in Chapter 7. Both works proclaim that art, including that art which they themselves manifest, is the polar opposite of subhuman despots and rotten states. Indeed, it may be that the magic creative and re-creative power of words, freshly imagined and imaginatively used, is the best and only defense available to Hamlet, to Krug, to their creators, and to us.

# Hurricane Lolita:
# The Nabokovian Tempest

In 1955, the London *Sunday Times* published one of those perennial articles wherein important literary and cultural figures are asked their choices of the best books of the past year. Graham Greene, a writer of high standing in literary circles in the mid-twentieth century, recommended as one of his choices Vladimir Nabokov's *Lolita*. The novel would not be published in England until 1959, nor in the USA until 1958, and was thus a virtually unknown book by an author not widely known in America or Western Europe outside of subscribers to *The New Yorker*, a handful of discriminating readers, and the small Russian émigré community when Greene praised it. *Lolita* had just appeared, in English, under the rather questionable imprimatur of the Olympia Press, Paris, an enterprise of a curious literary figure named Maurice Girodias. Because of its unconventional and somewhat shocking subject matter, *Lolita* had been spurned by all the publishing houses to which Nabokov had submitted it, but in the case of Olympia, this impediment was an asset. Girodias clearly knew good literature when he encountered it, and he knew pornographic trash too. He gleefully published both. He made a particular specialty of bringing out books of high literary quality, which dealt with taboo materials. Girodias published Henry Miller, Jean Genet, and Samuel Becket. Olympia also proudly brought out titles such as *Until She Screams* and *The Sexual life of Robinson Crusoe* (Appel, xxxiv). Although Nabokov's story of a sexual liaison between a young teenaged girl and a middle-aged predator would almost certainly have been controversial regardless of the circumstances of its publication, the fact that it initially appeared as the product of a firm which was known as a purveyor of pornography helped to cement its reputation as a naughty novel.

Immediately after Greene's recommendation, he, Nabokov, and *Lolita* became the center of a swirl of literary discord. Today, over a half-century later, that controversy generally seems more humorous than substantial. In the United States, Orville Prescott proclaimed in the *New York Times* that *Lolita* was "repulsive," while in England, John Gordon of the *Sunday Express* found it "unrestrained pornography" (as opposed, I guess, to "restrained pornography" …) (11,19). Equally strong words were spoken in defense of what today is recognized as a remarkable literary work, and, by the standards of twenty-first-century literature, an equally remarkably un-pornographic one, albeit a novel the subject matter and narrator of which still leaves many readers uncomfortable. Thus began the stormy career of the book which its creator later jokingly called (in *Pale Fire*) "hurricane Lolita" (41).

Even today, *Lolita* has a vague reputation as being a steamy book about sex (especially among those who have never read anything by Nabokov). After first reading, it seems much more clearly to be about love, as well as lust. And following careful study, most readers have concluded that it is actually about art as much or more than anything else.[1] In that subtle elevation of thematic response from the worldly to the aesthetic is the novel's first interesting resemblance to its Shakespearean analogs.

In Shakespeare's late drama *The Tempest* (1611) there is a parallel movement, in that the play begins as an action/revenge fantasy, is quickly distilled into a magical love story, and concludes as a meditation on forgiveness, redemption, and, again, art—the art of the magician and the art of the poet, and the moment those become one and the same. Before focusing more intensely on *The Tempest*, there are a number of other references to Shakespeare's works, his life, and his image and reputation to briefly survey.

- Some of those citations are merely games: for example, the character Clare Quilty claims automobile license plates "WS 1564" and "SH 1616," thus creating a rather truncated biography of the dramatist's birth and death years (251).

- Somewhat more serious citations can also be found. We learn of Humbert's attitude towards the stage, which is not incongruent with Nabokov's, when he declares:

  I detest the theatre as being a primitive and putrid form, historically speaking, a form that smacks of stone-age rites and communal nonsense despite those individual injections of genius, such as, say, Elizabethan poetry which a closeted reader automatically pumps out of the stuff (200).

- Humbert describes the aptly named headmistress Pratt of Beardsley School for girls, where he contemplates sending Dolly. He (and Nabokov) point out her educational philistinism—or rather, let her point it out for herself, using Shakespeare as an illustration:

  To put it briefly, while adopting certain teaching techniques, we are more interested in communication than in composition. That is, with due respect to Shakespeare and others, we want our girls to *communicate* freely with the live world around rather than plunge into musty old books. (177)

- Near the end of the novel, when Humbert is shooting Quilty, his victim raves "I propose to borrow—you know, as the Bard said with that cold in his head, to borrow and to borrow and to borrow" (301).
- Other miscellaneous references include an actor who "received stage training at Elsinore playhouse"; "Mona coming to practice … a scene from *The Taming of the Shrew*"; and "Shakespeare, a ghost town in New Mexico, where bad man Russian Bill was colorfully hanged seventy years ago" (31, 191, 157).
- Michael Maar finds several allusions in the novel to *King Lear*. Some of these are convincing; others, such as Humbert's use of the phrase "marb**le ar**ms" pointing to "lear" are less so. A clearer reference to *Lear* is Humbert's observation:

I have often noticed that we are inclined to endow our friends with the stability of type that literary characters acquire in the reader's mind. No matter how many times we reopen "King Lear," never shall we find the good king banging his tankard in high revelry, all woes forgotten, at a jolly reunion with all three daughters and their lapdogs. (265—Actually, some eighteenth-century rewritings of the play come perilously close to such a distortion!)

- Monica Manolescu argues that Humbert Humbert's description of his youthful Arctic adventures is a parallel to Othello's wooing of Desdemona by recounting his trials.
- A clear reference to *A Midsummer Night's Dream* and an important iteration of a dominant theme in the novel is Humbert's description of "thick tears that poets and lovers shed" (52).
- When Humbert Humbert comes across a book entitled *Who's Who in the Limelight*, a kind of encyclopedia of the stage, he notes the entry (with a Poe reference) to "Pym, Roland" who "Received stage training at Elsinore Playhouse, Derby, NY" (31).
- Yet another *Hamlet* reference is Humbert's aside: ("'elusive' is good, by Polonius!") (152—Humbert is comparing his warnings to Dolly to foolish Polonius's admonitions to his daughter Ophelia).

The pattern of allusions to *The Tempest*, though, is more thorough and pervasive. It touches deeply the thematic core of Nabokov's best-known novel.

\*\*\*

Two of the most important early passages in Lolita are connected to each other and to *The Tempest* through one of those Nabokovian coincidences which are, of course, not coincidence at all but a gentle reminder of the authorial consciousness which is patterning the fiction. In Chapter 3 of Part 1, Humbert Humbert makes his most serious attempt to define the objects of his desire: nymphets. He chooses, characteristically, a rather curious set of images:

> Now I wish to introduce the following idea. Between the age limits of nine and fourteen there occur maidens who, to certain bewitched travelers, twice or many times older than they, reveal their true nature which is not human, but nymphic (that is, demoniac); and these chosen creatures I propose to designate as "nymphets."
>
> It will be marked that I substitute time terms for spatial ones. In fact, I would have the reader see "nine" and "fourteen" as the boundaries— the mirror beaches and rosy rocks—of an enchanted island haunted by those nymphets of mine and surrounded by a vast, misty sea. (16)

The image of the "enchanted island of time" and its nymphic inhabitants and bewitched visitors is immediately repeated twice: "that intangible island of entranced time where Lolita plays with her likes" (17), and "that same enchanted island of time" (18).

An enchanted island surrounded by a misty sea, peopled by magical sprites and visited by bewitched travelers certainly might make us think of *The Tempest*, but then again, it might not. There are many such locales in literature and folklore. A considerably more explicit suggestion, however, reminds us of the enchanted island, and makes the connection with *The Tempest* much clearer six chapters later.

In Chapter 11, Humbert transcribes a list of Lolita's classmates at the Ramsdale school (51–2). The list begins with Angel, Grace (an invocation surely). It proceeds through such luminaries as "Fantasia, Stella;" the pair of "roses" who surround "Haze, Dolores" (Lolita's real name), Mary Rose Hamilton, and Rosaline Honeck; two other "roses" including the colorful Carmine, Rose (the opera *Carmen* plays an important role in the novel, too); and Emil Rosato. Humbert quite rightly announces that the list is "a poem, a poem, forsooth!" (52). There are four sets of twins in the class, a typical (and realistically improbable) illustration of Nabokovian mirroring. One is particularly interesting. Just after "McFate, Aubrey" are "Miranda, Anthony," and "Miranda, Viola." This is surely a Shakespearean duo, all three names being those of well-known Shakespearean characters. "Miranda, Anthony" evokes Prospero's daughter Miranda as well as Prospero's brother Antonio, who has usurped him as the Duke of Milan. (In addition to *Antony and*

*Cleopatra, Twelfth Night*, as noted above, also has an Antonio and a Viola, and *Lolita*'s is described as "an Italian schoolmate" [46].)

A careful reader would find "Miranda" a name with echoes elsewhere in *Lolita*. Humbert Humbert grew up amidst the sea vistas of the "splendid Hotel Mirana," a Mediterranean resort owned by his father and the site of his earliest sexual awakenings (10). Perhaps the oceanside "Mirana" delicately reinforces the image of the island-raised Shakespearean "Miranda."[2] And, in the first chapter of the novel's second part, Humbert asks "And do you remember, Miranda, that other 'ultrasmart' robbers' den with complimentary morning coffee ... (147)." Appel suggests the source of this line is a poem by Belloc, but it also surely alludes to Prospero's questioning of Miranda in 1. 2: "canst thou remember a time before we came unto this cell?" (38–9).

If by this verbal clue and the earlier stress upon the importance of the "enchanted isle" motif, Nabokov alerts us to be aware of resemblances between *Lolita* and *The Tempest*, we will not be disappointed.

***

One clear parallel between *Lolita* and *The Tempest* is that both feature in a central role characters who are "monstrous"—Shakespeare's Caliban and Nabokov's Humbert Humbert.

Nabokov's narrator describes himself in animalistic language:

My talons still tingling, I flew on. (206)

I am like one of those inflated pale spiders you see in old gardens. Sitting in the middle of a luminous web and giving little jerks to this or that strand. *My* web is spread all over the house as I listen from my chair where I sit like a wily wizard. (49)

Perhaps my ape-ear had unconsciously caught some slight change in the rhythm of her respiration. (48–9)

I was a pentapoid monster, but I loved you. (284)

Appel comments that Humbert "often characterizes himself as a predator" (356). While there are certainly elements of over-wrought mock-confession and parody in his professions of guilt and displays of self-abuse, it is clear that Humbert truly does recognize the bestial nature of his relationship with Dolores Haze. He does not, for example, appear to be joking when he describes himself in the third person as having "a cesspoolful of rotting monsters behind his slow boyish smile" (44). It seems particularly appropriate that his sense of his own degradation often takes the form of bestial self-imagery, since his crime—lust—is the most fleshly and animalistic of offenses. Humbert Humbert is no white-collar embezzler or fraud: he is a rapist and a child molester. (He is also, of course, a lover, a poet, and a lunatic.) Humbert's lust for his adoptive daughter is psychologically (and perhaps legally), if not physiologically, incestuous. While Dolores Haze is not Humbert's natural daughter, he did marry her mother, and his initial relationship to Dolly is, technically, that of parent to child.

All this, of course, is paralleled exactly to *The Tempest*. Caliban is a "thing of darkness" (5. 1. 275). As Humbert is figuratively, Caliban is literally—half-man, half-animal:

> What have we here? A man or a fish? A fish! He smells like a fish; a very ancient and fishlike smell; a kind of not of the newest Poor John. A strange fish! Were I in England now, as once I was, and had but this fish painted, not a holiday fool there but would give me a piece of silver. There would this monster make a man ... (2. 2. 24–31)

Caliban's most significant crime (at least before he hatches the murderous plot of Stephano and Trinculo to rule the island after slaying Prospero) is the attempted rape of a young girl, Miranda:

> PROSPERO:                    Thou most lying slave,
> Whom stripes may move, not kindness! I have used thee
> (Filth as thou art) with humane care, and lodged thee
> In mine own cell till thou didst seek to violate
> The honor of my child.
> CALIBAN: O ho, O ho, would't had been done!
> Thou didst prevent me; I had peopled else
> This island with Calibans.
> PROSPERO: Abhorred slave ... (1. 2. 346–53)

Just like Humbert's lust for Dolores Haze, Caliban's attempted rape of Miranda is psychologically but not literally, physically incestuous. When Prospero first came to his enchanted island, he attempted to treat Caliban as a son (which would make Miranda a sister-figure):

> CALIBAN:        ... When thou cam'st first
> Thou strok'st me and made much of me, wouldst give me
> Water with berries in't and teach me how
> To name the bigger light, and how the less,
> That burn by day and night; and then I lov'd thee
> And show'd thee all the qualities o' th' isle ...
> PROSPERO:        ... I pitied thee,
> Took pains to make thee speak, taught thee each hour
> One thing or other. (1. 2. 334–9, 355–7).

Nabokov reinforces the link between the pseudo-incestuous lust of *Lolita* and *The Tempest* cleverly. When Dolores says that "they are pretty bad, some of that school bunch," Humbert wants to know her definition of "pretty bad" when it comes to "heterosexual experience." She reveals that the Shakespearean Miranda twins Anthony and Viola, whom we had met in Humbert's recitation of the Ramsdale class list (above), "had shared the same bed for years" (136).

Caliban and Humbert are, of course, very different characters. But both combine human and bestial qualities and both are victims of uncontrollable lust for a young girl emotionally if not genetically within their family circle. Moreover, both have a kind of undeniable fascination for us. We may not very much *like* either of these characters, but we find their presence riveting. As many readers and critics have observed, Humbert Humbert has a kind of fascinating serpentine magnetism. The contemporary novelist David Mitchell observes "This is a lovable rogue, you think, this Humbert Humbert. How interesting life is in his company!"

Likewise, Caliban can be shockingly and enchantingly poetic:

> Be not afeared; the isle is full of noises,
> Sounds and sweet airs that give delight and hurt not.
> Sometimes a thousand twangling instruments
> Will hum about mine ears; and sometimes voices
> That, if I then had waked after long sleep,
> Will make me sleep again; and then, in dreaming,
> The clouds methought would open and show riches
> Ready to drop upon me, that, when I waked,
> I cried to dream again. (3. 2. 138–46)

And his claim to ownership of the island which is now Prospero's kingdom is clearly not unjustified: "This island's mine by Sycorax my mother, / Which thou tak'st from me" (1. 2. 333–4). We never agree with Humbert or Caliban, but we can't keep our eyes off them!

Finally both these characters seem to combine wickedness and naiveté in a curious manner. Caliban, for example, although sometimes remarkably articulate, cannot remember (in the lines cited above) the names "sun" and "moon." Humbert, for all his old-world sophistication, is shockingly uninformed about America, American teenage culture, and suburbia. Humbert and Caliban are both indeed monsters, but at times they are rather clumsy and uneducated monsters. Both of these masterfully drawn characters command our attention.

\*\*\*

Even more compelling than the connections between Caliban and Humbert Humbert are those that connect Prospero and Vladimir Nabokov himself. The first, of course, is a literary character, the second a real person. But in both cases, that seemingly straightforward identification demands reinvestigation and qualification. There is no character in any of Shakespeare's plays who so thoroughly controls the action of the work of which he is a part as Prospero. The most splendid emblem of this controlling dimension of Prospero is the Masque in Act 4, which functions as a play-within-a-play, staged by Prospero who overtly comments upon his role as creative dramatic artist. He introduces the Masque of Ceres as "some vanity of mine art" (4. 1. 41). Then, at the conclusion of the Masque, Prospero speaks what are surely some of the most touching lines ever written concerning the relationship between the artist and his or her art:

> Our revels now are ended. These our actors
> (As I foretold you) were all spirits, and
> Are melted into air, into thin air,
> And like the baseless fabric of this vision
> The cloud-capp'd towers, the gorgeous palaces,
> The solemn temples, the great globe itself,
> Yea, all which it inherit, shall dissolve
> And like this insubstantial pageant faded
> Leave not a rack behind. We are such stuff
> As dreams are made on, and our little life
> Is rounded with a sleep. (4. 1. 148–58)

This explicit linking between the world created by the artist/maker, and the world the artist himself inhabits is an essential theme in Nabokov's works. He seeks to create in art the patterns he finds, or seeks to find, in life itself:

> Neither in environment nor in heredity can I find the exact instrument that fashioned me, the anonymous roller that pressed upon my life a certain intricate watermark whose unique design becomes visible when the lamp of art is made to shine through life's foolscap. (*Speak, Memory* 25)

The following of such thematic designs through one's life should be, I think, the true purpose of autobiography (*Speak, Memory*, 27).

Prospero exerts a control over the action of *The Tempest* which goes far beyond his staged masque. Virtually everything which happens within the play happens because he makes it do so. Indeed, the very first words we hear spoken on the enchanted island, at the beginning of the second scene of the play make it clear that all the action we have witnessed thus far—the first scene of the storm at sea—was wholly Prospero's doing:

MIRANDA: If by your art, my dearest father, you have
Put the wild waters in this roar, allay them. (1. 2. 1–2).

Prospero affirms that he has in fact raised the tempestuous storm:

I have done nothing, but in care of thee
(Of thee my dear one, thee my daughter), who
Art ignorant of what thou art, nought knowing
Of whence I am, nor that I am more better
Than Prospero ... (1. 2. 16–19)

Prospero manipulates the visitors he has snared unto his island like a puppetmaster, using Ariel as his string. He dispatches one group here, another there. He brings Ferdinand and Miranda together, and fans the spark of affection between them:

PROSPERO: [Aside.] They are both in either's powers, but this swift business
I must uneasy make, lest too light winning
Make the prize light. (1. 2. 453–5)

Of course, there is a striking and important difference between an author acting as puppetmaster, visibly pulling the strings affixed to his characters, and a literary character who manipulates his fellow fictional creatures. But in the case of Prospero and Nabokov, *The Tempest* and *Lolita*, that distinction is not as clean-cut as reason would suggest. The reason for this blurring of the line between character and creator is the delicate and fascinating way in which the protagonists of both works can be, and have been, seen as partially autobiographical. And, conversely, in the ways in which Nabokov the author has toyed with making himself a fictional character.

There is a romantic and very attractive myth that Prospero is to be equated with the retiring Shakespeare; that when he leaves his magical art behind, he is speaking metaphorically for his creator who would shortly abandon his theatrical career and his art as well:

PROSPERO:      ... But this rough magic
I here abjure; and when I have requir'd
Some heavenly music (which even now I do)
To work mine end upon their senses that
This airy charm is for, I'll break my staff,
Bury it certain fathoms in the earth,
And deeper than did ever plummet sound
I'll drown my book. (5. 1. 50–7)

Frank Kermode notes that "by the time Saintbury wrote his chapter in *The Cambridge History* it had been accepted that *The Tempest* was a personal farewell and a personal allegory" (Introduction lxxxi). A typically florid nineteenth-century illustration is provided by James Russell Lowell, who found the play:

> A succession of illusions winding up with those solemn words of the great enchanter who had summoned to his service every shape of merriment and passion, every figure in the great tragic-comedy of life, and who was now bidding farewell to the scene of his triumphs. For in Prospero shall we not recognize the Artist himself ... (200) [Of course, the prototype of *Lolita* was entitled *The Enchanter*.]

In our more cynical age, it is generally agreed that the autobiographical reading of *The Tempest* can be and often is egregiously overstressed. Such readings have led to a mawkish and sentimentalized interpretation of the play as the Bard's allegorical farewell to the stage. As Samuel Schoenbaum has pointed out, if *The Tempest* was meant as a farewell to the theater, then Shakespeare, like many a lesser theatrical figure after him, opted not to keep his promise:

> How indifferent to sentimental yearnings that, having declared the revels ended, Shakespeare should several years later return to London to try his hand at yet another revel, *Henry VIII*, from which, alas, patient investigation has been unable to deduce any intimate revelation to rival those yielded by *The Tempest*. (64)

There is a more balanced middle view. It seems to make sense to suggest that Prospero's magic and Shakespeare's are not unrelated. The most obvious point of connection is Prospero's work as a creator of a dramatic spectacle—the Masque of Ceres noted earlier (but note that Bottom, too, in *A Midsummer Night's Dream* is also a dramatist!). Mike Frank comments upon the "parallel between Prospero's art and Shakespeare's." The Masque becomes:

> A paradigm for the evanescence of the society which [Prospero] has established on the island, of the theater in which the play *The Tempest* is being presented, and life in general. The word *globe* refers to the Masque, the island, the theater of the same name, and finally to the world itself, the globe that is the earth. (158–9)

We need not subscribe to the autobiographical myth (although I am reluctant to abandon it entirely) to recognize in Prospero the archetype of the creative artist, making something out of nothing: "these our actors, as I foretold you, were all spirits, and are melted into air, into thin air."

As Robert Alter reminded us, it is exactly the role that Prospero plays in *The Tempest* that Nabokov insists on playing in all his works: "Nabokov takes pains to remind us repeatedly that each scene has been arranged by a theatrical stage manager" (43). In his introduction to *The Annotated Lolita*, Appel has an entire section entitled "The Staging of the Novel," in which he explicitly compares Nabokov's role in his works to that of Prospero in *The Tempest*:

> Nabokov the protean impersonator is always a masked presence in his fictions: as impresario, scenarist, director, warden, dictator, landlord, and even as bit player (the seventh Hunter in Quilty's play within *Lolita*, a Young Poet who insists that everything in the play is his invention) [see also *The Tragedy of Mr. Morn*]—to name only a few of the disguises he has donned as a secret agent who moves among his own creations like Prospero in *The Tempest*. Shakespeare is very much an ancestor (he and Nabokov even share a birthday), and the creaking splintering noise made by the stage setting as it disintegrates at the end of *Invitation to a Beheading* is Nabokov's version of the snapping of Prospero's wand and his speech to the players ("Our revels now are ended …"). (xxx)

In this sense, there is also a way in which Humbert, too, can be equated with the possibly autobiographical figure of Prospero, as well as to the monstrous Caliban. Humbert is surely, in one very limited sense, a kind of parody of his creator—both are urbane, old-world expatriots, both are literary men, both have what Humbert himself proclaims to be a "fancy prose style" (11). It can be presumed that those 1950s critics of *Lolita* who characterized Nabokov as "perverted" were confusing the author for his narrator, mistaking the parody for the real thing. But, of course, Humbert is a sadly failed Prospero. He tries to control his world in the way Prospero manages his, but fails miserably. He cannot even begin to control himself, much less act as a puppetmaster for the novel's other characters.

Nowhere is Nabokov's own stage-managing of his novel more apparent than in some of the deliberately artificial, fantastic, coincidences he weaves into its fabric. These proclaim *Lolita* an artifice, remind us that it is fiction, not fact. There is, for example, the number "342." This number seems to have no particular thematic significance whatsoever: it could be "432" or "234." It appears, however, often in the novel, apparently just to remind us of the authorial presence behind the narrative. The Haze house is located at 342 Lawn Street. Humbert and Dolly spend the night in room number 342 at the Enchanted Hunters Hotel (itself an echo of the play "The Enchanted Hunters" by Clare Quilty). Humbert informs the readers that he and Lolita stopped at 342 hotels and motels during their year's travels.

Finally, it is noteworthy that for both Prospero and Nabokov, magic and art are inextricably linked. Prospero's "art" is magic:

> … Graves at my command
> Have wak'd their sleepers, op'd and let 'em forth
> By my so potent art. (5. 1. 48–50)

But likewise, his magic is artistic: the Masque of Ceres is "a vanity of mine art."

Nabokov's first literary stab at the themes and subjects of *Lolita* was in a long-unpublished and untranslated Russian novella entitled *The Enchanter*, which finally appeared in 1986.[3] This *Ur-Lolita* was written as early as 1939, and the child seducer who becomes, two decades later, Humbert Humbert describes his genitals as a "magic wand."

In *The Tempest* and in *Lolita*, Nabokov and Shakespeare emphasize the ways in which the literary creator is a kind of sorcerer. Through the autobiographical hints in the character of Prospero, and the intrusive authorial presence of Nabokov, we in the audience are made highly aware of the carefully *constructed* nature of the pageant we are witnessing. In the Epilogue of *The Tempest*, Prospero and the actor playing him observe that "Now my charms are all o'erthrown" (1), exactly as in the "epilogue" or "afterword" to *Lolita* Nabokov laments the loss of his original Russian, which "the native illusionist, frac-tails flying, can magically use to transcend the heritage in his own way" (317). But if both works end with a declaration that the magic has flown, that is only one more illusion, in which the enchanter reaches into his seemingly empty top hat, and pulls out a magical work of art.

***

These two masterpieces, three and a half centuries apart and in many ways so very different, share a number of other thematic points of contact which merit examination.

First, and perhaps most obvious, is the theme of exile. The story of *The Tempest* begins with Prospero's exile from Milan. One of the first events in the action of the play is his account of that event to Miranda:

> This king of Naples, being an enemy
> To me inveterate, harkens my brother's suit
> Which was, that he in lieu o' th' premises
> Of homage, and I know not how much tribute,
> Should presently extirpate me and mine
> Out of the dukedom, and confer fair Milan
> With all the honors on my brother … (1. 2. 121–7)

Prospero still smarts from the wound of expulsion, and yearns to be restored to his homeland: "By foul play … were we heav'd thence" (1. 2. 62) he tells his daughter. It is possible to describe the plot of *The Tempest* as Prospero's capturing those who exiled him, and working through the changes of heart—in them and in himself—which will enable him to be restored to his homeland and noble title.

While Prospero's exile has been bitter and heart-wrenching for him, it has also been fruitful, as he acknowledges when he tells his story to Miranda (and to the audience). The full passage containing the words above is as follows:

MIRANDA:          O the heavens,
What foul play had we, that we came from thence?
Or blessed was't we did?
PROSPERO:          Both, both, my girl.
By foul play (as thou say'st) were we heav'd thence,
But blessedly holp hither. (1. 2. 59–63)

It is during his exile that Prospero has been able to perfect his "art." Indeed, it was his preoccupation with his books of arcane magical lore and his neglect of the day-to-day matters of state which enabled his treacherous brother to usurp him and banish him. Freed of the burdens of the latter responsibilities, he has pursued his studies and polished his sorcery. When it is finally time for him to return to his homeland, it is not without regrets:

… and so to Naples
Where I have hope to see the nuptial
Of these our dear-belov'd solemnized
Ant thence to retire me to my Milan, where
Every third thought shall be my grave. (5. 1. 308–12)

Prospero has always been conscious of his status as an exile on his enchanted island, and that consciousness has been painful. But at the same time, the years away from Italy have been productive and enriching.

*Lolita*, too, is in many ways set in motion by the act of exile. Humbert Humbert is very much the "old-world" expatriate, adrift in mid-twentieth-century America. Like Prospero, he misses the world he has lost:

I grew, a happy, healthy child in a bright world of illustrated books, clean sand, orange trees, friendly dogs, sea vistas and smiling faces. Around me the splendid Hotel Mirana revolves as a kind of private universe, a whitewashed cosmos within the blue greater one that blazed outside. (10)

Humbert's status as a stranger in a strange land is, like that of Prospero, productive as well as sad. On one simple level, he exploits his exoticism as a cultivated European in the new world to win the awed affection of both Dolores and Charlotte Haze. Charlotte writes of his "dark romantic European way" (68), he notes his "queer accent" (44).

Humbert's status as an exile is the mechanism by which much of the social satire (a phrase Nabokov would not cherish) which enlivens *Lolita* takes place. Nabokov shows us middle-class, mid-twentieth-century America through the extremely idiosyncratic eyes of his narrator, a middle-aged, intellectual, old-world madman and covert criminal. A half-century later, much of that satiric vision still has sting:

> We passed and re-passed through the whole gamut of American roadside restaurants, from the lowly Eat with its deer head (dark trace of a long tear at the inner canthus), "humorous" picture postcards of the posterior "Kurot" type, impaled guest checks, life savers, sunglasses, adman visions of celestial sundaes, one half of a chocolate cake under glass, and several horribly experienced flies zigzagging over the sticky sugar-pour on the ignoble counter … (155)

It can be argued that only a consciousness alien to our society would see it this clearly and be able to depict it so strikingly. In this sense, Humbert, like Prospero, cultivates *his* "art"—his narrative and observational style, in exile.

Of course Humbert's creator was always conscious of *his* position as an exile, a status he cites in the "afterword" to *Lolita* when he laments the loss of his "untrammeled, rich, and infinitely docile Russian tongue" (317).

In both works, the theme of exile is closely related to the motif of imprisonment. Shakespeare and Nabokov make a clear link between forced exclusion and forced inclusion. There are a number of prisoners, literal and metaphoric, in both works.

In *The Tempest*, Ariel and Caliban both begin the play as prisoners of Prospero. Ariel, in fact, had been imprisoned by Caliban's mother, the witch Sycorax, in a cloven pine, then liberated by Prospero upon his arrival, only to become his servant. He addresses Prospero as "Master." Caliban, in turn, has become the slave of Prospero, "that Caliban whom now I keep in service" (1. 2. 386–7). In the course of the action he and others are imprisoned within a mire. At the conclusion of the play, Caliban receives Prospero's "pardon," and Ariel is told "be free, and fare thou well" (5. 1. 319). Of course, in a larger sense, all the victims of the shipwreck are Prospero's prisoners upon the island. And Prospero and Miranda are themselves imprisoned upon the enchanted island until they are liberated at the drama's conclusion. It is fitting, given this unusual panoply of imprisoning, that the very last words of the epilogue are "set me free" (20).

*Lolita* is equally a tale of entrapment—indeed, the novel includes a figure named "Trapp." The entire novel is written by Humbert while he is "in legal captivity" for the murder of Clare Quilty. Humbert has, in effect, kidnapped his own stepdaughter and keeps her captive until her escape. He recognizes his role as jailer, describing Dolly at one point as "Lo, a young captive" (157). In another way, he is a prisoner of hers, captivated by her nymphic enchantment. Or, more exactly, he is a prisoner of his own sexual obsession, trapped by his passion for young girls. Nabokov's account of the genesis of *Lolita* is a tale of imprisonment:

> As far as I can recall, the initial shiver of inspiration was somehow prompted by a newspaper story about an ape in the Jardin des Plantes, who, after months of coaxing by a scientist, produced the first drawing ever characoaled by an animal: this sketch showed the bars of the poor creature's cage. (311)

Humbert, of course, is that ape, the novel his work of art depicting the bars of his cage.

An important and major difference between the two works in the treatment of this theme of imprisonment is that in *The Tempest* the prisoners are set free. Caliban is pardoned, Ariel liberated, Prospero and Miranda returned from exile, and the shipwrecked sailors and nobles released. Prospero's magical art empowers him to create the ambience within which he can forgive his old enemies, and it is that act of selfless mercy (only partially reciprocated) which provides the key to open all the jail cells of *The Tempest*. The characters in *Lolita*, however, are only released from the confinements of their lives by death: Charlotte Haze is run over by a car; Quilty is killed by Humbert; Lolita "died in childbed, giving birth to a stillborn girl, on Christmas Day 1952" (4); and Humbert Humbert, we are told in the Foreword by the fictitious John Ray, Jr, "had died in legal captivity, of coronary thrombosis, on November 16, 1952, a few days before his trial was scheduled to start" (3). The magic-maker of *Lolita* is, finally, outside the work, while *The Tempest*'s sorcerer is within. The action of Shakespeare's play enables Prospero to aid his fellow characters, while Nabokov has built a novel in which the authorial presence manipulates the characters towards a mortal fate.

This is in part because Nabokov's prisoners, especially his narrator, are entrapped not so much by literal iron bars (although these, too) as by the walls of time. While Prospero works his magic on an enchanted island, set in a physical ocean, Humbert seeks an "enchanted island of time … I substitute time terms for spatial ones" (16–17).

Nabokov's most straightforward description of the prison of time occurs not in *Lolita* but in his autobiography. The opening sentences of *Speak, Memory* evoke this concept in a series of remarkable images:

> The cradle rocks above an abyss, and common sense tells us that our existence is but a brief crack of light between two eternities of darkness. That this darkness is caused merely by the walls of time separating me and my bruised fists from the free world of timelessness is a belief I gladly share with the most gaudily painted savage. I have journeyed back in thought—with thought hopelessly tapering off as I went—to remote regions where I groped for some secret outlet only to discover that the prison of time is spherical and without exits. (19–20)

A strikingly similar statement, using the same words and grappling with the same concepts, occurs in *The Tempest*—perhaps to some degree a source of Nabokov's statement:

> PROSPERO:                    But how is it
> That this lives in thy mind? What seest thou else
> In the dark backward and abysm of time? (1. 2. 48–50)

As Shakespeare liberates his characters at the conclusion of *The Tempest*, Nabokov's prisoners of time are not, finally, without a way out. The author of *Speak, Memory* does recapture his past—by writing *Speak, Memory*. At the very end of *Lolita*, Humbert at last does gain a kind of entrance to his enchanted island of entranced time. The last words of the novel are:

> I am thinking of aurochs and angels, the secret of durable pigments, prophetic sonnets, the refuge of art. And this is the only immortality you and I share, my Lolita. (309)

It is legitimate to interpret this passage as Humbert Humbert's claim that his retelling of the story of his life with Dolly has given that story a kind of timelessness—the timelessness of sonnets and paintings. But the phrase "my Lolita" is an ambiguous one, permitting another equally valid interpretation of the passage. At the conclusion of the novel (as in many of his others) Nabokov partially throws off his narrative disguise, comes forward, and speaks directly as author to his readers. So, "my Lolita" is not only Humbert's little girl—it is Nabokov's big book. The author and his words, like the lovers, ascend to immortality through the magic of art. The fictional Lolita died in 1952; the fiction *Lolita* is still fresh decades later, and will live a long, long time. Nabokov makes this claim that literature is a gateway to immortality citing "prophetic sonnets." Shakespeare's sonnets, many of which peer into the future, make exactly this same powerful assertion about art:

Sonnet 18

Shall I compare thee to a summer's day?
Thou art more lovely and more temperate.
Rough winds do shake the darling buds of May,
And summer's lease hath all too short a date.
Sometime too hot the eye of heaven shines,
And often is his gold complexion dimmed;
And every fair from fair sometimes declines,
By chance, or nature's changing course, untrimmed.
But thy eternal summer shall not fade,
Nor lose possession of that fair thou ow'st,
Nor shall Death brag thou wand'rest in his shade,
When in eternal lines to time thou grow'st.
    So long as men can breathe or eyes can see
    So long lives this, and this gives life to thee.

Shakespeare's *The Tempest* also ends with a bravura movement into the realm in which art and life are strangely confused, and the speaker is simultaneously both a fictional character and a "real" person. The Epilogue addresses a plea to the audience in the voices of Prospero the character, the actor playing that character, and the creator of Prospero:

Now my charms are all o'erthrown,
And what strength I have's mine own
Which is most faint. Now 'tis true
I must be here confin'd by you
Or sent to Naples. Let me not
Since I have my dukedom got,
And pardon'd the deceiver, dwell
In this bare island by your spell,
But release me from my bands
With the help of your good hands.
Gentle breath of yours my sails
Must fill, or else my project fails,
Which was to please. Now I want
Spirits to enforce, art to enchant,
And my ending is despair,
Unless I be reliev'd by prayer,
Which pierces so, that it assaults
Mercy and frees all faults.
    As you from crimes would pardon'd be,
    Let your indulgence set me free. (Epilogue, 1–20)

Evoking the magical release made possible through art, the character asks to be freed from his island; the actor, from the play; the dramatist to the immortality of *The Tempest*.

*Lolita* is a unique work of art. It is certainly not a "version" of *The Tempest* nor of anything else. Nabokov does not imitate Shakespeare, nor does he try to write a twentieth-century retelling of the play. But Nabokov weaves a web of evocation between his work and Shakespeare's which adds complexity and richness to his novel, and enhances our understanding of both masterpieces. *Lolita*'s deep and strong links to *The Tempest* enable us to experience the play, too, from a new perspective. In both, we enter a world of exile, an enchanted island, a prison of time. We see a father and daughter, a lustful monster, and the escape made possible by the sorcery of art.

# 6

# Tempest Point on the Bohemian Sea: *Pnin*

*Pnin* appeared in 1957, between *Lolita* and *Pale Fire*. It is Nabokov's most accessible novel, and his sweetest. Its protagonist, a Russian émigré college teacher, while certainly not without his flaws, is lovable, charming, brave, bright, and decent. Some parts of the novel were originally published separately in *The New Yorker* as free-standing short stories. Consequently, each chapter of the novel seems both to stand alone as a self-contained literary work and to dovetail neatly with the other chapters, making up an integrated novel. In one sense, it is a kind of picaresque novel, a series of adventures, linked together by the character who undergoes them: Pnin has a difficult time traveling to a lecture he is scheduled to deliver; he rents a room near Waindell College where he teaches Russian and Russian culture; we learn of, and meet, his ex-wife and his son; he recreates with other émigrés at a New England summer home; we learn of the tragic death of his first love at the hands of the Nazis; we follow his career at the college; he gives a party; and so on. As the novel progresses, we discover gradually that its narrator had a connection with Pnin in Russia, that their relationship is far from cordial, and, at the conclusion, that Pnin refuses to work with the narrator, who has been offered a position at Waindell. We come to realize that from the outset the narrator has tended to emphasize Pnin's comic, idiosyncratic, or even incompetent characteristics; that we are being told Pnin's story by a teller who wants to make his subject appear foolish. In many ways, it is the character of this narrator, more than that of Timofey Pnin, who seems the typical Nabokovian protagonist. The novel can be heartbreaking, particularly when Pnin remembers his lost love, and his Russian past. It can also be achingly funny, especially as Pnin habitually massacres the English language:

> If his Russian was music, his English was murder. He had enormous difficulty ("dzeefeecooltsee" in Pninian English) with depalatization, never managing to remove the extra Russian moisture from *t*'s and *d*'s before the vowels he so quaintly softened. His explosive "hat" ("I never go in a hat even in winter") differed from the common American pronounciation of "hot" (typical of Waindell townspeople, for example)

only by its briefer duration, and thus sounded very much like the German verb *hat* (has). Long *o*'s with him inevitably became short ones: his "no" sounded positively Italian, and this was accentuated by his trick of triplicating the simple negative ("May I give you a lift, Mr. Pnin?" "No-no-no, I have only two paces from here"). He did not possess (nor was he aware of this lack) any long *oo*: all he could muster when called upon to utter "noon" was the lax vowel of the German "*nun*" ("I have no classes in after*nun* on Tuesday. Today is Tuesday."). (66)

Many scholars see a real-life model for Timofey Pnin in Nabokov's fellow émigré and colleague at Cornell University, the historian Marc Szeftel, a connection explored fully in Galya Diment's *Pniniad*. The strength of that connection has been debated, but most agree that Pnin is not just a renamed, thinly disguised version of Szeftel (e.g., Szeftel is Jewish and Pnin is not; Szeftel's story is considerably sadder than Pnin's); however, most also agree that Nabokov's protagonist clearly is linked to Szeftel. The evidence suggests that Nabokov found Szeftel's naiveté both charming and comic (Diment, *passim*). In some ways, the relationship between the rather cruel narrator of *Pnin* and his title character parallels and parodies the relationship between Nabokov and Szeftel. While the details of this biographical link are interesting, they are probably not essential to an understanding and appreciation of the novel.

Rather like the novel itself, some of *Pnin*'s Shakespearean citations seem gently humorous. There is, for example, the amusing twist on *Othello* found in the character of Pnin's landlord's cleaning woman. She is Desdemona, but instead of being a young, Caucasian woman who weds an older African man, she herself is old, and an African-American:

> Desdemona, the old colored charwoman, who came on Fridays and with whom at one time God had gossiped daily ("'Desdemona,' the Lord would say to me, 'that man George is no good.'"), happened to glimpse Pnin basking in the unearthly lilac light of his sun lamp, wearing nothing but shorts, dark glasses, and a dazzling Greek-Catholic cross on his broad chest, and insisted thereafter that he was a saint. (40)

This choice of name seems to me more whimsical than of thematic import.

Sometimes, Shakespeare is used in the service of some of the novel's clever, and accurate, academic satire:

> murals displaying recognizable members of the faculty in the act of passing on the torch of knowledge from Aristotle, Shakespeare, and Pasteur to a lot of monstrously built farm boys and farm girls ... (9)

One of Pnin's better students in his Russian classes (and his enrollments are always rather slight) is a Charles Macbeth, "whose prodigious memory had already disposed of ten languages and was prepared to entomb ten more" (9) and whom Pnin describes as "A madman, I think, judging by his compositions" (34).

A final whimsical Shakespearean citation involves a device which Pnin's son Victor uses to lull himself to sleep. He fantasizes a tale in which he is pacing:

> A beach on the Bohemian Sea, at Tempest Point, where Percival Blake, a cheerful American adventurer, had promised to meet him with a powerful motorboat. (85—This soporific device is, of course, closely related to the plot of *Pale Fire*.)

Here, Nabokov conjoins the marine settings of two of the darker Shakespearean comedies, *The Winter's Tale* and *The Tempest*. The latter, of course, is set on an island, not a point. The former, famously, is set on "the seacoast of Bohemia" ("Thou art perfect then our ship hath touched upon / The deserts of Bohemia?" (3. 3. 1–2). As one editor (Frank Kermode in *The Complete Signet Classic Shakespeare*) puts it plainly, "Bohemia, as is notorious, had no seacoast" (1516). Thus, Nabokov turns Prospero's magical island into a point of land, set upon a sea which does not exist!

There is also, in *Pnin* a thread of more serious allusions to *Hamlet*. The first, rather faint echo of *Hamlet* comes when the narrator gives as an example of Pnin's classroom digressions, the tale of his arrival in the United States. He is quizzed by an immigration official:

> He asks: "Are you anarchist?" I answer—time out on the part of the narrator for a spell of cozy mute mirth—"First what do we understand under 'Anarchism'? Anarchism practical, metaphysical, theoretical, mystical, abstractical, individual, social? When I was young," I say, "all this had for me signification." So we had a very interesting discussion in consequence of which I passed two whole weeks on Ellis Island— abdomen beginning to heave; heaving; narrator convulsed. (11)

Although the subject is quite different, Pnin's description of the conversation which keeps him on Ellis Island for two weeks derives from Polonius's description of the wandering players in *Hamlet*:

> The best actors in the world, either for tragedy, comedy, history, pastoral, pastoral-comical, historical-pastoral, tragical-historical, tragical-comical-historical-pastoral; scene individable, or poem unlimited. (2. 2. 403–7)

*Pnin*'s narrator's version of Pnin's description of his arrival in the United States is clearly an imagined example of the protagonist's classroom digressions—digressions which the narrator, who was teaching at another college could not possibly have heard. So, it is not Pnin, but the narrator who chooses language which is reminiscent of Shakespeare's "foolish prating knave." It is certainly possible that the eternally optimistic and often ridiculously pedantic Pnin might have told such a story, and might even have found a two-week confinement at Ellis Island something to laugh about.[1] But the figure of fun we see here is not Pnin, but the narrator's version of him.

Later, we learn a bit about Pnin's acquisition of the English language:

> Except for such not very helpful odds and ends as "the rest is silence," "nevermore," weekend," who's who," and a few ordinary words like "eat," "street," "fountain pen," "gangster," "Charleston," "Marginal utility," he had no English at all at the time he left France for the States. (14—As an academic émigré steeped in the arcania of Slavic culture, Pnin himself might be said to have only "marginal utility")

Pnin might not have much English, but he has read *Hamlet* and remembers that his very last words are "the rest is silence." That line is followed by Horatio's "Now cracks a noble heart. Good night, sweet prince, / And flights of angels sing thee to thy rest" (5. 2. 360–2). The hint of mortality here is reiterated by the fact that the second word Pnin apparently knows, "nevermore," would surely come from Poe's *The Raven*. Although the protagonist's health remains good throughout the novel, mortality is never far away in Pnin. Timofey himself has a frightening seizure in Chapter 1, and the deaths of his family, acquaintances and loved ones is always lurking in the background. Less seriously, these lines seem to suggest that he has apparently studied, at some point, some of the more arcane points (at least to literary scholars, if not economists) of economic theory, such as "marginal utility!"

As Pnin conducts his unending and somewhat obscure research on Russian culture, he encounters a description of "old pagan games that were still practiced at the time, throughout the woodlands of the Upper Volga, in the margins of Christian ritual" (77):

> Peasant maidens would make wreaths of buttercups and frog orchises; then, singing snatches of ancient love chants, they hung these garlands on riverside willows; and on Whitsunday the wreaths were shaken down into the river, where, unwinding, they floated like so many serpents while the maidens floated and chanted among them.

A curious verbal association struck Pnin at this point; he could not catch it by its mermaid tail but made a note on his index card … (77).

The verbal association is, of course, Shakespearean—Ophelia's suicide in *Hamlet*.

> Pnin pocketed his index card and, while doing so, recalled without any prompting what he had not been able to recall a while ago:
>  ... *plila I pela, pela I plila*
>  ... she floated and she sang, she sang and floated.
> Of course! Ophelia's death! *Hamlet*! In good Andrey Kroneberg's Russian translation, 1844—the joy of Pnin's youth, and of his father's and grandfather's young days. And here ... there is, we recollect, also a willow and also wreaths. But where to check properly? Alas, *"Gamlet" Vil'yama shekspira* ... was not represented in Waindell College library, and whenever you were reduced to look up something in the English version, you never found this or that beautiful, noble, sonorous line that you remembered all your life from Kroneberg's text in Vengerov's splendid edition. Sad! (78–9—Kroneberg's translation is real).

The description of Ophelia's death, in Shakespeare's version, not Kroneberg's, comes from Queen Gertrude:

> There is a willow grows askant the brook,
> That shows his hoar leaves in the glassy stream:
> Therewith fantastic garlands did she make
> Of crowflowers, nettles, daisies, and long purples,
> That liberal shepherds give a grosser name,
> But our cold maids do dead men's fingers call them.
> There on the pendant boughs her crownet weeds
> Clamb'ring to hang, an envious sliver broke,
> When down her weedy trophies and herself
> Fell in the weeping brook. Her clothes spread wide,
> And mermaidlike awhile they bore her up,
> Which time she chanted snatches of old lauds
> As one incapable of her own distress,
> Or like a creature native and indued
> Unto that element. But long it could not be
> Till that her garments, heavy with their drink,
> Pulled the poor wretch from her melodious lay
> To muddy death. (4. 7. 166–83)

This scene from *Hamlet* is one which seems to have played an important part in Nabokov's imagination. As we shall see, it is of crucial importance in the later novel, *Ada*. It is interesting to note that Nabokov spent most of his life living on or very near rivers or inland lakes: the Neva, the Charles, Lac

Léman. In particular, the Nabokov family summer home Vyra is nestled next to the Ordezh, which Nabokov describes in his autobiography as following a "winding, branching and looping course" (*Speak, Memory*, 61). The Ordezh is exactly the kind of heavily vegetated lazy watercourse one imagines sucking Ophelia to her death by water. The connection is made stronger by another passage from *Speak, Memory*:

> There came a July day—around 1910, I suppose—when I felt the urge to explore the vast marshland beyond the Ordezh. After skirting the river for three or four miles, I found a rickety footbridge. While crossing over, I could see the huts of a hamlet on my left, apple trees, rows of tawny pine logs lying on a green bank, and the bright patches made on the turf by the scattered clothes of peasant girls, who, stark naked in shallow water, romped and yelled, heeding me as little as if I were the discarnate carrier of my present reminiscences. (137–8)

It is not difficult to associate these innocently lewd peasant girls with those who give a grosser name to Queen Gertrude's long purples. Nor is it difficult to imagine that when Nabokov thought of *Hamlet* and Ophelia's suicide, it brought into his mind's eye the lazy Ordezh, the family estate of Vyra, and "a summer morning, in the legendary Russia of my boyhood" (*Speak, Memory*, 119).

Timofey Pnin concludes his ruminations on the scene of Ophelia's drowning by exclaiming "Sad!" What makes him sad is not, of course, the death of Shakespeare's character, but the loss of the mid-nineteenth-century Russian translation of Shakespeare's English. He has remembered all his life, in Russian then in English-speaking exile, the sonorous line in Kroneberg's translation— not the lines which Shakespeare wrote in English. In one sense, this is funny: to lament having to read Shakespeare in English is like grieving at having to drink wine in France. But in another way, Pnin is right; it is indeed sad. He has lost the language of his youth, and now has to live with his awkward and adopted English. This is, of course, a sentiment shared by Pnin's creator:

> My private tragedy, which cannot, and indeed should not, be anybody's concern, is that I had to abandon my natural idiom, my untrammeled, rich, and infinitely docile Russian tongue for a second-rate brand of English, devoid of any of those apparatuses—the baffling mirror, the black velvet backdrop, the implied associations and traditions—which the native illusionist, frac-tails flying, can magically use to transcend the heritage in his own way (*Lolita*, 317).

One of the characteristics of Shakespeare's greatness is that his tragedies are never wholly tragic, and his comedies are never without darker moments.

The drunken Porter in *Macbeth* or the gravediggers in *Hamlet* are examples of the former. The final disposition of Malvolio or of Bottom in *Twelfth Night* and *A Midsummer Night's Dream* illustrate the latter. Nabokov shares this characteristic, and nowhere is it more evident than in *Pnin*, overall his lightest English novel. But the comic world of this work is given depth and texture by its moments of despair and heartbreak. The *Hamlet* thread in *Pnin* plays a significant part in giving to Nabokov's novel the fullness, variety, and complexity of life.

# 7

# The Lunatic, the Lover, and the Poet:
## *Pale Fire* and *Timon of Athens*

*Pale Fire* is perhaps Nabokov's most formally experimental novel. The book takes the shape of a long narrative poem, written by a modestly successful poet and professor, John Shade. The name "Shade" suggests both "shadow" and "ghost." The plot includes an (invented) group of terrorist regicides called "The Shadows," and the action of the novel takes place after Shade is murdered, and, thus, a ghost. The poem is preceded by a preface, and followed by a commentary by a fellow professor and scholar, Charles Kinbote, who tells us he is an exile from the land of Zembla. Shade is a somewhat hoary New England poet, who appears to be (if it is possible to imagine the combination) a cross between Robert Frost and Vladimir Nabokov. The poem (which occupies pages 33 to 69 of the novel) is entitled, like the whole book, "Pale Fire." (In the text below, the poem will appear in quotation marks—"Pale Fire"—and the novel in italics—*Pale Fire*.) It is written in loose but regular heroic couplets and tells the story of the suicide of Shade's daughter, Hazel, and of the poet's search for an understanding of the riddle of her death—and thus, to some comprehension of all human life and death. The poet believes he finds that meaning through an odd coincidence (a misprint of the word "fountain" for "mountain") which, he concludes, is no coincidence at all, but a clue the world is a patterned and ordered creation, presided over by some kind of creative deity or deities:

> But all at once it dawned on me that *this*
> Was the real point, the contrapuntal theme;
> Just this: not text but texture; not the dream
> But topsy-turvical coincidence,
> Not flimsy nonsense, but a web of sense.
> Yes! It sufficed that I in life could find
> Some kind of link-and-bobolink, some kind
> Of correlated pattern in the game,
> Plexed artistry ... (63)

One of the several areas in which readers and critics have disagreed sharply is the intrinsic worth of Shade's "Pale Fire" as a poem. This controversy was reignited by the publication in 2011 of the poem as a free-standing literary work, stripped of the remainder of Nabokov's novel, as *Pale Fire: A Poem in Four Cantos by John Shade* (edited and with commentary by Brian Boyd and R. S. Gwynn). Some, such as Alvin Kernan and George Cloyne, found the poem weak. Michael Wood sees "Pale Fire" as "Not quite grand or strong enough" (180). In a *New Yorker* review of the Boyd/Gwynn edition, Giles Harvey cites both negative and positive reactions to Shade's poem. Dan Chiasson, the *New Yorker's* poetry critic, declared that "to say it's great poetry is just absurd." Chiasson's unenthusiastic reaction to "Pale Fire" and *Pale Fire* parallels that of Dwight Macdonald at the time of original publication. On the other hand, the contemporary novelist (and avid Nabokov partisan) Arthur Phillips states:

> My strongest impression on this nth re-reading is that the poem is really a novel in verse. Vivid and thoroughly drawn characters, scenes, themes, tragedies large and small, recurring images and motifs. Even without the marvels of the novel *Pale Fire*, the poem "Pale Fire" is a little novel in itself. And, as a rhyming novella, there's really no question who wrote it. Only the novel makes it a poem by Shade; without the Commentary, the poem could only be by Nabokov. The language, the languages, the butterflies, the literary jokes (Chapman's homer will make me happy until I am a walking shade). And, as such, it deserves to be published on its own, as a poem by Nabokov. The greatest poem of its century? I'm not ready to go that far, even as I'm ready to call its proper housing the greatest novel of the century.

Similarly, Martin Amis in the *TLS* says the new version reveals what he praises as "the poem in all its innocence."

The poem is preceded by a Foreword by Charles Kinbote, who tells us that he was, until shortly before he began his work on the text of "Pale Fire," a professor at Waindell, a small, New England college, and a colleague of John Shade's. Kinbote is extremely tall and sports a huge beard, which earns him the mocking nickname "The Beaver" from his students. He is also flamboyantly homosexual and sharply resents Shade's steadfast and devoted marriage to Sybil Shade. He is, nonetheless, a zealous admirer of Shade as a person and a poet. As Brian Boyd points out in *Nabokov's Pale Fire: The Magic of Artistic Discovery*, the effort to achieve a tone of cool, disinterested literary scholarship in the Foreword disintegrates immediately: "The second paragraph continues in the same apparently bloodless critical vein but its pulse soon starts to twitch erratically" (18). That twitch becomes a spasm when, at the end of the third paragraph of the Foreword, Kinbote injects: "There is a very loud amusement park right in front of my present lodgings" (13).

The Commentary as well as an Index and the Foreword, all created by Kinbote, do not in fact comment much at all upon the poem, but rather use it as a springboard for Kinbote's narration of his relationship with John Shade, and even more for his telling the tale of the strange deposition, escape, and exile of one Charles the Beloved, King of a distant Northern land, Zembla. At the conclusion of the novel—the end of Kinbote's notes and index—it turns out that he is himself Charles, a secret the careful reader has guessed several scores of pages earlier. Or, at least, Kinbote *thinks* he is King Charles. Or, at least, Kinbote wants *us* to think he is King Charles. Or, at least, *somebody* wants us to think that Kinbote thinks he is King Charles!

In any event, it is clear that Kinbote is a wildly unreliable narrator, and obviously insane. Shade, it turns out, was (probably) killed just after (or just before) finishing writing his poem "Pale Fire." Kinbote claims that the murderer was a Zemblan regicide. The police and everyone else connected with the case seem sure it was an American criminal lunatic, Jack Grey, who confused Shade for his neighbor, the judge who had sentenced him to the Institute for the Criminally Insane (or "ICI," a chilling French acronym), and whose house Kinbote is renting. The judge is known to resemble John Shade. After the murder, Kinbote apparently pilfers the manuscript of "Pale Fire" and flees to the American West (Cedarn, Utana) where he puts together his edition of the poem and commentary, that is, the edition which is Nabokov's novel *Pale Fire*.

Once the basic surface structure, plot, and characters of *Pale Fire* are apprehended (which in itself takes a while), other interpretative questions emerge. While these questions are only of tangential relevance to this investigation of Nabokov's Shakespeareanisms, they need to be noted briefly.

*Pale Fire* has often seemed to readers (and re-readers and re-re-readers) to be a challenging literary puzzle. For many, that challenge has led to ingenious "solutions" to the core questions of the novel: who, within the fictional universe of the literary work, really wrote the poem and the commentary? Is Shade really dead? Who is Kinbote? An excellent survey of the many and various theories seeking to solve the puzzles is provided by Rene Alladaye in *The Darker Shades of* Pale Fire: *An investigation into a Literary Mystery*. One theory which emerged soon after the novel was published posited that "Kinbote" was really one "Botkin," cited in the "Index" as "an American scholar of Russian descent" who has crossed the line between sanity and lunacy, and has fantasized that he is an imaginary king of an imaginary country. On the other hand, many careful readers have noted seemingly inexplicable similarities between the poem and commentary, and that has led them to conclude that the same author is responsible for both (of course, finally, such is the case: that author is Vladimir Nabokov!). If there is a single author within the fiction, who is it? Some have argued that John Shade wrote both the poem and the commentary, and that his death is part of his own fictional construct. Others believe that whoever wrote the commentary (Kinbote? Botkin?) also wrote the poem. One theory, briefly held by Brian Boyd, is that the ghost of John Shade is a major influence on the commentary to his own poem. Another reading, subsequently held by Boyd, is that the spirit of Hazel Shade, John and Sybil's daughter, has returned from the dead, and helps to shape both poem and commentary.

All these clever and creative explanations and readings of the novel are not without evidence and merit. But perhaps it is the case that Nabokov made *Pale Fire* a puzzle without any definitive solution. It seems to me at least possible that he injected into the work clues which point in a number of different directions, but that none of them leads to a single "right" answer … or perhaps all of them do.

***

One puzzle Nabokov playfully but seriously injects into *Pale Fire* which does have a clear solution is the source of the title of the poem and novel, the words "pale fire." That source is Shakespeare's *Timon of Athens*. In both Shade's and Kinbote's sections of the work, Nabokov injects a series of hints and jokes related to the title. These clues, and the answer to which they point, prove to have thematic import as well as entertainment value. They are worth pursuing.

In the first version of her glowing and perceptive review of *Pale Fire*, Mary McCarthy confessed herself unable to decipher the clues pointing to the derivation of the novel's title (in a revised version, she had figured it out). Others, including Dwight McDonald in his negative comments in *Partisan Review*, were quick to unravel the mystery. Here is a quick retracing of the pathway leading to this solution.

First, Shade, within the poem, discusses his search for a title:

> *Dim Gulf* was my first book (free verse); *Night Rote*
> Came next; then *Hebe's Cup*, my final float
> In that damp carnival, for now I term
> Everything "Poems," and no longer squirm
> (But *this* transparent thingum does require
> Some moondrop title. Help me, Will! *Pale Fire*.). (68)

(Of course, *Transparent Things* became the title of another Nabokov novel, years after John Shade called his poem a "transparent thingum.")

The connection between Shakespeare ("Help me, Will!") and the moon ("some moondrop title") might remind the careful reader of *A Midsummer Night's Dream*, certainly an appropriate association, given the play's well-known linking of lunatics, lovers, and poets—a linking in keeping with John Shade's description of Kinbote as a "poet" rather than a "loony." Early in his commentary, Kinbote also had some observations regarding Shakespeare and the moon:

> These lines are represented in the drafts by a variant [the "variants" Kinbote reveals are often of suspiciously dubious authorship; assuming a dual authorship understanding, Kinbote himself clearly wrote some of Shade's "variants"] reading:
>
> 39 ... and home would haste my thieves,
> 40 The sun with stolen ice, the moon with leaves
>
> One cannot help recalling a passage in *Timon of Athens* (Act IV, Scene 3) where the misanthrope talks to the three marauders. Having no library in the desolate log cabin where I live, like Timon in his cave,[2] I am compelled for the purpose of quick citation to retranslate this passage into English prose from a Zemblan poetical version of Timon which, I hope, sufficiently approximates the text, or is at least faithful to its spirit:
>
> The sun is a thief: she lures the sea          *See  p 90*
> and robs it. The moon is a thief:
> he steals his silvery light from the sun
> The sea is a thief: it dissolves the moon.
>
> For a prudent appraisal of Conmal's translations of Shakespeare's works, see note to line 962. (79–80)

This passage raises a number of questions, all of which Nabokov answers subsequently in the text. For example, we may want to know where Kinbote acquired the Conmal translation of *Timon of Athens* into Zemblan, from which he retranslates this passage back into English.

Later in his commentary, Kinbote tells of an earlier childhood escapade in which Charles the Beloved discovers a secret passage out of the Zemblan palace in which he lives. That passage is entered through a closet, in which, on a shelf, is a "thirty-twomo edition of *Timon of Athens* translated into Zemblan by his [Kinbote is still attempting to disguise the fact that he is Charles: hence the 'his'] Uncle Conmal" (125). Then, Kinbote narrates how, years later, he escaped from the same palace, utilizing the same passage, reached through the same closet. He reconnoiters, discovering now that the closet is empty, "save for the tiny volume of *Timon Afinsken* still lying in one corner" (128). Later, in the dark, making his exit, he picks up a souvenir: "As he was removing the second shelf, an object fell with a miniature thud: he guessed what it was and took it with him as a talisman" (132). The "miniature thud" of course, is caused by the tiny thirty-twomo edition of *Timon*.

A first-time reader now knows:

1. That John Shade has found the title of his poem "Pale Fire" in Shakespeare's works.
2. That Kinbote possesses a miniature version of *Timon of Athens* translated into Zemblan by Conmal.
3. That a line from a variant of Shade's poem reminded Kinbote of a passage from *Timon*.

These threads come together in Kinbote's note to Shade's line about the name of the poem ("Help me, Will! *Pale Fire.*"):

> Paraphrased, this evidently means: Let me look in Shakespeare for something I might use for a title. And the find is "pale fire." But in which of the Bard's works did our poet cull it? My readers must make their own research. All I have with me is a tiny vest pocket edition of *Timon of Athens*—in Zemblan! It certainly contains nothing that could be regarded as an equivalent of "pale fire" (if it had, my luck would have been a statistical monster. (285)

The reader doing her or his own research, though, discovers that Kinbote's "luck" is just such a monster—and doubly so. The title does come from *Timon of Athens*, and even more statistically monstrous, it comes from the very lines Kinbote had quoted earlier, but in translated, then retranslated form. The Shakespearean original is:

> The sun's a thief, and with his great attraction
> Robs the vast sea; the moon's an arrant thief,
> And her pale fire she snatches from the sun;
> The sea's a thief, whose liquid surge resolves
> The moon into salt tears. (4. 3. 437–41)

For comparative purposes here, again, is the passage as Kinbote quoted it some 150 pages earlier, filtered through the translations of Conmal (Shakespeare's English into Zemblan) and Kinbote (Conmal's Zemblan back into English):

> The sun is a thief; she lures the sea
> and robs it. The moon is a thief:
> he steals his silvery light from the sun
> The sea is a thief: it dissolves the moon.

Shakespeare's "pale fire" emerges as Conmal/Kinbote's "silvery light."

Amusingly, Kinbote criticizes Shade (and Nabokov) for indulging in the custom of naming works of literature after quotations from other earlier works: Shade entitled a collection of essays "The Untamed Seahorse" and Kinbote's note reads:

> See Browning's *My Last Duchess*.
>
> See it and condemn the fashionable device of entitling a collection of essays or a volume of poetry—or a long poem, alas, with a phrase from a more or less celebrated poetical work of the past. Such titles possess a specious glamor acceptable maybe in the names of vintage wines and plump courtesans but only degrading in regard to the talent that substitutes the easy allusiveness of literacy for original fancy and shifts onto a bust's shoulders the responsibility for ornateness since anybody can flip through a *Midsummer Night's Dream* or *Romeo and Juliet*, or, perhaps, the *Sonnets* and take his pick. (240)

It appears that, in the final sentence here, Kinbote is perhaps guessing at the source of Shade's title. Later, in the index, he has another guess. Under the (very long) entry for "*Kinbote, Charles, Dr.*" we find "his severe criticism of quotational titles, from *The Tempest* etc., such as 'pale fire,' etc." (309).

***

In addition to presenting the solution to an amusing literary puzzle, the discovery of the correct passage points to several important considerations in the novel.

The amusing game of tracking down the source of the novel's title reaffirms Nabokov's very serious and recurring thematic consideration of "coincidence." Kinbote/Charles just happened to discover the escape passage as a child, note therein a copy of *Timon of Athens*; to pick up that copy fifteen years later while making his escape; to write a commentary on a poem which had as its title a line from *Timon*, at that point the only book in his possession; and to have already cited that specific line in his notes but in an unrecognizable twice-translated version. This is quite a sequence of accidents, and Nabokov invites the discerning reader to ponder their improbability with Kinbote's unconsciously ironic statement about "a statistical monster." Of course, the point we are meant to realize is that this chain of events is not accidental nor coincidental nor monstrous at all—it only seems that way to Charles Kinbote. From our more knowledgeable perspective, it is clear that everything has been planned and carefully wrought. The "pale fire"—*Timon of Athens*' sequence is not part of some random life; it is part of a novel's plot, imagined, structured, and built by Nabokov. The author of *Pale Fire* is using Shakespeare's play to remind us that the novel is an aesthetic construct, not "reality" but an artifice created by an artificer. This effect is like that at the conclusion of *A Midsummer Night's Dream*: as the actors playing the Athenian court sit and chuckle at the acting of the rude mechanicals, we, in the second tier audience chuckle at them, but might have a moment in which we wonder what audience is amused by our antics.

This persistent reminder that the work of art is a created object, which was made by a creator, points to a larger, metaphysical theme which pervades much of Nabokov's work, including *Pale Fire*.

Nabokov criticism since the 1980s has often focused upon aspects of the moral and spiritual world of his *oeuvre*. In 1979, the author's widow, Vera Slonim Nabokov, contributed a foreword to a posthumous collection of Nabokov's Russian poems. She startled the small world of Nabokov scholars and significantly changed the course of Nabokov scholarship by announcing that "potustoronnost," which is usually translated as "the other-worldly" or "the hereafter," is the "main theme" of her late husband's works, and that it "permeates all that he has written and characterizes it like a kind of watermark."[3] (Of course, otherworldliness does not necessarily equate with theism.) Since we know that Mrs. Nabokov was deeply engaged in her husband's artistic creative process, her declaration was taken very seriously by students of Nabokov's works. The 1980s and 1990s saw several books and articles which focused upon the motif of the Otherworld or the other-worldly, including books by D. Barton Johnson, Vladimir E. Alexandrov, and W. W. Rowe. And the author's few and often enigmatic words on theological subjects have been resurfaced and re-examined. Perhaps foremost among those remarks was his teasing and mysterious response to the final question of Alvin Toffler in a January 1964 interview, which Nabokov included in *Strong Opinions*:

> Q: Man's understanding of these mysteries is embodied in his concept of a Divine Being. As a final question, do you believe in God?
> A: To be quite candid—and what I am going to say now is something I never said before and I hope it provokes a salutary little chill—I know more than I can express in words, and the little I can express would not have been expressed, had I not known more. (45)

The first and most obvious manner in which a theist theme appears in Nabokov's works is in the parallel he so often emphasizes between the creative artist and a creative deity. This trope is hardly unique to Nabokov, and has frequently been noted in his work and that of others. But it is a surpris-ingly pervasive and important element in his authorial stance. Alexandrov remarks that "Nabokov's characteristic aesthetic practices resurrect the

Romantic idea that the artist is God's rival, and that man's artistic creations are analogues to God's Natural World" (18). Rowe describes Nabokov's authorial presence in his works, such as the titular puzzle in *Pale Fire* as "the author, as a Creator who can turn backward and forwards at will the file cards upon which he composes … [and who thus] transcends the time of his unsuspecting characters' world" (108). Nabokov himself explicitly invokes this theme of the creative artist as a parallel to the divine creator. In the preface he wrote for the *Time* reprinting of *Bend Sinister* he speaks of "an anthropomorphic deity impersonated by me," and he describes that novel's ending in similar theological terms: "Krug returns unto the bosom of his maker." To me, this recurrent motif (Nabokov is to his created world as God is to his) makes no sense if there was to Nabokov no God. The writer's insistence on comparing himself to the Everlasting is meaningless in a non-theist context. Alexandrov puts it neatly. For Nabokov, "the metaliterary is camouflage for, and a model of, the metaphysical" (18). Of course, not all metaphysics are theistically oriented. But if Nabokov's image of himself as a creative artist leads us to conclude that he compared himself to God, in the matter of arranging things into a beautiful and coherent order—not topsical turvical coincidence, but a web of sense—might we not conclude that Nabokov believed in God … and God believed in Nabokov? We are wise to recall the writer's charming description of his childhood as an embryonic artist: "I used to be a little conjurer when I was a boy. I loved doing simple tricks—turning water into wine, that sort of thing" (*Strong Opinions*, 11). In a discussion with a potential publisher of *Bend Sinister*, Nabokov wrote:

> [Krug] realizes suddenly the presence of the Author of things, the Author of him and of his life and of all the lives around him,—the Author is *I*, the man who writes the book of his life. This singular apotheosis (a device never yet attempted in literature) is, if you like, a kind of symbol of the Divine Power. (*Selected Letters*, 49–50)

Thus, in a metamorphosis which I find fascinating, the amusing search for the source of the title of *Pale Fire* finally leads us into metaphysics: it not only leads to Shakespeare, but to the Lord.

***

In addition to finding the source of the Shakespearean passage which gives John Shade's poem and Vladimir Nabokov's novel their titles, it is important to note what that passage actually says. In a paraphrase even more awkward than Conmal's, the clause containing the words "pale fire" means "the moon steals its dim light from the sun." "Pale fire" then is reflected illumination. *Pale Fire* is, in fact, a novel of reflections. We have already seen that one of its major characters is named Shade. Another (Gradus) is allegedly a mirror maker by profession. And "Gradus" is in turn reflected by a character whose name is his alphabetic mirror image, "Sudarg." The political faction which supports the exiled King Charles is the "Shadows." Kinbote's imaginary country is "Zembla," and much is made of the "Zembla–Resemble" verbal pairing:

> I negligently observed that all bearded Zemblans resembled one another—and that, in fact, the name Zembla is a corruption not of the Russian *zemlya*, but of Semberland, a land of reflections, of "resemblers." (265)

Nabokov even suggests that there are some ways in which Kinbote is a reflection of his own creator. At the very end of his notes, Kinbote remarks that "I may turn up yet, on another campus, as an old, happy, healthy, heterosexual Russian, a writer in exile, sans fame, sans future, sans audience, sans anything but his art" (300–1). (This echoes, of course, *As You Like It*, 2. 7. 165, Jacques' "All the world's a stage" speech, which ends with "second childishness and mere oblivion, / Sans teeth, sans eyes, sans taste, sans everything.") It is certainly impossible not to equate that happy, healthy, heterosexual Russian writer in exile sans everything but his art with Vladimir Nabokov. Kinbote, a crazy, homosexual, unperceptive, and unattractive man is a distorted image of his maker. The lunatic and the poet both create coherent worlds of fascination and beauty. Kinbote creates himself and his Zembla; Nabokov creates Kinbote, Zembla, and *Pale Fire*. The novel is full of twins, doubles, curious pairings, and similar reiterations of the "reflections" theme embodied by the title. There are, for example, Kinbote's ping pong-playing "charming identical twins and another boy, another boy" (23) or the half-brothers Odon and Nodo.

Nabokov choose for the title of his novel a phrase from Shakespeare which invokes the notion of a lesser light reflecting a greater one. It seems to me that the unavoidable conclusion is that *Pale Fire* is explicitly meant to stand in just such a relationship to Shakespeare's incandescence in *Timon of Athens*.

***

The tiny (thirty-twomo) Zemblan edition of *Timon of Athens* as translated by Kinbote/Charles's uncle Conmal affords Nabokov an opportunity for commentary on the art and craft of translation, in particular the translation of Shakespeare. Conmal is a hilariously inept translator of Shakespeare, seriously hampered by fact that he doesn't know the English language. As he is dying, "his last words in his last delirium were "*Comment dit-on 'mourir' en anglais?"*—a beautiful and touching end" (285). It is difficult to excuse a translator of Shakespeare who cannot remember how to say "die." Once, when the accuracy of his translations was questioned, Conmal fired off:

> "an extraordinary sonnet composed directly in colorful, if not quite correct, English, beginning:
>
> > 'I am not slave! Let be my critic slave, I cannot be.
> > And Shakespeare would not want thus.
> > Let drawing students copy the acanthus
> > I work with Master on the architrave!'" (286—In classical architecture, the "acanthus" is the leaf shaped decoration on the top of a column; "architrave" the lintel which runs across a series of columns)

Even his name suggests that "con mal" does a bad job with his literary hobby.

The motif of "translation" in *Pale Fire* is particularly telling, because at the exact moment Nabokov was creating Conmal and Kinbote, "Pale Fire," and *Pale Fire*, he was simultaneously laboring on completing the publication of his own monumental, occasionally Kinbotian translation and annotation of Pushkin's *Eugene Onegin*. Nabokov's *Onegin* is a four-volume tome, of which only a small part of the first volume is actually Pushkin; the remainder is Nabokov's overwhelming commentary. This work appeared in 1964, only two years after the publication of *Pale Fire*. Seen in this light, *Pale Fire* has something of the status of a Greek Satyr play: it is the comic relief, the parody of a related literary task of great weight and high seriousness. Nabokov had developed, and came to hold fiercely, a theory of literary translation which was quirky, and was the subject of intense criticism. He believed, and proclaimed the belief aggressively, that only the strictest, most literal, word-for-word translation was legitimate: "My translation is, of course, a literal one, a crib, a pony. And to the fidelity of transposal I have sacrificed everything: elegance, euphony, clarity, good taste, modern usage, and even grammar" (*Strong Opinions*, 38). It was on this issue that Nabokov's long and close friendship with Edmund Wilson finally foundered. In the figure of Conmal, then, and his hilariously inept versions of Shakespeare, Nabokov is making a most serious statement about his own intense and deeply felt efforts to translate Russian into English, an enterprise which had taken most of his attention and energy over a period of years. Like Conmal, he had translated parts of *Hamlet* into Russian, in part in response to what he felt was the irresponsibly loose translation of Pasternak, whose philosophy of translation Nabokov felt was Conmal-esque.

Moreover, to Nabokov, "translation" was no dry academic enterprise—it was a gateway into the quintessence of his being. It is both a literary exercise, and a biographical fact. His art and his life (which seem impossible to separate) were "translated" from Russian to English, a movement which was clearly one of the defining aspects of his existence. In the amusing minor character of Conmal in *Pale Fire*, Nabokov creates and opens a tiny door into a rich, complex, and serious room within the mansion of his literary consciousness.

\*\*\*

Charles Kinbote repeatedly compares his situation to that of Shakespeare's Timon. Timon spends the second half of Shakespeare's play living like a hermit in a cave outside Athens. Kinbote, although he is apparently living in a cabin-style motel in the American West, to which he has fled after pilfering the manuscript of Shade's "Pale Fire," repeatedly refers to his residence as a "cave":

> Instead of answering a month-old letter from my cave in Cedarn ... (18)

> Having no library in the desolate log cabin where I live like Timon in his cave ... (79)

> I believe I can guess (in my bookless mountain cave) what poem is meant ... (194)

> [In the "Index" under the entry for "Kinbote, Charles, Dr."]: his having no library in his Timonian cave. (308)

Kinbote's version of his life story parallels that of Shakespeare's protagonist. Both began as wealthy, famous, prominent, and irresponsible men, surrounded by flatterers and admirers. Both became, with lightning suddenness, friendless exiles, living in bitter and eccentric isolation. Timon and Kinbote share some of the blame for their downfalls. In particular, they share their naïve assumptions concerning the permanency of their lofty positions; their even more naïve faith in the sincerity of the sycophants who surround them; and their blindness to the dangers just before them. But both men are equally victims of external malignancy: Kinbote/Charles is the victim of a Soviet-style revolution, just as Timon's loss of fiscal fortune is the consequence of bad advice and bad luck, as well as folly and poor planning.

Both heroes are deranged by their changed status. Timon is reduced to grubbing in the woods for roots, after his frenzied final confrontation with his supposed friends. He rants:

> [*Throws the water in their faces.*]
> Live loathed and long,
> Most smiling, smooth, detested parasites,

Courteous destroyers, affable wolves, meek bears,
You fools of fortune, trencher-friends, time's flies
Cap-and-knee slaves, vapors, and minute-jacks.
Of man and beast the infinite malady
Crust you quite o'er. What, dost thou go?
Soft, take physic first; thou too and thou.
Stay, I will lend thee money, borrow none.
[*Drives them out.*]
What? All in motion? Henceforth be no feast
Whereat a villain's not a welcome guest.
Burn house! Sink Athens! Henceforth hated be
Of Timon man and all humanity. (3. 6, 94–106)

Kinbote's sanity, alas, is never really in question. As noted earlier, Kinbote's pose of rationalist literary executor and commentator degenerates before the end of the third paragraph of his Foreword— "There is a very loud amusement park right in front of my present lodgings." The senior member of John Shade's department describes Kinbote as "known to have a deranged mind" (195). Later, at an academic party, Kinbote comes up on a group chatting about him just after one of them has called him a "lunatic," to which Shade responds "That is the wrong word," he said. "One should not apply it to a person who deliberately peels off a drab and unhappy past and replaces it with a brilliant invention" (238). In the Foreword Kinbote confronts "a certain ferocious lady" who remarks:

> "You are a remarkably disagreeable person. I fail to see how John and Sybil can stand you," and, exasperated by my polite smile, she added: "What's more, you are insane." (25)

Kinbote himself remarks that "Whatever energy I possessed has quite ebbed away lately, and these excruciating headaches now make impossible the mnemonic effort and eye strain that the drawing of another such plan would demand" (107). And later, even more dramatically, he reveals he suffers from "these dark evenings that are destroying my brain" (123).

Kinbote and Timon have quite similar images of themselves—both believe they have been wronged (which is true) and that they are entirely blameless (which is false). Moreover, both take a kind of obsessive delight in proclaiming their innocence, and their victimhood.

As a consequence of their situations in life, and their mental and emotional chaos, the two characters speak in rather similar tones: self-pitying, intolerant, overwrought, and hysterical.

KINBOTE: … that young roomer of mine who snapped the picture. A week later he was to betray my trust by taking sordid advantage of my

absence on a trip to Washington whence I returned to find he had been
entertaining a fiery-haired whore from Exton who had left her combings
and reek in all three bathrooms. (17)

TIMON:                              Matrons, turn incontinent!
Obedience, fail in children! Slaves and fools
Pluck the grave wrinkled Senate from the bench
And minister in their steads! To the general filths
Convert o' th' instant, green virginity!
Do't in your parents' eyes. (4. 1. 3–8)

Shakespeare's play and Nabokov's novel both force the reader to confront,
center-stage, as it were, very loud, intelligent, madmen, blind to their
own failings but acutely sensitive to all the flaws of others around them.
Both characters strive mightily to persuade their audiences that theirs
is an accurate vision of the world, and both fail, as a consequence of the
extremity of that vision. Timon and Kinbote respond to their status as exiles
with curses, hysteria, plots, and self-pity. We share some of the pity, but it
is tempered by a more objective view of their responsibility for their own
downfall, and the excesses of their reactions to it.

***

Yet another revealing connection between *Pale Fire* and *Timon of Athens* is
structural: both works adopt an unusual bifurcated form.

There has been some critical controversy regarding the structure of
*Timon of Athens*, focusing not upon the issue of the play's split structure,
but upon the intentionality and functionality of that two part organization.
All agree that the play divides at the point of Timon's self-imposed exile
from Athens after Act 3. For some critics, such as Frank Kermode, this
division makes thematic sense: "The play was evidently designed to consist
of two halves illustrating contrasting modes of excess" (14). Other readers
see this split as a major compositional weakness in *Timon*. One strong
statement of this position was offered, somewhat hyperbolically, by Mark
Van Doren:

If Aristotle was right when he called plot the soul of tragedy, *Timon
of Athens* has no soul ... The play is two plays, casually joined in the
middle. (249–53)

In any event, there is no question that the play has a sharp split between an
Athenian half and an exile half.

Those same descriptors could be applied to the two, equally sharply
divided segments of *Pale Fire*. Kinbote's commentary and the associated

critical paraphernalia is certainly an "exile" segment of the novel. It describes the condition of Kinbote as an exile. And it presents, in some detail, his version of how he was exiled from Zembla to the United States (like Timon, on his own initiative) and then re-exiled from his comfortable teaching post in New England to the isolated tourist cabin in "Cedarn, Utana." Shade's poem might be seen as "Athenian" in its contemplative, philosophical temper. It is certainly worlds apart from Kinbote's frenetic sections of *Pale Fire*. Indeed, to some readers, the two may seem so far removed as to seem impossibly yoked together into one novel.

Such sharply divided literary structures are a "high risk/high gain" aesthetic gamble. The risk, of course, is that the work becomes so deeply bifurcated as to lose its wholeness and, in effect, fall apart. Some critics have felt this to be the fate of *Timon*, and some have made similar comments about *Pale Fire*. Dwight Macdonald's sharply negative review, cited earlier, found Nabokov's work "unreadable" in part for this reason.

On the other hand, the potential gain of such an aesthetic tactic is the achieving of a kind of "triangulation effect." If a work can present the same plot, characters, and thematic materials from two very divergent points of view, the audience, if it can assimilate both perspectives, can gain a far sharper and more accurate view of that material. (Contemporary examples might include novels like Arthur Phillips' *Angelica* or David Mitchell's *Cloud Atlas*.). This effect is similar to viewing, say, a mountain peak from one spot, then moving 10 miles away and viewing it again: if the beholder can keep both vistas in mind, there will emerge a fuller and "truer" image of the actual pinnacle.

Similarly, we first explore Timon's view of himself, his friends, and the world of Athens when he is at the top of Fortune's wheel. Then, when his situation is reversed, we see those same elements of his world from his radically shifted point of view. By keeping both visions within our consciousness, we emerge with an enhanced understanding of both this character and his surrounding culture. That vision is neither that of the first, nor the second half of the play, but combines them both.

The same aesthetic phenomenon can occur with readers of *Pale Fire*. In the novel, we hear two very, very different voices (both of which are, of course, the masked voice of Vladimir Nabokov). Shade seems a reasoned, comfortable, serious, somewhat avuncular philosophic regional poet. Kinbote is a brilliant, insane, touchy, and wild eccentric. (These characterizations apply whether one adopts the "one author" or the "two authors" reading.) To a great extent, in *Pale Fire*, both see, react to, and write about many of the same things. They teach at the same college, know many of the same people, live in adjacent houses, and the like. More importantly, both are engaged, for quite different reasons, on a rather desperate search for some sense of their own mission or purpose in life. Shade is grappling with the recent and inexplicable death of his only child; Kinbote tries to cope with his growing isolation, mental disorientation, and geographical uprooting. Both explore the same areas in their individual searches: conventional theology, the world of nature, love and sex, scholarship, and art. It is through the latter, in the creation of the poem "Pale Fire" at least in part, that Shade finds enough of the answer to his questions to satisfy him. Then he is murdered. Kinbote creates "his" *Pale Fire*, the critical edition of Shade's poem and is left alive at the work's conclusion, but he is still far from satisfied. He has not found in his creation the peace which John Shade discovered through his. Perhaps this is because Kinbote, through the King Charles/Zembla history, is attempting to create a "real" life for himself, while Shade is content with a poem.

Shakespeare utilizes the bifurcated structure of *Timon of Athens* to illuminate the extremities of character within his protagonist, and the radical hypocrisy of the society which surrounds him, first as a wealthy patron, then as an impoverished hermit. Nabokov employs a similar organization in *Pale Fire* to highlight both the similarities and the disparities between Kinbote and Shade, lunatic and poet.

***

Although *Timon of Athens* is the chief Shakespearean referent in *Pale Fire*, it is by no means an exclusive source of allusions for Kinbote, for Shade, for Nabokov. One passage of particular relevance to the study of Nabokov and Shakespeare takes place in a conversation between Shade and Kinbote, narrated somewhat in the style of Boswell, by Kinbote:

> Shakespeare at college level having been introduced: [*Shade speaks*] "First of all, dismiss ideas, and social background, and train the freshman to shiver, to get drunk on the poetry of *Hamlet* or *Lear*, to read with his spine and not with his skull." Kinbote: "You appreciate particularly the purple passages?" Shade: "Yes, my dear Charles, I roll upon them as a grateful mongrel on a spot of turf fouled by a Great Dane." (155)[5]

The reference to the "Great Dane" is an appropriate one as there is an important and revealing chain of *Hamlet* citations and allusions in the novel. While these do not, perhaps, have the core structural significance of the *Timon of Athens* pattern, they merit attention.

Kinbote's (and Nabokov's) imagined country of Zembla appears to be quite close to Denmark: the assassin Gradus takes a commercial flight from Zembla to Copenhagen on the way to Paris (163); the extremist "Shadows" communicate in Danish (252); King Alfin was a wretched linguist who spoke "only a few phrases of French and Danish" (102); and the like. (The "real" Nova Zembla or Novaya Zemlya is in the Arctic Ocean, north of Russia.)

*Hamlet* figures importantly in the novel as it illuminates the theme of suicide, in at least two ways. First is a string of references to "Ophelia" and her self-destruction, one of the Shakespearean scenes to which Nabokov returns time and again. The major event in the poem "Pale Fire" is the death by suicide of Shade's daughter Hazel. Like Hamlet's intended, Hazel kills herself by drowning:

> ... and some say
> She took her poor young life. I know. You know.
> It was a night of thaw, a night of blow,
> With great excitement in the air. Black spring
> Stood just around the corner, shivering
> In the wet starlight and on the wet ground
> The lake lay in the mist, its ice half drowned
> A blurry shape stepped of the reedy bank
> Into a cackling, gulping swamp, and sank. (50–51)

Later, Kinbote reiterates obviously the Ophelia motif, while discussing various means of suicide: "drown with clumsy Ophelia" (220). Less clearly, the theme recurs when Kinbote, listing Shakespearean trees, notes: "two willows, the green, likewise from Venice, the hoar-leaved from Denmark" (291). He is echoing, consciously or unconsciously, Gertrude's description of Ophelia's drowning, in a passage we have seen Nabokov using earlier, in *Pnin*:

> There is a willow grows askant the brook,
> That shows his hoar leaves in the glassy stream ...
> There on the pendent boughs her crownet weeds
> Clamb'ring to hang, an envious sliver broke,
> When down her weedy trophies and herself
> Fell in the weeping brook ...
> ... her garments, heavy with their drink,
> Pulled the poor wretch from her melodious lay
> To muddy death. (4. 7. 166–83)

Kinbote, as well as Shade, spends considerable time and thought on suicide. He says admiringly of Hazel that she "deserves great respect, having preferred the beauty of death to the ugliness of life" (Index 312). Indeed, Kinbote—like Hamlet—is obsessed with self-destruction. In the passage where he remarks on Ophelia's clumsy drowning, he discusses other methods of suicide:

> There are purists who maintain that a gentleman should use a brace of
> pistols, one for each temple, or a bare botkin (note the correct spelling)
> ... (220)

This, of course, refers to Hamlet's most famous brooding upon the same
issue as Kinbote in what is probably the most famous speech in English
dramatic literature: whether to kill himself or not.

> To be, or not to be; that is the question ...
> For who would bear the whips and scorns of time,
> Th' oppressor's wrong, the proud man's contumely
> The pangs of despised love, the law's delay,
> The insolence of office, and the spurns
> That patient merit of th' unworthy takes
> When he himself might his quietus make
> With a bare **bodkin**? (3. 1. 56–76)

Both agree that it would be very desirable to put an end to the tortures of
life; both decide not to do so. As noted earlier, many scholars believe that
"Charles Kinbote" is actually "V. Botkin," who has tipped into insanity and
invented a new identity as Kinbote/Charles the Beloved for himself. The
Index entry for "Botkin" is tantalizing:

> Botkin, V., American scholar of Russian descent, 894; king-bot, maggot
> of extinct fly that once bred in mammoths and is thought to have
> hastened their phylogenetic end, 247; bottekin-maker, 71; *bot*, plop, and
> boteliy, big-bellied (Russ.); botkin or bodkin, a Danish stiletto.

The careful reader, faced with all these "botkins" will note that this suicidal
stiletto is a syllabic anagram of "Kinbote." Indeed, the narrator himself has
earlier reported a conversation in which an academic colleague remarks to
him "I was under the impression you were born in Russia, and that your
name was a kind of anagram of Botkin or Botkine?" (267). The Professor V.
Botkin cited in the index appears in the notes in a rather curious, Kinbotian,
aside:

> Speaking of the Head of the bloated Russian Department, Prof. Pnin, a
> regular martinet in regard to his underlings (happily, Prof. Botkin, who
> taught in another department, was not subordinated to that grotesque
> "perfectionist") (155).

Why "happily"? This remark, which seems to come out of the blue, makes
little sense unless we entertain the idea that Kinbote is, indeed, perhaps
Botkin, and thus his not being under the yoke of martinet Pnin is a "happy"

fact. Of course, if we assume *Pale Fire*'s Professor Pnin is essentially the same character as *Pnin*'s Pnin, we might also question the "martinet" designation ...

If we are searching the novel for a "real solution" to its puzzles, the Kinbote = Botkin theory makes good sense (but is not, to me, dramatically more persuasive than several other solutions). Certainly Nabokov suggests that Kinbote's fantasy about the crazed killer Gradus, who kills Shade by accident while attempting regicide, is not "real." The actual killer (and some readers do not believe that there is an "actual killer") is surely Jack Grey. Grey was sentenced to the Institute for the Criminally Insane by Judge Goldsworth, Kinbote's landlord. Grey does seem to kill the wrong man by mistake, but he mistakes Shade for the judge, rather than accidentally missing Kinbote/Charles with his bullet. On this level, it may well be that "Kinbote" is the crazed émigré professor, Botkin, not the deposed monarch of a distant northern land.

On the other hand, the fantasy world Kinbote creates is far more powerful than the flimsy "reality" which must undergird it somehow. We readers of *Pale Fire* know that there is no Zembla, nor a Charles the Beloved. But we know equally well that there is no "real" John Shade, Charles Kinbote, or V. Botkin. All are the products of Nabokov's imagination, and in this sense (as in one or two others) Kinbote resembles his inventor: he has come up with a "brilliant invention" (238).

More importantly, Kinbote shares Hamlet's morbid preoccupation with self-destruction, and he connects himself to Hamlet through the Kinbote/Botkin link, a theme which points with the directness of a sharp Danish stiletto at the suicidal link between Nabokov's and Shakespeare's protagonists.

\*\*\*

There are brief citations of other Shakespearean works in *Pale Fire* which point in interesting directions. Kinbote cites the cryptic dedication to Shakespeare's sonnets in discussing the link between his commentary and Shade's poem: "it is the underside of the weave that entrances the beholder and only begetter ..." (17). Since some have found in Shakespeare's dedication to Mr. W. H. as the "only begetter" of the sonnets hints of the homosexual attraction depicted in the earlier sonnets in particular, this seems an apt description of Kinbote's (purely platonic) attraction to Shade. Too, Kinbote deplores works (other than *Pale Fire*) which take their names from Shakespearean plays and poems: "anybody can flip through a *Midsummer Night's Dream* or *Romeo and Juliet*, or, perhaps, the *Sonnets* and take his pick" (240). Conmal's first botched Shakespearean translation, too, was the *Sonnets*. Other plays which are briefly mentioned, but which seem to have no major thematic significance include *Othello* (Shade's Aunt Maud's verse book is open to the index at "moor"—36), *Macbeth* (Kinbote calls one of the "hags" who serve in the college cafeteria "The third in the witch row" 267), *Lear*, *A Midsummer Night's Dream*, *The Tempest*, *As You Like It*, and *Twelfth Night*. Just as a random sample, at one point late in the novel, Kinbote suggests that he may "assume other disguises" and "turn up yet, on another campus" as "a writer in exile, sans fame, sans future, sans audience, sans anything but his art" (300–1). As noted above, this is an obvious reference to the famed "All the world's a stage" speech made by Jacques in *As You Like It* which ends with a description of second childhood as "Sans teeth, sans eyes, sans taste, sans everything" (2. 7. 165).

A curious feature of the Wordsmith College campus on which Kinbote and Shade both teach is its famous avenue of trees mentioned by Shakespeare. Kinbote calls our attention to this arboreal street several times:

The famous avenue of all the trees mentioned by Shakespeare ... (92)

At the end of the the so-called Shakespeare Avenue, on the campus (93)

In a black notebook that I fortunately have with me I find, jotted down ... the inscriptions on the trees in Wordsmith's famous avenue ... (154)

one of the most famous avenues in Appalachia ... I can enumerate here only a few kinds of those trees: Jove's stout oak and two others, the thunder-cloven from Britain, the knotty-entrailed from a Mediterranean island; a weather-fending line (now lime) a phoenix (now date palm), a pine and a cedar, all insular; a Venetian sycamore tree (*Acer*); two willows, the green, likewise from Venice, the hoar-leaved from Denmark; a midsummer elm, its barky fingers enringed with ivy, a midsummer mulberry, its shade inviting to tarry; and a sad clown's cypress from Illyria (291). [This list includes trees from, at least, *The Tempest*, *Twelfth Night*, *Mid-Summer Night's Dream*, *Othello*, *Hamlet*, and *Coriolanus*. *The Tempest* dominates. That Venetian Sycamore is from Othello, and refers to the European Sycamore, which is a type of maple (Acer), not the American variety.]

Curiously, there is another Shakespearean street, "Coriolanus Lane" in Zembla, where Kinbote says he had an apartment (76), and under which ran the tunnel through which King Charles escaped (126).

Of the other citations, perhaps the most intriguing comes from an early poem of John Shade called "The Nature of Electricity," which Kinbote includes. The first lines are:

The dead, the gentle dead—who knows?—
In tungsten filaments abide

And on my bedside table glows
Another man's departed bride
And maybe Shakespeare floods a whole
Town with innumerable lights,
And Shelley's incandescent soul
Lures the pale moths of starless nights. (192)

Shakespeare indeed floods the whole of *Pale Fire*, and the lights which
illuminate the greatest part of the novel are *Hamlet* and especially *Timon of
Athens*.

# "O What a Noble Mind:" *Ada* and *Hamlet*

Nabokov's *Ada* was published in 1969, just as its author was turning 70. It is a work of astonishing vigor for a writer of any age. *Ada* is, by a substantial margin, Nabokov's longest novel—the Vintage edition runs to 606 pages, and the same publisher's *Lolita* a mere 317. It is richly enhanced by Shakespearean references, containing some 60 citations or parodies of Shakespeare, allusions to his works, life, or repute—nearly one every ten pages throughout its massive length.[1] In the pages which follow, I make a few general comments about the reception the novel has received, from critics and general readers alike; note the wide range of Shakespearean works to which it makes reference; then focus specifically on the links between *Ada* and *Hamlet*. *Ada* is also Nabokov's most densely allusive novel overall, filled with hundreds of references to European, Russian, and American authors—a very abbreviated sample list might include Maupassant, Tolstoy, Chateaubriand, Balzac, Goethe, Cocteau, H. G. Wells, Joyce, Lewis Carroll, Borges, Chekhov, Mandelshtam, Blok, Proust, Poe, Milton, and, perhaps most importantly, Pushkin.

The novel is set in a fantasy fictional world, Antiterra or Demonia, which is akin to but quite different from Terra, our world. In *Ada*'s cosmos, electricity is replaced by water (characters converse on "dorophones"); there exists a kind of gliding flying carpet called "jikkers." Not only technology, but political geography seems to the first-time reader a kind of crazy quilt:

> Van's maternal grandmother Daria ("Dolly") Durmanov was the daughter of Prince Peter Zemski, Governor of Bras d'Or, an American province in the Northeast of our great and variegated country, who had married, in 1824, Mary O'Reilly, an Irish woman of fashion. Dolly, an only child, born in Bras, married in 1840, at the tender and wayward age of fifteen, General Ivan Durmanov, Commander of Yukon Fortress and peaceful country gentleman, with lands in the Severn Tories (Severniya Territorii), that tessellated protectorate still lovingly called "Russian" Estoty, which commingles, granoblastically and organically, with "Russian" Canady, otherwise "French" Estoty, where not only

French but Macedonian and Bavarian settlers enjoy a halcyon climate under our Stars and Stripes. (3)

This is the work's second paragraph. Surely many a reader, especially those not already familiar with the dense texture of Nabokov's prose, encounters this startlingly revised globe and, with no pages to its left and some 600 to its right, gives up immediately. Parker observes that "Some readers will read no further [than Chapter 1]" (106). It is amusing and sobering, and I think useful, to scan some of the comments on *Ada* posted by readers who are not literary professionals. Here is a random but representative sample of such comments from the internet review site www.goodreads.com:

"so beautiful and lush"

"undoubtedly a masterpiece"

"65 % of the time I did not know what was going on in it"

"I couldn't stand this"

"morally repugnant"

"just about my favorite book of all time."

The responses of sophisticated literary critics to the novel vary as wildly as those of non-professional readers. Some find it a major masterpiece of modern fiction; others have a vehement negative reaction. An example of the former is the review in the *New York Times* by Alfred Appel, Jr (the annotator of *Lolita*):

"Ada," Nabokov's 15th novel, is a great fairy tale, a supremely original work of the imagination. Appearing two weeks after his 70th birthday, it provides further evidence that he is a peer of Kafka, Proust and Joyce, those earlier masters of totally unique universes of fiction.

"Ada, or Ardor: A Family Chronicle" (its full title ... spans 100 years. It is a love story, an erotic masterpiece, a philosophical investigation into the nature of time. Almost twice as long as any previous Nabokov novel, its rich and variegated prose moves from the darkest to the lightest of sonorities as Nabokov sensually evokes the widest range of delights. Nabokov the lepidopterist once said that he was "born a landscape painter," and he has never "painted" more luminous landscapes than in "Ada."

On the other side of the spectrum is Martin Amis, who commented in *The Guardian* that *Ada* is "a waterlogged corpse at the stage of maximum bloat." Elsewhere, in an interview, he elaborated:

[*Ada* is] all genius and no talent. It's impossible to read. The love of the reader ... becomes onanistic. It's a hand-job, basically, that sort of novel. It's self-loving.

John Updike, usually an admirer of Nabokov, wrote in *The New Yorker*:

> When a book fails to agree with a reader, it is either because the author has failed to realize his intentions or because his intentions are disagreeable. Since Vladimir Nabokov is, all in all, the best equipped writer in the English speaking world ... the opening chapter of his new novel *Ada* must be taken as intentionally repellant. (67)

Some have seen the work as a glorification of incest (e.g. John Updike's unflattering review in *The New Yorker* in 1969). To others, though, it is a serious philosophical investigation: in *Nabokov's Ada: The Place of Consciousness*, Boyd argues that this novel's core theme is the celebration of free and unfettered consciousness, set against the limitations and temporal entrapments of the present moment. In *Ada*, Boyd contends, as in much of his fiction and non-fiction, Nabokov seeks a world which transcends the limits of time and matter, allowing consciousness to expand infinitely in both time and space.

The full title of the novel is *Ada or Ardor: A Family Chronicle*. But here again, Nabokov makes the unwary reader work: it turns out that the novel's primary ardors are between Van and Ada. They, and the reader, discover that they are actually brother and sister. At the beginning of the novel, when Van is 14 and Ada is 11, they believe they are cousins. But soon they discover that both are the children of Demon Veen and Marina. This discovery does nothing to dampen their raging erotic passion, which lasts (with some agonizing interruptions) for 80 years.

***

In keeping with its encyclopedic nature, Ada makes reference to a remarkable number of Shakespeare's works, in addition to general allusions to his life. By my count, 16 plays are invoked, significantly more than in any other novel (*Pale Fire* is the runner-up with 12). *Hamlet*, with some 21 citations, is clearly the dominant drama, but it is intriguing and important to survey some of the others:

- *The Tempest*: "Bathwater (or shower) was too much of a Caliban to speak distinctly" (24). [This is part of a description of Aqua Veen's madness, in which she thought she could hear water speak. Water is a major theme of *Ada*, especially in regard to Lucette, Marina Veen's daughter (see below section VI).]

- *The Merchant of Venice* and *King Lear*: "'I read to her twice Segur's adaptation in fable form of Shakespeare's play about the wicked usurer.' 'She also knows my revised monologue of his mad king,' Said Ada: Ce beau jardin fleurit en mai, mais en hiver jamais, jamais, jamais, jamais, jamais, n'est vert, n'est vert, n'est vert, n'est vert, n'est vert" (92–3).[2] [A brilliant play on King Lear's lament for Cordelia, that he will see her "never, never, never, never, never." The same speech is echoed later by Van: "N'est vert, n'est vert, n'est vert … Never never shall I hear again her 'botanical' voice …" (300). Another amusing reference to *King Lear* comes when Van and Ada peruse a photo album put together by a peeping tom. They "skip nature shots—of skunklike squirrels, of a striped fish in a bubble tank, of a canary in its pretty prison" (399—Lear: "Come, let's away to prison: / We two alone will sing like birds i' th' cage …" 5. 3. 8–9).

- *Antony and Cleopatra*: Squeeze, you goose, can't you see I'm dying?" (119—noted by Boyd in *Ada Online*). In 4. 15, Antony says "I am dying, Egypt, dying" (18).

- *Romeo and Juliet*: "Naively ready to embrace him the way Juliet is recommended to receive her Romeo" (121). "She [Ada] did not want him to see her in the role of a moribund Romeo" (169).

- *Othello*: "'My sister, do you recollect that turret, 'of the Moor' yclept?" (141).

- *A Midsummer Night's Dream*: "She fondled him, she entwined him: thus a tendril climber coils round a column" (141—*MND*: Titania—"So doth the woodbine the sweet honeysuckle / Gently entwist; the female ivy so / Enrings the barky fingers of the elm." 4. 1. 43–5). Van: "we are lost in another part of the forest" (153—also *As You Like It*).

- *I Henry IV*: "this cannot be taken away, can it? (it will, it was)" ([53—*I H IV*: Falstaff—"Banish plump Jack, and banish all the world!" Hal—"I do, I will" 2. 4. 485–6. This is one of the relatively few references in Nabokov to the History Plays).[3]

- *Much Ado About Nothing*: "an English 'bull' had become a New England 'bell'" (4—suggested by Boyd in *Ada Online*].

DON PEDRO: Well, as time shall try:
"In time the savage bull doth bear the yoke."
BENEDICK: The savage bull may; but if ever the sensible Benedick bear it, pluck off the bull's horns and set them in my forehead, and let me be vilely painted; and in such great letters as they writer "Here is good horse to hire" let them signify under my sign "Here you may see Benedick the married man" (1. 1. 260–8).

- *The Winter's Tale* and *Measure for Measure*: Bodies of water and fishing as images of unfaithful wives, cited by Boyd in *Ada Online* (5).
- *As You Like It*: "We are lost 'in another part of the forest'" (153). [Stage direction at 3.5 and 5.2. Demon Veen has a secretary with the intriguing name of "Rosalind Knight," which sends the alert reader back to the Shakespearean names of *The Real Life of Sebastian Knight* and to *As You Like It's* Rosalind. Van parodies Touchstone's "an ill-favored thing, sir, but mine own" (5. 4. 58–9) when he says "a poor pun, but mine" (271)].
- *Pericles*: "Yes—*Mytilene, petite isle*, by Louis Pierre" (165) [the heroine of *Pericles* is sold into bondage in Mytilene].
- *Julius Caesar*: "*E tu?*" Pedro asked Marina as he walked past her chair, 'Again screwdriver?'" (200). [Caesar's much-parodied last words are "Et tu, Brute? Then fall Caesar" (3. 1. 77)].
- *Macbeth*: "a stable boy who, I suspect, was impersonated by the youngest of the three demoiselles de Tourbe, witches all" (335). Of course, a play on the three weird sisters of the "Scottish Play." The witches return when Van is at one point diagnosed as sterile, which he describes as a "Hecatean diagnose" (394).

This is but a sample. Some of these references are obvious (e.g. Juliet's embrace of Romeo), others much less so or somewhat dubious (e.g. the English Bull alluding to Benedick in *Much Ado About Nothing)*. Taken altogether, they certainly give a sense of the range Nabokov's familiarity with the Shakespeare canon, and his eagerness to insert a substantial portion of that canon into his longest novel.

There are also about 14 general references to Shakespeare's life and works in *Ada*. These seem to me to fall into three groups.

First are quite casual, not infrequently humorous, asides. For example, the rather obvious pseudo-Shakespeareanism (described by Boyd as Shakespearean mock banter) "And how goes it with you, sweet cousin?" (167). Nabokov mentions the actress Duse, who was famed for her Shakespearean performances, especially Juliet (164). And then, in an amusing parody of Shakespeare's will which left his second-best bed to his wife, we read "nurse Bellabestia ('Bess') to whom he bequeathed a trunkful of museum catalogues and his second-best catheter" (438—"Bess" may also remind us of the diminutive of Queen Elizabeth).

Second, Shakespeare's birthday (and, as we have noted before, by some rather convoluted calculating, Nabokov's as well) is cited three times:

"On April 23, 1869 in drizzly and warm, gauzy and green Kaluga, Aqua, aged twenty-five and afflicted with her usual vernal migraine, married Walter D. Veen." (4)

"ever since Shakespeare's birthday on a green rainy day." (26)

"When had Demon visited Ardis in recent years? April 23, 1884 (the day Van's first summer stay had been suggested, planned, promised)." (237)

These citations are significant in their self-referential aspect, and, rather like the repetition of the number "342" in *Lolita*, function as a kind of gentle reminder of the made, artificial, patterned character of the novel.

Third, and most often and typically, Nabokov frequently cites Shakespeare as a kind of lodestar of literary excellence. Occasionally in *Ada*, those citations also contain a touch of satirical humor:

"genius is not all gingerbread even for Billionaire Bill with his pointed beardlet and stylized bald dome." (73)

"the greatest international shows—English blank-verse plays, French tragedies." (172)

"a theatrical club that habitually limited itself to Elizabethan plays, with queens and fairies played by pretty boys." (181)

"'Look, I can swear I never have, by—by William Shakespeare' (extending dramatically one hand toward a shelf with a set of thick red books)." (371)

"I feel cuddled in the embrace of puzzled Will." (426)

"I love Flemish and Dutch oils, flowers, food, Flaubert, Shakespeare, shopping, scheeing [*sic*], swimming." (464)

(After death) "and if you land on Terra Caelestis, with your pillow and chamberpot, you are made to room not with Shakespeare or even Longfellow, but with guitarists and cretins." (585)

\*\*\*

In spite of this remarkable anthology of citations of plays and biography, the dominant Shakespearean presence in *Ada* is *Hamlet*. Although many of the citations to *Hamlet* are of profound seriousness in *Ada*, and point to its deepest themes, some are considerably more lighthearted. For example, near the Veen residence is a small town named "Gamlet, a hamlet" (35, 87). Van, discussing Ada and Lucette's sexual experimentation, refers to "punning in an Ophelian frenzy on the feminine glans" (394). A prominent politician makes "fairly regular visits to Cuba or Hecuba" (329). Ada has "a three volume *History of Prostitution* which she had read at the age of ten or eleven, between *Hamlet* and Captain Grant's Microgalaxies" (220).

Van inverts syllables when he jests that "he had to travel ... to a hamlet the opposite way from Letham" (178). But most of this novel's references to Nabokov's most-cited Shakespearean drama are anything but "lighthearted."

Something is rotten in the world in which Nabokov's novel takes place: a world called "Demonia."[4] Yet much of what we see of this world seems hardly demonic. Indeed, especially during their first summer together, Van and Ada seem to live in a world which looks like Nabokov's fond memories of pre-revolutionary Russia, early twentieth-century Europe, and mid-twentieth-century America. Life in the country is idyllic and, for the young lovers, sensuous. As they age, even as they are often and sadly parted, they live lives of aristocratic indulgence. And yet they are living on a world which is named for demons, and called as well "Antiterra." Van's (and Ada's) father is named "Demon." And the name "Ada" itself is Russian for "of Hell." Some critics, John Updike among them, see Van and Ada as unappealing characters; certainly many have seen their vigorous and unabashed incestuous sex life as morally tainted.[5] Demonia is not heaven. With Shakespeare in mind, then, it is not difficult to see a link between the world of Nabokov's novel, and that of *Hamlet*. Marcellus, one of the Officers of the Watch who with young Hamlet see the Ghost of old Hamlet on the ramparts of Elsinore castle, famously observes: "Something is rotten in the state of Denmark" (1. 4. 90—a line very commonly misattributed to the protagonist).

In *Hamlet*, of course, one thing which is wrong, rotten, is murder, premature death, the extinguishing of consciousness. The Ghost of Old Hamlet tells his son:

> But know, thou noble youth,
> The serpent that did sting thy father's life
> Now wears his crown.
> HAMLET:                 O my prophetic soul!
> My uncle?
> GHOST:          Ay that incestuous, that adulterate beast,
> With witchcraft of his wits, with traitorous gifts—
> O wicked wit and gifts, that have the power
> So to seduce!—won to his shameful lust
> The will of my most seeming-virtuous queen. (1. 5. 38–46)

As Boyd notes, one aspect of the demonic which taints the world of *Ada* is the prison of time. The novel covers nearly a century of its protagonists' lives, but the very first few years take up half the manuscript, and time seems to accelerate more and more rapidly towards the dissolution of life.

The prison of time is a recurrent theme throughout Nabokov's fiction and non-fiction. He begins his autobiography with an invective against the imprisoning walls time builds around human life:

> Nature expects a full-grown man to accept the two black voids, fore and aft, as stolidly as he accepts the extraordinary visions in between. Imagination, the supreme delight of the immortal and the immature, should be limited. In order to enjoy life, we should not enjoy it too much. I rebel against this state of affairs. I feel the urge to take my rebellion outside and picket nature. Over and over again, my mind has made colossal efforts to distinguish the faintest of personal glimmers in the impersonal darkness on both sides of my life. That this darkness is caused merely by the walls of time separating me and my bruised fists from the free world of timelessness is a belief I gladly share with the most gaudily painted savage. (*Speak, Memory*, 20)

In the "Afterword" to *Lolita*, Nabokov spells out his view of that free world of timeless consciousness:

> For me a work of fiction exists only insofar as it affords me what I shall bluntly call aesthetic bliss, that is a sense of being somehow, somewhere connected with other states of being where art (curiosity, tenderness, kindness, ecstasy) is the norm. (315)

In the concluding chapter of *Speak Memory* Nabokov describes his "confirmed non-unionist" metaphysics:

> When that slow-motion, silent explosion of love takes place in me, unfolding its melting fringes and overwhelming me with the sense of something much vaster, much more enduring and powerful than the accumulation of matter or energy in any imaginable cosmos, then my mind cannot but pinch itself to see if it is really awake. I have to make a rapid inventory of the universe, just as a man in a dream tries to condone the absurdity of his position by making sure he is dreaming. I have to have all space and all time participate in my emotion, in my mortal love, so that the edge of its mortality is taken off, thus helping me to fight the utter degradation, ridicule, and horror of having developed an infinity of sensation and thought within a finite existence. (297)

Hamlet, too, broods on the relationship between mortality and infinity, between what it is "to be" and what it is "not to be":

> What a piece of work is a man, how noble in reason, how infinite in faculties, in form and moving how express and admirable, in action how

like an angel, in apprehension how like a god: the beauty of the world, the paragon of animals; and yet to me, what is this quintessence of dust? (2. 2. 311–6)

There is something rotten in Demonia and in Denmark. It is death, the finite boundaries of mortality, which imprison humankind's infinity of sensation, thought, faculties, and apprehension.

***

The other malaise at the core of Hamlet's Denmark and Van's Demonia is incest. From a contemporary American legal standpoint, Claudius's marriage to Gertrude is not technically incest: it is not prohibited in modern America to marry the widow of one's brother. But there is no doubt whatsoever that to Hamlet (both young Hamlet and the ghost of his father) and to Shakespeare, this union is incestuous. When he names Claudius as his murderer, the Ghost describes him as "that incestuous, that adulterate beast" (1. 5. 42). He urges young Hamlet:

Let not the royal bed of Denmark be
A couch for luxury and damned incest. (1. 5. 82–3)

Even before he learns that his uncle has murdered his father, Hamlet regards the Claudius/Gertrude union as incestuous: "O, most wicked speed, to post / With such dexterity to incestuous sheets!" (1. 2. 156–7).

In Christian canon law in Shakespeare's culture, wedding the widow of one's brother was clearly forbidden as incest. For example, Leviticus 18:16 reads "You shall not uncover the nakedness of your brother's wife: she is your brother's nakedness" and Leviticus 20:21 states "If a man takes his brother's wife, it is impurity." The marriage of Claudius and Gertrude has infected the Danish court with the pollution of incest.

Less clearly, a number of critics and directors have seen Hamlet's wild rage at his mother's re-marriage as a sign he himself is in the grip of an Oedipal response to Gertrude. This emerges most clearly in the scene (3. 4) in Gertrude's closet, when Hamlet confronts her with her crimes, shows her the pictures of her past and present husbands, and exhorts her violently not to "let the bloat king tempt you again to bed" (183). The classic 1948 film of *Hamlet* directed by and starring Sir Laurence Olivier clearly suggests an incestuous motif in this scene, as Hamlet and Gertrude confront each other lying on her bed. Even more explicit was the 1990 film directed by Franco Zeffirelli and starring Mel Gibson as Hamlet and Glenn Close as a quite young Gertrude, whose behavior toward her son is close to explicitly sexual.

In *Ada*, we are first given to understand that Ada and Van are cousins: the (misleading) family tree which precedes the text shows Van as the son of Dementiy (Demon) Veen and Aqua Durmanov; and Ada the daughter of Demon's cousin Daniel and Aqua's sister Marina. Don Johnson nicely unravels what he calls the "tangled skein of incest" (224) in the novel. At a very young age, during their first summer together at Ardis Hall, the sibling lovers realize that Demon and Marina had a passionate affair, and that Daniel was out of the country nine months before Van's birth. Then, they realize that Aqua had lost a baby at the same time Marina gave birth to Ada, and that Ada had been substituted for that lost child. Thus, both Van and Ada are the natural children of Marina and Demon Veen. Lucette is their uterine half-sister, the child of Dan and Marina. The siblings are not the least put off by their discovery, although, much later, when he discovers their sexual relationship, their father Demon Veen is. Indeed, before they realize they are more than cousins, Van and Ada make jokes about "incest," including anagrammatic word-play such as "scient" and "nicest." As discussed below, Van does draw the line at having sex with Lucette, his half-sister, although later both he and Ada think that his qualms in that regard were probably a cruel mistake. Van himself makes the connection to inappropriate sexual relations in *Hamlet* when he remarks "Claudius, at least, did not court Ophelia" (202).

Does Nabokov romanticize or glorify or at least look kindly on incest, or at least this particular incestuous relationship? Some readers have thought so (just as some readers have thought, with less cause, that he romanticizes pedophilia in *Lolita*). Updike, in his negative review of *Ada*, wrote: "Rape is the sexual sin of the mob, adultery of the bourgeoise, and incest of the aristocracy" (72). It is certainly true that the ferocious sexual passion of the novel's central lovers is matched by the depth of a genuine love which lasts for most of a century. Most readers of the novel would, I believe, agree that Van and Ada's mutual attraction is powerful, lasting, and in many ways admirable. It is also true that both suffer for their life-long incestuous relationship, in ways that would not have arisen if they were, say, distant cousins. They have to hide their affair, Ada eventually marries another man, and they endure long, sometimes very long, periods of enforced separation. I think it is clear that *Ada* is not a novel about how Nabokov is "for" or "against" incest. The fact that the lovers are siblings makes them in many ways closer than unrelated lovers could be. I do think that *Ada* is about love and much, much more, and the fact is that the core sexual love story which runs through the entire work is one of incest.

\*\*\*

In many ways, Van Veen echoes, or at least reminds us, of young Hamlet. Both are, for example, brilliant and original thinkers. We know that Hamlet was a student at Wittenburg University (now Martin Luther University of Wittenburg-Halle). More importantly, Shakespeare shows us his mind mulling and seeking light on some of the deepest and most important questions of human existence: the famed "to be or not to be" speech, for example, probes the nature of human life and death, the differences between "dying" and "being dead." He looks deep into himself, entangles himself in psychological and metaphysical questions, and never stops thinking. He thinks about the morality of blood revenge, about filial duty, about the fate of the kingdom of Denmark, the nature of ghosts and spirits. He spends a great deal of time thinking about himself: what is he feeling and thinking? What should he do? When should he do it? How? Indeed, it is a platitude of Hamlet commentary that he thinks too much, too deeply, too much of the time, and is thus paralyzed from taking action.

Van, too, is a student, at Chose University, and then has a career as a professor. He earns a Ph.D., and is a student of Psychology and Philosophy. "Chose" is generally seen as the Demonian equivalent of Cambridge University, so, like Hamlet, his formal academic training is at a venerable European university. Like Hamlet, Van Veen is no stilted academic. His mind ranges widely across a range of subjects. Perhaps most clearly, we see his scholarly brilliance in Part 4 of the novel, in which Van is simultaneously composing his opus "The Texture of Time" as he is driving across Europe to meet Ada. "The Texture of Time" is a dense, and for many readers difficult, psycho-philosophical speculation on the nature of past, present, and future. Van himself describes it as "a difficult, delectable and blessed work [in which] I wish to examine the essence of Time, not its lapse" (536–7). Nabokov's juxtaposition of Van's monograph and his driving trip is a remarkable literary feat. An important part of Van's philosophical speculation comes straight from *Hamlet*: "'To be' means to know one 'has been.' 'Not to be' implies the only 'new' kind of (sham) time: the future" (559).

Hamlet and Van, then, both are students of human nature, including their own nature. They are psychologists and philosophers, pondering some of the biggest and most baffling questions of human life. Their thoughts are often brilliant, they are often tortured by the difficulty of the questions and issues they insist on raising. What is the nature of Time? What is the nature of Being and Not Being? Surely these are two characters of intellectual brilliance.

In some ways, as well, both seem to exemplify the ideal of the scholar athlete (an ideal today, alas, more often honored in the breach than the observance). Hamlet appears to have been working on his swordsmanship: when Horatio suggests he will lose the duel with Laertes, Hamlet responds,

"I do not think so. Since he went into France I have been in continual practice. I shall win at the odds" (5. 2. 211–13).[6]

Van's physical prowess is a bit more obvious. He masters the art of walking on his hands: "fourteen-year-old Van treated us to the greatest performance we have ever seen a brachiambulant give" (82). Later, under the name of "Mascodagama," Van performs this odd stunt in music hall settings, to the amazement of audiences when, at the conclusion of his act, he flips himself right-side-up, and what had seemed to be his legs were revealed to be his arms (181–6). Parker also describes Van as a "sexual athlete" (107). Given his many, frequent, and varied amorous activities, this seems an apt description.

It appears that neither Van nor Hamlet has allowed the philosophical life of scholarship to lead them into inactivity!

Although for much of the action, neither Van nor Hamlet has much to joke about, these protagonists have a similar sense of humor. Perhaps reflecting their respective creators' skills as wordsmiths, both have a taste for puns and word games. Given their intellectual brilliance, they often seem to exhibit a kind of convoluted humor which sometimes eludes those with whom they are speaking. And, not infrequently, both show a kind of sardonic streak in their words. Famously, Hamlet's very first three lines in *Hamlet* are exactly that sort of sardonic, punning, wordplay:

KING: But now, my cousin Hamlet, and my son—
HAMLET: [*aside*] A little more than kin, and less than kind!
KING: How is it that the clouds still hang on you?
HAMLET: Not so, my lord. I am too much in the sun. ꞇo ᴺ
QUEEN: Good Hamlet, cast thy nighted color off,
And let thine eye look like a friend on Denmark.
Do not forever with thy vailed lids
Seek for thy noble father in the dust.
Thou know'st 'tis common; all that lives must die,
Passing through nature to eternity.
HAMLET: Ay, Madame, it is common (1. 2. 64–74—the puns of course are "kind" = natural/amiable; "sun" = light/son; and "common" = frequent/low class).

Van's jokes, too, can be quite cutting (he calls old age, in which one forgets to finish one's sentences "dot-dot-dotage" 109). They can also sometimes be a bit obscene. When, for example, he is about to engage in a duel we are treated to this quick dialog between Van and his opponent's second:

The merest adumbration of an apology on Baron Veen's part would clinch the matter with a token of gracious finality [*says the second*].

"If," said Van, "the good Captain expects that, he can go and stick his pistol up his gracious anality." (306)

Perhaps a better example of Van's customary habit of speaking of even the most important of things in a cruelly flip manner is provided later in this incident. Anticipating that he may be killed in the forthcoming duel (he has just left Ada after discovering her infidelity to him), he writes to his father:

> Dear *Dad*,
>
> In consequence of a trivial altercation with a Captain Tapper, of Wild Violet Lodge, whom I happened to step upon in the corridor of a train, I had a pistol duel this morning in the woods near Kalugano and am now no more. Though the manner of my end can be regarded as a kind of easy suicide, the encounter and the ineffable Captain are in no way connected with the Sorrows of Young Veen. In 1884, during my first summer at Ardis, I seduced your daughter who was then twelve. Our torrid affair lasted till my return to Riverlane; it was resumed last June, four years later. That happiness has been the greatest event in my life, and I have no regrets. Yesterday, though, I discovered she had been unfaithful to me, so we parted. Tapper, I think, may be the chap who was thrown out of one of your gaming clubs for attempting oral intercourse with the washroom attendant, a toothless old cripple, veteran of the first Crimean War. Lots of flowers, please!

He carefully reread his letter – and carefully tore it up. The note he finally placed in his coat pocket was much briefer.

> *Dad*,
>
> I had a trivial quarrel with a stranger whose face I slapped and who killed me in a duel near Kalugano. Sorry!
>
> *Van* (308–9)

Van's cruel humor sometimes has a Shakespearean twist. Responding to a sweet request from Ada to visit the grave of "the late Krolik," Van explodes "I refuse to stare at a stone under which a roly-poly old Pole is rotting, let him feed his maggots in peace" (297), echoing Hamlet's "We fat all creatures else to fat us, and we fat ourselves for maggots" (4. 3. 21–3).

Hamlet makes puns about the death of his father and the over-hasty re-marriage of his mother; Van writes in a tone of saucy insouciance about what may be his immediately forthcoming death, and the loss of the love of his life.

Surely part of the reason for both these protagonists' often sardonic humor is a clear sense of entitlement felt by them both. Neither Hamlet nor Van could ever be accused of being "humble." Hamlet, for example, reveals in the play's very last scene his belief (which is probably correct) that upon the death of his father he, not Claudius, should have become king of Denmark. Claudius has "Popped in between th' election and my hopes" (5. 2. 65). Likewise, Van Veen tends to assume unthinkingly the privileges of aristocracy:

> Van revisited Ardis Hall in 1888. He arrived on a cloudy June afternoon, unexpected, unbidden, unneeded; with a diamond necklace coiled loose in his pocket. (187)

> Of their many houses, in Europe and in the Tropics, the chateau recently built at Ex, in the Swiss Alps, with its pillared front and crenelated turrets, became their favorite. (567)

> He contemplated the pyramids of Ladorah (visited mainly because of its name) under a full moon that silvered the sands inlaid with printed black shadows. He went shooting with the British Governor of Armenia, and his niece, on Lake Fan. From a hotel balcony in Sidra his attention was drawn by the manager to the wake of an orange sunset that turned the ripples of a lavender sea into goldfish scales and was well worth the price of enduring the quaintness of the small striped rooms he shared with his secretary, young Lady Scramble. On another terrace, overlooking another fabled bay, Eberthella Brown, the local Shah's pet dancer (a naïve little thing who thought "baptism of desire" meant something sexual), spilled her morning coffee ... (449)

The humor and the sense of entitlement of both Van and Hamlet speak to another important, and not particularly attractive characteristic of both: they can be casually and cuttingly and at times mortally cruel. Indeed, in *Strong Opinions* Nabokov said that he loathed Van (120), and yet, of course, made him the narrator and protagonist of his most ambitious novel! Both characters can be cruel to those who might be seen to merit their distaste; to those who are merely innocent bystanders; but most importantly, both can be cruel to those who love them, and to whom there is a special obligation to be kind.

So, for example, Hamlet is responsible for the deaths of Rosencantz and Guildenstern when he changes the letter they are bearing to the King of England so as to call for their immediate "sudden death, / Not shriving time allowed" (5. 2. 46–7). In fact, his two ex-schoolmates had agreed to spy on Hamlet for Claudius and Gertrude, but sudden and unshriven death seems a harsh punishment. As Tom Stoppard suggests in *Rosencrantz and*

*Guildenstern are Dead*, these two seem to many to be baffled bystanders, in the grip of forces way beyond their control, or even understanding. But that is not how they seem to Hamlet:

> Why, man, they did make love to this employment.
> They are not near my conscience; their defeat
> Does by their own insinuation grow. (5. 2. 58–9)

Similarly, there is no doubt that old Polonius is a foolish, self-important courtier who causes considerable mischief. Hamlet taunts him mercilessly:

> POLONIUS: My lord, I have news to tell you.
> HAMLET: My lord, I have news to tell you. When Roscius was an actor in Rome—
> POLONIUS: The actors are come hither, my lord.
> HAMLET: Buzz, buzz.
> POLONIUS: Upon my honor—
> HAMLET: Then came each actor on his ass—. (2. 2. 396–402)

Then, mistaking the old courtier for the usurping and incestuous King, he kills him, and again shows little remorse:

> POLONIUS: O, I am slain!
> QUEEN:                  O me, what hast thou done?
> HAMLET: Nay, I know not. Is it the king?
> QUEEN: O, what a rash and bloody deed is this!
> HAMLET: A bloody deed – almost as bad, good Mother,
> As kill a king, and marry with his brother.
> QUEEN: As kill a king?
> HAMLET:                  Ay, lady, it was my word.
> [*Lifts up the arras and sees POLONIUS.*]
> Thou wretched, rash, intruding fool, farewell!
> I took thee for thy better. Take thy fortune.
> Thou find'st to be too busy is some danger—. (3. 4. 26–34)

And then, famously,

> I'll lug the guts into the neighbor room.
> Mother, good night. Indeed, this counselor
> Is now most still, most secret, and most grave
> Who was in life a foolish prating knave. (3. 4. 213–16)

Hamlet's most unforgivable acts of cruelty, however, arise from his relationship with, and treatment of Ophelia, a motif considered at length in the following section.

Van, too, is not overly tender in his relations with many of those he encounters. With women other than those of his station, he can be brutal. He encounters a young anonymous chambermaid:

> Her cameo profile, her cute pink nostril, her long, French, lily-white neck, the outline, both full and frail, of her figure (male lust does not go very far for descriptive felicities!), and especially the savage sense of opportune license moved Van so robustly that he could not resist clasping the wrist of her raised tight-sleeved arm (48—This move does not actually result in anything more than a conversation).

At a picnic at Ardis, Lucette and Marina are having an awkward conversation with Greg Erminin about the latter's Jewish ancestry. Marina suggests, bizarrely, that "It's not a very old religion, anyway, as religions go, is it?" and Van snaps "Who cares—" (90–1). And here is how he describes Percy de Prey, whom he discovers has wooed Ada. He writes looking back on Percy's death from nearly 70 years' perspective:

> Percy, you were to die very soon—and not from that pellet in our fat leg, on the turf of a Crimean ravine, but a couple of minutes later when you opened your eyes and felt relieved and secure in the shelter of the macchie; you were to die very soon, Percy; but that July day in Ladore County, lolling under the pines, royally drunk after some earlier festivity, with lust in your heart and a sticky glass in your strong blond-haired hand, listening to a literary bore, chatting with an aging actress and ogling her sullen daughter [*Ada, of course*], you reveled in the spicy situation, old sport, chin-chin, and no wonder. Burly, handsome, indolent and ferocious, a crack Rugger player, a cracker of country girls, you combined the charm of the off-duty athlete with the engaging drawl of a fashionable ass. (273)

He is not much kinder to another rival, Mr. Rack, a musician, whom he visits on his death bed, and taunts:

> Hospital records put your age at thirty; I thought you were younger, but even so that is a very early age for a person to die—whatever he be *tvoyu mat*—half-baked genius or full-fledged scoundrel, or both. As you may guess by the plain but thoughtful trappings of this quiet room, you are an incurable case in one lingo, a rotting rat in another. No oxygen gadget can help you to eschew the "agony of agony"—Professor Lamort's felicitous pleonasm [*the use of extra words to express an idea*]. The physical torments you will be, or indeed are, experiencing, must be prodigious, but are nothing in comparison to those of a probable hereafter. (314)

We have already seen Van's duel with a more-or-less innocent and irrelevant military officer, Tapper, whom he accidentally brushes past in a train corridor:

> Upon reaching the vestibule he glanced back at her with a wave of the glove he held—and crashed into somebody who had stooped to pick up a bag: *"On n'est pas goujat a ce point,"* observed the latter: a burly military man with a reddish mustache and a staff captain's insignia.
>
> Van brushed past him, and when both had come down on the platform, glove-slapped him smartly across the face. (304)

Van can even be cruel to his beloved Ada. When, in their late middle age, they discover that her husband, Andrey Vinlander, is mortally ill, she begins to cry. "'Part of the act?' [Van] inquired coldly" (529). And when Ada explains she cannot leave her husband to resume her affair with Van while he is ill, Van again comments, "sort of patching up a bloke before hanging him" (529).

But Van's greatest cruelty is to Lucette, his and Ada's half-sister (all share the same mother, Marina, but Lucette's father, Dan, is a cousin of Demon, the father of the sibling lovers). Lucette is to Van as Ophelia is to Hamlet, and it is to these two doomed young women we now turn.

***

It is never really clear what the nature of Hamlet's relationship with Ophelia ?Lucette was before the loss of his father and the remarriage of his mother. Has their romance ever gone beyond words? Shakespeare does not come near to suggesting there has ever been a physical relationship between the two, but neither does he imply there has not. The first we hear about their courtship is when Ophelia's brother Laertes warns her against taking too seriously Hamlet's protestations of love:

> For Hamlet, and the trifling of his favor,
> Hold it a fashion and a toy in blood,
> A violet in the youth of primy nature,
> Forward, not permanent, sweet, not lasting.
> The perfume and suppliance of a minute,
> No more. (1. 3. 5–10)

She seems to indicate that she will take this brotherly advice seriously: "I shall the effect of this good lesson keep / As watchman to my heart" (1. 3. 45–6). When Laertes leaves, their father Polonius steps in with some more discouraging advice. He demands to know what is between them, and Ophelia responds "He hath, my lord, of late made many tenders / Of his affection to me" (1. 3. 99–100), and after Polonius responds unceremoniously "pooh!" reiterates:

> OPHELIA: My lord, he hath importuned me with love in honorable fashion.
> POLONIUS: Ay, fashion you may call it. Go to, go to.
> OPHELIA: And hath given countenance to his speech, good my lord
> With almost all the holy vows of heaven.
> POLONIUS: Ay, springes to catch woodcocks. (1. 3. 110–15)

Then, in Act 2, Ophelia tells Polonius of her frightening meeting with Hamlet, in which he acts bizarrely, shakes her arm, and leaves without a word (2. 1. 77 ff.). Polonius then reports to Claudius and Gertrude that Hamlet is mad for love of his daughter. Finally, in 3. 1, just after the renowned "To be or not to be," we actually see these two together for the first time. It is not a pretty sight. He verbally berates her: "Are you honest? Are you fair?" (3. 1. 102–104). First he claims "I did love you once" 3.1.115) and then immediately declares "I loved you not" (3. 1. 119). He urges her to cloister herself in a nunnery, and then he insults her whole gender:

> I have heard of your paintings, well enough. God hath given you one face, and you make yourselves another. You jig and amble, and you lisp. You nickname God's creatures and make your wantonness your ignorance. Go to, I'll no more on't; it hath made me mad. I say we shall have no moe marriage. Those that are married already—all but one—shall live. The rest shall keep as they are. To a nunnery, go. [*Exit.*] (3. 1. 143–50)

Ophelia responds with her lament "O what a noble mind is here o'erthrown!" (3. 1. 151).

In the very next scene, Hamlet behaves equally cruelly and inexplicably to Ophelia. As they settle in to watch the play-within-the-play, Hamlet offers up a series of suggestive and lewd comments to and about Ophelia, culminating in his rather lame joke:

> OPHELIA: I think nothing, my lord.
> HAMLET: That's a fair thought to lie between maid's legs.
> OPHELIA: What is, my lord?
> HAMLET: Nothing. (3. 2. 119–22)

Pyles points out in an essay entitled "Ophelia's Nothing" that if Hamlet offers the standard hand sign for "nothing" (the thumb and the first finger making the shape of a zero) it makes the joke even clearer—and more offensive.

The very next time we see Ophelia, she has been driven mad by Hamlet's murder of her father, and in her distraction, she is singing sexually suggestive songs:

Then up he rose and donned his clothes
   And dupped the chamber door
Let in the maid, that out a maid
   Never departed more …
By Gis and by Saint Charity
   Alack, and fie for shame!
Young men will do't if they come to't
   By Cock, they are to blame. (4. 4. 52–62)

Rejected by the man she loves, who then accidentally murders her father, thinking him his better, the mad Ophelia drowns herself. This is the third of Nabokov's novels (after *Pnin* and *Bend Sinister*) in which we have encountered this story and the emblem of the mournful willow. Gertrude describes Ophelia's sad end:

There is a willow grows askant the brook,
That shows his hoar leaves in the glassy stream:
Therwith fantastic garlands did she make
Of crowflowers, nettles, daisies, and long purples,
That liberal shepherds give a grosser name,
But our cold maids do dead men's fingers call them.
There on the pendent boughs her crownet weeds
Clamb'ring to hang, an envious sliver broke
When down her weedy trophies and herself
Fell in the weeping brook. Her clothes spread wide,
And mermaidlike awhile they bore her up
Which time she changed snatches of old laude,
As one incapable of her own distress
Or like a creature native and indued
Unto that element. But long it could not be
Till her garments, heavy with their drink,
Pulled the poor wretch from her melodious lay
To muddy death. (4. 7. 166–83)

Hamlet certainly does not mean to kill Ophelia, and his grief when he learns of her death in Act 5 is deep and genuine:

I loved Ophelia. Forty thousand brothers
Could not with all their quantity of love
Make up my sum. (5. 1. 269–71)

But his brusque indifference to the woman who loved him, his public mockery of her gender, and his accidental slaying of her father have surely and directly led to her self-inflicted watery death.

NB

In very much the same ways, Van Veen's treatment of the half-sister of his lover leads unwittingly but unerringly to Lucette's demise, a connection Nabokov makes explicit.

Red-haired Lucette is four years younger than Ada. In any other family, one imagines, she would be considered a prodigy, but compared to Ada's dark beauty and stunning intellect, she seems unexceptional. Even as a young girl, she has a childish crush on Van, constantly follows him around, wants to play with him, and spies on his trysts with Ada. The lovers, in turn, devise increasingly complex, and semi-successful, tactics to sneak away from her and enjoy their romance, their making love, in relative privacy. Once, for example, they plop her in a bath tub and tell her: "don't you dare get out of this nice warm water until bell rings or you'll die" (144). This device works, but not well:

> The two elder children, having locked the door of the L-shaped bathroom from the inside, now retired to the seclusion of its lateral part, in a corner between a chest of drawers and an old unused mangle, which the sea-green eye of the bathroom looking glass could not reach; but barely had they finished their violent and uncomfortable exertions in that hidden nook, with an empty medicine bottle idiotically beating time on a shelf, when Lucette was already calling resonantly from the tub … (144–5)

On another occasion, Van tries to bribe Lucette, offering to give her a book of poetry if she will sit quietly for an hour and memorize one short poem, while he and Ada sneak off.

She clings to the lovers constantly:

> Lucette, the shadow, followed them from lawn to loft, from gatehouse to stable, from a modern shower booth near the pool to the ancient bathroom upstairs. Lucette-in-the-Box came out of a trunk. Lucette desired they take her for walks. Lucette insisted on their playing "leaptoad" with her—and Ada and Van exchanged dark looks. (213)

As Lucette grows older, her crush on Van begins to take on an increasingly sexualized character:

> Lucette fondly admired his long long lashes while pitying his tender skin for the inflamed blotches and prickles between neck and jaw where shaving caused the most trouble … Lucette, always playing her part of the clinging, affectionately fussy lassy, placed both palms on Van's hairy chest … Lucette kissed his hand, then attacked him. (204–5)

When she is 15, Lucette sends Van "a rambling, indecent, crazy, almost savage declaration of love in a ten-page letter" (366). Shortly thereafter she visits Van in his collegiate residence, and reveals that she knew from an early point that Ada and Van kept trying to leave her behind and "appeased your lust, had allayed your fire" (370). She also reveals that she and her half-sister had indulged in childish sex games for years. Van is sorely tempted by Lucette's efforts to seduce him. Although he is unaccustomed to overcoming his sexual appetites, he does manage not to make love, at least technically, to the half-sister of his one and only true lover. But a bit later, in Chapter 8 of Part II, Van, Ada, and Lucette do have a tripartite sexual encounter, which Van calls a "nasty prank" (421), but does not involve literal intercourse. That scene, which could probably be described accurately as a "sex scene" is depicted in spectacularly lavish Nabokovian prose:

> Thus seen from above, as if reflected in the ciel mirror ... we have the large island of the bed illumined from our left (Lucette's right) by a lamp burning with a murmuring incandescence on the west-side bedtable. The top sheet and quilt are tumbled at the footboardless south of the island where the newly landed eye starts on its northern trip, up the younger Miss Veen's pried-open legs ... (418–19)

Lucette and Ada caress Van, he has a climax, Lucette runs from the room.

A few years later (1901 on Demonia) they meet again, again Lucette begs Van to have sex with her, and again he declines:

> "Why, Van? Why, Why Why?"
> "You know perfectly well why. I love her, not you, and I simply refuse to complicate matters by entering into yet another incestuous relationship."
> (467)

A few days later, Van departs on the ship *Admiral Tobakoff* from England back to the States. Lucette is on board, they spend a day on board ship, have a romantic dinner, and it is clear Lucette plans to have, at last, Van's ardors all to herself that night and, at that moment, so does Van. They attend the evening movie playing in the ship's theater, and, in an emotional jolt which derails Van's surrender to Lucette's life-long effort to make love to him, the movie features Ada playing a leading role. Van flees the movie theater, dashes to his room and "vigorously got rid of the prurient pressure as he had done the last time seventeen years ago" (490). He masturbates a second time "for the sake of safety" (491), turns off the light and tries to go to sleep. His phone rings, it is Lucette asking "can I come now" to his room, and he responds, cruelly and untruthfully, "I'm not alone" (491). Lucette hangs up, takes a handful of sleeping tablets which a helpful couple has given her, goes to the bar and has a few drinks, drags herself on deck, and throws herself overboard. In a quick reference to Hamlet's "To be or not to be" soliloquy ("For who would bear the whips and scorns of time … When he himself might his quietus make / With a bare bodkin?" 3. 1. 69–76), those sleeping pills given to the suicidal Lucette are named "Quietus Pills" (487). The passage describing her suicide, written by Van with aid from Ada, clearly shows the usually hyperarticulate lovers distraught and rendered nearly speechless by their grief:

> Although Lucette had never died before—no *dived* before, Violet [*the manuscript's typist*]—from such a height, in such a disorder of shadows and snaking reflections, she went with hardly a splash through the wave that humped to welcome her. That perfect end was spoiled by her instinctively surfacing in an immediate sweep—instead of surrendering under water to her drugged lassitude as she had planned to on her last night ashore if it ever came to this … she could not make out the lights of the liner, an easily imagined many-eyed bulk receding in heartless triumph … the sky was also heartless and dark, and her body, her head, and particularly those damned thirsty trousers felt clogged … At every slap and splash of cold wild salt, she heaved with anise-flavored nausea and there was an increasing number, okay, or numbness, in her neck and arms. As she began losing track of herself, she thought it proper to inform a series of receding Lucettes—telling them to pass it on and on in a trick-crystal regression—that what death amounted to was only a more complete assortment of the infinite fractions of solitude. She did not see her whole life flash before her as we all were afraid she might have done. (493–5)

Van sees clearly and accepts the blame for Lucette's suicide. He writes to Ada and her husband, in rather thinly disguised, and obviously Shakespearean terms:

> I know the unsoundness of speculation as to whether Ophelia would not have drowned herself after all, without the help of a treacherous sliver, even if she had married her Voltemand. Impersonally I believe she would have died in her bed, gray and serene, had V. loved her; but since he did not really love the wretched little virgin, and since no amount of carnal tenderness could or can pass for true love, and since, above all, the fatal Andalusian wench [*Ada, in the movie they watched just before Lucette's suicide*] who had come, I repeat into the picture, was unforgettable, I am bound to arrive … at the conclusion that whatever the miserable man could have thought up, she would have … put an end to herself all the same. In other more deeply moral worlds than this pellet of muck, there might exist restraints, principles, transcendental

consolations, and even a certain pride in making happy someone one does not really love; but on this planet Lucettes are doomed. (497–8)

["Voltemand" is an unremarkable courtier in *Hamlet*, and the name Van adopts as a *nom de plume* in some of his writings: "'I also know,' said Lucette as if continuing their recent exchange, 'who *he* is.' She pointed to the inscription 'Voltemand Hall' on the brow of the building from which they now emerged. Van gave her a quick glance – but she simply meant the courtier in *Hamlet*" (386). Reinforcing the *Hamlet* motif, one of "Voltemand's" books, *Letters from Terra* is reviewed by "First Clown in *Elsinore*, a distinguished London weekly." (343) The gravediggers at Elsinore Castle are identified as two "clowns."]

Lucette herself hints at the link to Ophelia when she writes to Van: "You may call it a document in madness or the herb of repentance, but I wish to come and live with you, wherever you are, for ever and ever" (384). This surely reminds us of the madness of Ophelia, and her similar floral allusion: "There's rue for you, and here's some for me. We may call it herb of grace o' Sundays" (4. 5. 181–2).[7]

At the very end of the novel, Ada speaks for herself and for Van:

Oh, Van, oh Van, we did not love her enough. That's whom you should have married, the one sitting feet up, in ballerina black, on the stone balustrade, and then everything would have been all right—I would have stayed with you both in Ardis Hall, and instead of that happiness, handed out gratis, instead of all that we *teased* her to death. (586)

Indeed, since *Ada* is a memoir, written by Van (and Ada) in their old age, we can even discover in early mentions of Lucette their consciousness of her Ophelian fate:

Lucette, in passing, stopped to pick up her sister's [*bathing*] cap and sunglasses ... My tidy little Lucette (I shall never forget you ...). (203)

Early in the novel, Lucette's link to Ophelia is perhaps foreshadowed when Van describes Ada as smelling like "nenuphars, like mad Ophelia." (199—"nenuphars" are water lilies)

Her death-by-drowning is surely also foreshadowed by the liquid names of her mother and aunt, Marina and Aqua. This is reinforced by the fact that Marina, an actress, had appeared as Polonius' daughter in *Hamlet*: "'Yes, indeed,' began Marina, 'When I was playing Ophelia, the fact that I had once collected flowers—'". (63)

As these examples illustrate, the links between Hamlet/Ophelia and Van/Lucette/Ada are indeed many, deep, and crucially important to the novel.

***

The Lucette–Ophelia connections between *Hamlet* and *Ada* are noteworthy, and, indeed, the links between the two works and between Shakespeare's other writings and the novel are an important part of the texture of Nabokov's longest and most complex novel. And yet, such is the character of *Ada* that its ties to *Hamlet* are not as central as, say, those of *Bend Sinister* to the same play, or *Pale Fire* to *Timon of Athens*. This is not because the Shakespeareanisms are less intense, or less vital to the development of theme, character, and style in the novel; it is because here, even more than elsewhere in the Nabokov canon, there is such a richness of literary allusion that Shakespeare does not play a central role that dramatically outshines other influences and sources. So, for example, *Ada*'s opening paragraph parodies and reverses Tolstoy's aphorism about happy and unhappy families in *Anna Karenina*, and also refers to his *Childhood*. In between is a sly reference, as a pseudo bibliographic note, to the Transfiguration of Christ and, probably, the opening of His tomb following the Crucifixion ("transfigured into English by R. G. Stonelower, Mount Tabor Ltd., 1880"—3). [Mt. Tabor is often associated with the mountain upon which the miracle of Christ's transfiguration took place; the first sign of his resurrection was the removal of the stone which blocked the entrance to his tomb.]

*Ada* is indeed "encyclopedic"—it is an encyclopedia of the life and learning and mind of Nabokov. This anthology of the understandings of a genius is too broad to be dominated by any single source. But within this rich constellation of historical and literary stars, none burns with steadier and greater intensity that that of Shakespeare, and his *Hamlet*.

# The Last Novels

After the massive and encyclopedic *Ada* (1969), Nabokov wrote two and a half much slimmer novels: *Transparent Things* (1972), *Look at the Harlequins!* (1974), and *The Original of Laura*, on which he was working at the time of his death in 1977, and which was published, with significant controversy, in 2009.[1] *The Original of Laura* has only a few Shakespearean references: given that novel's status as a "work in progress," it does not seem productive to set it next to completed works which Nabokov saw through publication.

## Transparent Things

*Transparent Things* follows *Ada* in the Nabokov canon. After the voluminous collection of literary (and historical and cultural) references of *Ada*, Nabokov seems to have turned more inward. Both *Transparent Things* and *Look at the Harlequins!* feature characters who clearly have much in common with Nabokov himself. In the former novel, it is one "R," a magisterial author and relatively minor character visited in Switzerland by the work's protagonist, an American publishing executive, Hugh Person. In the latter, it is Vadim Vadimovich N. It is as though Nabokov decided after *Ada* that hereafter the primary literary influence on his new writing would be … himself.[2]

*Transparent Things* tells the story of Hugh Person's four trips to Europe and his ill-fated romance with his wife Armande. Person is a bright but glum and clumsy publisher's representative. On his second trip to Switzerland, to discuss publication terms with the Nabokov-like "R", he meets and falls in love with Armande. Theirs is an eccentric courtship and marriage. She is not undemanding, has rather peculiar sexual tastes, and makes little effort to assume a pose of faithfulness. Hugh remains "monstrously in love" (51). (He is not a very adequate lover, and often his sexual efforts end in disappointment.) Person also suffers from a lifelong trait of sleepwalking, a trait which soon proves tragic.

There has been considerable critical discussion of the narrative voice(s) of *Transparent Things*. The novel is told from the perspective of what seems to be a group of specters, with the curious ghostly ability to drift below the surface of objects and individuals they examine:

> When *we* concentrate on a material object, whatever its situation, the very act of attention may lead to our involuntarily sinking into the history of that object. Novices must learn to skim over matter if they want matter to stay at the exact level of the moment. Transparent things, through which the past shines! (1)

This curious ability is demonstrated in Chapter 3, which is virtually entirely given over to the history of a stray pencil Hugh Person finds abandoned in a drawer—the tale of the graphite which fills the pencil, the tree from which its wood derives, etc. The narrative sinks deeper and deeper into the history and character of this insignificant object.

Hugh's marriage comes to an abrupt and tragic end, as a consequence of his sleepwalking. At their home in New York, Person accidentally murders his wife while he sleeps. He dreams that their house is on fire, and, trying to save Armande in his dream from a deadly fall from a window, he strangles her. He spends some time in jail, some time in an insane asylum, is ultimately freed, and makes a final trip to Europe hoping to revisit the scenes of his early days with Armande. But on his last night in the hotel where they had stayed together, there is a real—not dream—fire, in which Hugh Person perishes. The novel's final sentences seem to suggest that Person moves from the world of the living, which he has not navigated very well, to that of the ghostly narrators of the novel:

> This is, I believe, *it*: not the crude anguish of physical death but the incomparable pangs of the mysterious mental maneuver needed to pass from one state of being to another.
>
> Easy, you know, does it, son. (104)

The most important Shakespearean referent in *Transparent Things* is, not surprisingly, *Romeo and Juliet*, which of course also tells the story of an ill-fated romance, which ends in bungled, accidental deaths.

The scene in which Hugh Person accidentally murders Armande is saturated with references to *Romeo and Juliet*. Here, in somewhat abbreviated form, is much of that section:

> Flames spurted all around and whatever one saw came through scarlet strips of vitreous plastic. His chance bedmate had flung the window wide open. Oh, who was she? ... Giulia Romeo, the surname means "pilgrim" in archaic Italian, but then we are all pilgrims, and all dreams are anagrams of diurnal reality. He dashed after her to stop her from

jumping out ... Giulia, or Julie, wore a Doppler shift over her luminous body and prostrated herself on the sill, with outspread arms still touching the wings of the window ... poor Hugh did all he could to restrain Juliet ... he had clamped Julia nicely and would have saved her from certain death if in her suicidal struggle to escape from the fire she had not slipped somehow over the sill and taken him with her into the void. What a fall! What a silly Julia! What luck that Mr. Romeo still gripped and twisted and cracked that crooked cricoid as X-rayed by the firemen and mountain guides in the street. How they flew! (81)

The fire dream, which results in the death of Armande, and the real hotel fire, which results in the death of Hugh, are foreshadowed several times in the text of *Transparent Things*. There is, for example, a film entitled *Golden Windows* (32); during their honeymoon, Armande "decided that last nights were statistically the most dangerous ones in hotels without fire escapes, and their hotel looked indeed most combustible" (64), Hugh notes that he can draw "a silhouette of human panic in the blazing windows of a villa ..." (28).

Given the sudden burst of Romeo and Juliet references in the strangulation scene, and the fact that both Armand's death and Hugh's involve looking out an upper-story window, it is easy to see a kind of sly Nabokovian reference to the opening line of *Romeo and Juliet*'s (and, indeed, perhaps Shakespeare's) most famous scene:

> But soft! What light through yonder window breaks?
> It is the East, and Juliet is the sun!
> Arise fair sun, and kill the envious moon ... (2. 2. 1–3)

Except, of course, the light breaking through the window in *Transparent Things*, which does in fact kill and is not the sun, is a burning hotel.

That sort of grotesque and twisted parody of Shakespeare's line seems to me to emblematize the way in which *Transparent Things* relates to *Romeo and Juliet*. Shakespeare's relatively early (1594–6) drama has entered the mythos of the Western literary and cultural tradition as the archetypical story of pure, transcendent young love, destroyed by an uncomprehending adult society. That is not an undeserved reputation, although it does, perhaps, oversimplify somewhat a play by an author who never oversimplified. The love of Romeo and Juliet is pure, it is all-consuming, it is flamboyantly youthful. How different is the courtship, marriage, and end of the relationship between Hugh and Armande. Hugh is 32 when he meets his future wife, and she is hardly an inexperienced girl. She turns to Hugh when a former lover, one Jacques:

had demanded her presence at the onanistic sessions he held with the
Blake twins at their chalet. Once already he had made Jack show her
his implement but she had stamped her foot and made them behave
themselves. Jacques had now presented her with an ultimatum—either
she join them in their nasty games or he would cease being her lover.
She was ready to be ultramodern, socially and sexually, but this was
offensive, and vulgar, and as old as Greece. (53)

Hugh himself is sexually inept—halfway through their initial attempt to
make love, Armande remarks "'Well, bad luck,' she said finally ...'" (54).
Once they are married, their amorous life "perplexed and distressed Hugh."
Indeed, it seems to resemble a scene from the theater of the absurd:

> Armande decreed they regularly make love around teatime, in the
> living room, as upon an imaginary stage, to the steady accompaniment
> of casual small talk, with both performers decently clothed, he wearing
> his best business suit and a polka-dotted tie, she a smart black dress
> closed at the throat. In concession to nature, undergarments could
> be parted, or even undone, but only very, very discreetly, without
> the least break in the elegant chit-chat: impatience was pronounced
> unseemly, exposure, monstrous. A newspaper or coffee-table book hid
> such preparations as he absolutely had to conduct, wretched Hugh,
> and woe to him if he winced or fumbled during the actual commerce;
> but far worse than the awful pull of long underwear in the chaos of his
> pinched crotch or the crisp contact with her armor-smooth stockings
> was the prerequisite of light colloquy about acquaintances, or politics,
> or zodiacal signs, or servants, and in the meantime, with visible hurry
> banned, the poignant work had to be brought surreptitiously to a
> convulsive end in a twisted half-sitting position on an uncomfortable
> little divan. (66)

In startling contrast, in *Romeo and Juliet*, between Act 2, scene 5, when
Friar Lawrence marries them, and Act 3 scene 5, when Romeo must leave
Juliet, they have but one single night to spend together as a married couple.
Shakespeare, of course, discretely leaves to the imagination of playgoers the
actions of that night, but even the most puritanical or pallid of imaginations
knows that Romeo and Juliet did not make love fully clothed, while chatting
of politics!

It is significant that in both works, all four of the lovers die as a result of
a tragic mistake, and they perish one at a time. Armande dies because the
sleeping Hugh dreams he is rescuing her from a fire. Then he dies because
he insists on spending an extra night at his hotel in Switzerland, and doesn't

understand until it is too late that the hotel is burning. Romeo dies "with a kiss," thinking the drugged Juliet is already dead because he never received the message that she was feigning death. Then, when she awakes, Juliet kills herself when she discovers the body of Romeo.

If there is a spectrum of heterosexual married sexual love, then passionate Romeo and pure Juliet stand at one extreme, and awkward, impotent Hugh Person and quirky, faithless, promiscuous Armande at the other. The love story of *Transparent Things* is a sadly distorted reflection of the pure passion of Shakespeare's youthful lovers in *Romeo and Juliet*.

## *Look at the Harlequins!*

*Look at the Harlequins!*, Nabokov's last completed work, is also a sad and distorted reflection. It is, surely, his most self-parodic, and it is also interestingly and widely Shakespearean.

The novel is narrated by a Russian–American author named "Vadim Vadimovich N.," easily but incorrectly confused with "Vladimir Vladimirovich Nabokov." At the beginning of the work is a list of "Other Books by the Narrator," including many which are obviously variants of Nabokov's own novels. For example, Vadim's Russian novels include *Tamara*, a story of first love like Nabokov's *Mary*; *Pawn Takes Queen*, a play on *King, Queen, Knave*; and *The Red Top Hat*, which is, obviously, the reflection of *Invitation to a Beheading*. The English books listed include *See under Real* (*The Real Life of Sebastian Knight*); *Dr. Olga Repnin* (*Pnin*); *A Kingdom by the Sea* (an early title of *Lolita*) and *Ardis* (*Ada*).

Other characters in the novel confuse Vadim with Vladimir: a bookseller named OKS, for example, says,

> "I am deeply honored," finished at last OKS, "to welcome to this historic house the author of *Camera Obscura*, your finest book in my modest opinion!"
>
> "It ought to be modest," I said, controlling myself (opal ice in Nepal before the avalanche), "because, you idiot, the title of *my* novel is *Camera Lucida*" (92). [OKS, interestingly, is described as "a tall, bony, elderly man with a Shakespearean pate ..."] (91)

Of course, "Camera Obscura" was the original title of Nabokov's *Laughter in the Dark*. Just a few pages later, he makes another similar error, when he speaks of "*Mary*—damn it, I mean *Tamara*" (94). And OKS describes, rather exactly, Vladimir's father, thinking he is the parent of Vadim, whose father died six months before Vadim was born.

Indeed, sometimes Vadim himself seems to wonder if he is Vladimir:

> I now confess that I was bothered that night, and the next and some time before, by a dream feeling that my life was the non-identical twin, a parody, an inferior variant of another man's life, somewhere on this or another earth. A demon, I felt, was forcing me to impersonate that other man, that other writer who was and would always be incomparably greater, healthier, and crueler than your obedient servant. (89)

Later, when his consciousness is being restored after a rather complete mental breakdown, he says:

> Yes, I definitely felt my family name began with an *N* and bore an odious resemblance to the surname or pseudonym of a presumably notorious (Notorov? No) Bulgarian, or Babylonian, or, maybe, Betelgeusian writer with whom scatter brained émigrés from some other galaxy constantly confused me; but whether it was something on the lines of Nebesnyy or Nabedrin or Nablizde (Nablidze? Funny) I simply could not tell. (248–249)

A few lines later, Vadim discusses Russian patronymics, and observes "the hardly utterable, tapeworm-long 'Vladimir Vladimirovich' becomes colloquially similar to 'Vadim Vadimych'" (249).

Sometimes, however, Vadim seems like not the creator but a character from a Nabokov novel—for example, while conducting an affair with a woman named "Dolly," he identifies himself and his address as "Dumbert Dumbert, Dumbeton" (143). He used to drive an "Icarus" auto. He stops at the Lolita Lodge in Texas (156).

Yet it is clear that in many ways Vadim is NOT Vladimir. As mentioned above, Vadim's father "was a gambler and a rake" (96); Vladimir's was a patriot, a leading figure in Russia's aborted democratic reforms, and a committed anti-anti-Semite. Vadim knows, and cares, nothing about butterflies ("I know nothing about butterflies, and indeed do not care for the fluffier night-flying ones; and would hate any of them to touch me" 34); he is often cruel and has a rather violent temper. Most importantly, Vadim is, by his own account, insane. He describes his "mental health" (39) as a "humble morbid condition." It consists, at first, of his being unable to imagine proceeding from point A to point B and turning around to return to point A. He has no trouble actually performing such a reversal, but he cannot *imagine* it. At the end of *Look at the Harlequins!*, however, he has an episode of complete breakdown, in which the inability to imagine turning about becomes reality, and he is, in effect, mentally and physically paralyzed. As far as we know, Vladimir Nabokov never suffered any such debilitating mental condition.

It is interesting, though, to speculate on a metaphorical connection between Vadim's mental defect and Vladimir's life. The former cannot imagine himself moving in one direction, then turning and moving back. In some ways, Nabokov's life must have seemed to himself to have moved along a certain trajectory—cultivated, intellectual, creative Russian aristocrat—and then to have abruptly, in a kind of biographical knight's move, veered off entirely. Could the Nabokov we meet in *Speak, Memory* imagine the American Nabokov: penniless professor, controversial author of *Lolita*, distinguished novelist? Perhaps something of Vadim's disorientation reflects the sharp and unpredictable turn-arounds in his creator's life and career.

In addition to describing the writings, adult life and times of Vadim Vadimovich N., *Look at the Harlequins!* details his amorous life. In cavalier fashion, the very first sentence of *Look at the Harlequins!* begins: "I met the first of my three or four successive wives in somewhat odd circumstances …" (3). His first wife is the sister of an old acquaintance named Iris; the last is (like Vera Nabokov in *Speak, Memory*) only identified in the text as "you." In between he is enamored of one of his typists, then much taken with her daughter Bel, with whom he travels, Humbert Humbert-like, from motel to motel across America. It is not entirely clear how fully Vadim's affection for Bel is consummated. Ultimately, she runs away from Vadim, and moves to Soviet Russia with a pro-Communist young rebel. Vadim's first marriage ends when Iris is killed by a Russian émigré; the second and third marriages fail; the last, with "you," is ongoing as the book is written.

Given its relatively short length, the range of Shakespeareanisms in *Look at the Harlequins!* is remarkably catholic: at least nine plays are referenced, as are the sonnets, some miscellaneous citations (e.g., one character—as we have seen—has a "Shakespearean pate"), and a few general allusions to Shakespeare and his life.

Among the latter are two mentions of the Shakespeare/(Nabokov) birthday:

On the morning of April 23, 1930, the shrill peal of the hallway telephone caught me in the act of stepping into my bathwater. (65)

During my three Cambridge years (1912–1922) and thereafter, till April 23, 1930, my domestic tongue remained English, while the body of my own Russian works started to grow and was soon to disturb my household gods (124). [On April 23, 1930, Vadim rendezvous with his friend and mentor Ivor, the brother of Vadim's wife Iris, they go out to lunch together, and afterward, Iris is shot to death.]

It does not seem to me that this "coincidence" has any particular thematic importance, other than to remind us that Vladimir Nabokov is lurking behind the life of Vadim Vadimovich N., and that Shakespeare is lurking behind Nabokov.

As in other works, *Hamlet* is to be found in *Look at the Harlequins!*, but infrequently, and fairly insubstantially. Several times we meet a character named "Hamlet Godman," who seems remarkably parallel to Mr. Goodman, the biographer of Sebastian in *The Real Life of Sebastian Knight*:

> The story of his ["an English novelist, a brilliant and unique performer"] life was being knocked together by the uninformed, coarse-minded malevolent Hamlet Godman, an Oxonian Dane ... [*sic*: "Dane," not "don"]. (121; also 172 and 226)

Another interesting *Hamlet* allusion comes when Vadim discusses a character in one of his works, *Esmeralda and her Parandrus* (see below): a "mad scholar in *Esmeralda and Her Parandrus* wreathes Botticelli and Shakespeare together by having Primavera end as Ophelia with all her flowers" (162). In Botticelli's painting *Primavera*, Spring is born surrounded with flowers; in the play, Ophelia dies wreathed in them.

Among the other plays receiving mention are *The Tempest* ("In the meantime Miranda, the daughter of the house" 19); *Othello* ("She listened to me like Desdemona" (21) and "Oh, but I too can speak of 'deserts idle rough quarries, rocks'" 108); *King Lear* ("the shiver caused ... by one line in *King Lear*" 23); *The Merchant of Venice* ("He conceals our ancestry like a dark treasure, yet will flare up publicly if someone calls someone a Shylock" 43); *A Midsummer Night's Dream* (O. B. Long—"This I could expand into, say, Oberon Bernard Long ..." 203); and *Macbeth* ("her old Hecate convertible" 186).

Given the diversity of references to Shakespearean dramas in *Look at the Harlequins!*, it is striking how many allusions the novel contains that could refer to more than one play. For example, a minor character is named "Sebastian" (5), a character name in both *The Tempest* and *Twelfth Night*. Perhaps for that reason Vadim appends to the name Sebastian "whoever that was" (5). Similarly, the phrase "another part of the forest" (10), which occurs when Vadim is fleeing Russia and shoots a border guard, might be from *As You Like It*, or from *2 Henry IV*. And when Vadim discovers a photograph of "two girls in a fancy frame, obliquely inscribed as 'The Lady Cressida and thy sweet Nell, Cambridge, 1919 ...'" (31–2), the reference could well be to "Nell" in *Troilus and Cressida*, but it could also refer to the Nell in *Comedy of Errors* (who is the opposite of "sweet"), Nell in *Romeo and Juliet*, Nell in *Henry V*, or the Nell in *2 Henry VI*, who is twice called "sweet Nell" by the Duke of Gloucester.

In *Troilus and Cressida*, Helen of Troy is twice called "Nell" by Paris. (Their relationship is made clear to any who are not familiar with Greek epic within the first 10 lines of the play, when the Prologue describes "The ravished Helen, Menelaus' queen, / With wanton Paris sleeps" (Prologue, 9–10). Shakespeare's problematic play *Troilus and Cressida* is hardly mentioned in Nabokov's other writings, but it plays an important and interesting role in *Look at the Harlequins!*.

The story of Troilus and Cressida, in Shakespeare's version, in Chaucer's, and other variants such as that of Henryson, is a tale of inconstancy in love. Its view of the world seems acidic and far more cynical than that of most of Shakespeare's other works. *Troilus and Cressida* is filled with characters who take a bitter and satirical view of their fellows, the Trojan War, and humankind in general: the foul-mouthed Thersites, Achilles and his friend/lover Patroclus, Pandarus, Diomedes. Even the wise Ulysses bases much of his wisdom on a low view of humankind:

> Time hath, my lord, a wallet at his back,
> Wherein he puts alms for oblivion,
> A great-sized monster of ingratitudes.
> Those scraps are good deeds past, which are devoured
> As fast as they are made, forgot as soon
> As done. (3. 3. 145–50)

The play's only heroic character, Hector, is ambushed, butchered, and dragged around Troy by the treacherous Achilles. And, of course, after swearing her "truth" to Troilus, Cressida is rapidly won over by Diomedes once she has been bartered from the Greek camp to that of the Trojans. The play concludes with Pandarus cursing the audience:

> Some two months hence my will shall here be made
> It should be now, but my fear is this,
> Some galled goose of Winchester would hiss.
> Till then I'll sweat and seek about for eases,
> And at that time bequeath you my diseases. (5. 10. 51–5)

This is surely quite a way from, say, *A Midsummer Night's Dream*'s "Give me your hands, if we be friends, / And Robin shall restore amends" (5. 1. 436–7). At the end of *Troilus and Cressida* one would want to wash those hands! It is little wonder that this drama has not been very popular on the stage, nor a favorite of many critics or readers. Its cynicism and bitterness has not been without resonances in the last century, and its themes and mood add a darker tone to parts of Nabokov's final complete novel.

As *Look at the Harlequins!*'s protagonist Vadim is walking (naked) around the house of Ivor and Iris, he "seeks distraction in the baubles of my love's lavender-scented bedroom" (31). Among these is:

a color photograph of two girls in a fancy frame, obliquely inscribed as "The Lady Cressida and thy sweet Nell, Cambridge 1919"; I mistook the former for Iris herself in a golden wig and a pink make-up; a closer inspection, however, showed it to be Ivor in the part of that highly irritating girl bobbing in and out of Shakespeare's flawed farce. (31–2)

Ivor later cites this same photo:

Ivor said that if ever we wanted to sell Villa Iris he knew someone who would snap it up any time. Iris, he said, knew him too: David Geller, the actor. "He was (turning to me) her first beau before you blundered in. She must still have somewhere that photo of him and me in *Troilus and Cressida* ten years ago. He's Helen of Troy in it, I'm Cressida." (67)

Ivor's citation of the *Troilus and Cressida* photo is foreshadowed, lightly, by the fact that the conversation takes place in a restaurant named the "Paon d'Or" which is "much patronized by American tourists, who called it "Pander" or "Pandora" (67).

A similar slip of the tongue links one of Vadim's English works to Shakespeare's play. On a trip to the New York Public Library, Vadim encounters Dolly von Borg, with whom he shortly has sex on the desk of his (shared) office at the university where he teaches. Dolly introduces Vadim to her boyfriend:

"Oh, Terry: this is *the* writer, the man who wrote *Emerald and the Pander*." (138)

The actual title of Vadim's novel is *Esmeralda and Her Parandrus*. This work is mentioned with his other English books at the start of *Look at the Harlequins!* It is, of all those, perhaps the hardest to identify. A Parandrus is a mythical beast, able to change shape or color. Esmeralda is most famously a gypsy maiden in *The Hunchback of Notre Dame*, but also a character in at least two works by Thomas Mann: *Death in Venice* and *Doctor Faustus*. Brian Boyd identifies *Esmeralda and her Parandrus* with *Lolita*:

Lolita is associated with Carmen, with gypsies (as she is repeatedly in *Ada*, too): when Humbert first sees her, it's as if she's "some little princess (lost, kidnaped, discovered in gypsy rags)"; Esmeralda's parandrus seems a close image of the chameleonic car in which Quilty follows Lo and Hum. A parandrus is an enchanted stag; and the centrality of Diana's stag as an element of *Lolita* is something I note in my discussion of *Lolita*'s hunter hunted motif (centering on the Enchanted Hunters, of course) in *Lolita* in *Stalking Nabokov* p. 331–4. Esmeralda is also linked with Lolita in "Lines Written in Oregon," written in the last year of

Lolita's composition and with, as subject, European enchantment rediscovered in America (as Annabel's is in Lo, for instance).[3]

Others, including Jansy Mello and Omry Ronen, connect *Esmeralda and her Parandrus* with *Bend Sinister*. Ronen writes:

> Nabokov's contempt for the myth of the 20th century was both artistic and moral. He found tasteless Thomas Mann's image of Hetaera Esmeralda in *Doctor Faustus* as part of Mann's myth of the diabolic nature of modernism, based on false racial and aesthetic presuppositions (cf. *Lines Written in Oregon* and the title of Vadim Vadimovich's novel in *Look at the Harlequins!*: *Esmeralda and her Parandrus*).[4]

In any event, at least one character in *Look at the Harlequins!* confuses "Parandrus" with "Pandar" or "Pandarus," which at least slightly reinforces the *Troilus and Cressida* link.

*Look at the Harlequins!* does have many thematic and character affinities  with *Troilus and Cressida*. Vadim, and many of those who surround his life, is certainly a model of inconstancy in love. Two of his marriages end in separation, and there are numerous liaisons. Not often, but occasionally, he can be as scurrilous as Shakespeare's Thersites: at one point he refers to "my Negro maid, little Nefertitty as I had dubbed her …" (160). And like so many of the characters in Shakespeare's play, Vadim and his colleagues can be acerbic in their comments on others:

> I closely observed podgy dour Basilevski—not because he had just had or was about to have a row with his young mistress, a feline beauty who wrote doggerel verse and vulgarly flirted with me, but because I hoped he had already seen the fun I had made of him in the last issue of a literary review in which we both collaborated. (76–7)

> Still restraining myself, though aware of the uncontrollable cloud of black fury growing within my brain, I said: "You are mistaken. You are a somber imbecile." (218)

> A familiar symptom of my complaint, not its gravest one but the toughest to get rid of after every relapse, belongs to what Moody, the London specialist, was the first to term the "numerical nimbus" syndrome. His account of my case has been recently reprinted in his collected works. It teems with ludicrous inaccuracies. (15)

And, as Shakespeare's drama turns the heroic myth of the Trojan War topsy-turvy, Nabokov's novel seems to mock the myth of memory and the genre of artistic autobiography—both of which Nabokov takes very seriously in other settings, particularly in his artistic autobiography which invokes the muse of memory, *Speak, Memory.*

But taken as a whole, *Look at the Harlequins!* is *not* as bitter, negative, and cynical as *Troilus and Cressida.* Perhaps most obviously, this is because the face of Vladimir Vladimirovich Nabokov keeps peeking out from behind the mask of Vadim Vadimovich N. Although there are, as noted earlier, many similarities between the two V. V. N.s, there are also many differences, and the differences make the fictional character seem not so much a doppelganger of his creator, but a parody, a portrait of the artist through a glass, very darkly.

Nabokov's last two completed novels, *Transparent Things* and *Look at the Harlequins!* have revealing links to two of Shakespeare's works—*Romeo and Juliet* and *Troilus and Cressida.* The former is a relatively early drama, the latter from Shakespeare's middle period of creative activity. More importantly, *Romeo and Juliet* is a work which invites us to admire the power of pure young love, while *Troilus and Cressida* adopts a bitter and cynical perspective on amorous relations. Neither of Nabokov's novels could be said to embody a blithe or romantic view of human love. *Transparent Things* seems to parody the naiveté of Shakespeare's star-crossed lovers; *Look at the Harlequins!* draws upon the theme of inconstancy in love embodied in Shakespeare's Greeks and Trojans.

# A Miscellany of Other English Works

As he first became and then matured as a writer of English prose, Vladimir Nabokov turned to Shakespeare not only in his masterpiece novels, but in a host of other, minor but still important and interesting, prose works. These include short stories, book reviews, unpublished notes, translations, autobiography, and non-fiction. In this chapter, I examine a cluster of these miscellaneous writings which seem to me to incorporate Shakespearean materials most interestingly and deeply.

## "*That in Aleppo Once ...*"

Two of Vladimir Nabokov's works of fiction have titles taken directly from Shakespeare plays. The most important, of course, is the novel *Pale Fire*. The second is the short story "That in Aleppo Once ..." The reference is to Othello's magnificent closing soliloquy:

Soft you, a word or two before you go.
I have done the state some service, and they know't.
No more of that. I pray you, in your letters,
When you shall these unlucky deeds relate,
Speak of me as I am. Nothing extenuate,
Nor set down aught in malice. Then must you speak
Of one that loved not wisely, but too well;
Of one not easily jealous, but, being wrought,
Perplexed in the extreme; of one whose hand,
Like the base Judean, threw a pearl away
Richer than all his tribe; of one whose subdued eyes,
Albeit unused to the melting mood,
Drops tears as fast as the Arabian trees
Their med'cinable gum. Set you down this,
And say besides **that in Aleppo once**,
Where a malignant and turbaned Turk

Beat a Venetian and traduced the state
I took by the th' throat the circumcised dog
And smote him—thus.
　　　　[He stabs himself.] (5. 2. 337–55)

Othello has just murdered the innocent Desdemona, then realized he has been terribly duped by Iago, and now destroys himself.

Nabokov's story has puzzled readers and critics since it was published in 1943, not long after he began writing in English after his move to America. The narrator is an author, speaking to another writer named "V." Fleeing the Nazi invasion of France, the narrator and his wife are separated when her train unexpectedly leaves him behind at the station. Later, when they are reunited, she tells him she has conducted a torrid affair with a brute she met on the train. But abruptly she reverses herself, and says the affair never took place. When the narrator leaves her to acquire their tickets to emigrate to the new world, she disappears again; he travels alone to New York; they are never reunited. The narrator becomes convinced that his wife never existed, although he has encountered several individuals who met her.

This enigmatic story has teased readers into several variant interpretations. Did the narrator, like Othello, actually murder his wife when he suspected her of infidelity during their first separation? Is he going to kill himself, again like Othello? Has he perhaps already done so? Priscilla Meyer suggests the possibility of this last, ghostly, reading:

> the story may mean that, like Othello, the narrator has killed himself, tormented by his own suspicion, his wife's possible infidelity, the wrong he has done her. (130)

"That in Aleppo Once ..." not only echoes *Othello*, but it also invokes a similar literary precedent, that of Pushkin, the author who, with Shakespeare, Nabokov most admired. Early in the story, the narrator describes his missing wife:

> She was much younger than I—not as much younger as was Nathalie of the lovely bare shoulders and long earrings in relation to swarthy Pushkin, but still there was a sufficient margin for that kind of retrospective romanticism which finds pleasure in imitating the destiny of a unique genius (down to the jealousy, down to the filth, down to the stab of seeing her almond-shaped eyes turn to her blond Cassio behind her peacock fan) even if one cannot imitate his verse." (557)

Here, Nabokov conflates two stories: that of Shakespeare's *Othello*, and that of the end of Pushkin's life. Pushkin was, on his maternal side, descended in part from an African slave, Abram Gannibal. He was, as Nabokov says, "swarthy." He was married to Natalya Goncharova. Although he himself was not a faithful husband, Pushkin challenged to a duel the man who was accused of being (or trying to be) his wife's lover. That man, Georges d'Anthes, shot Pushkin fatally through the spleen, and he died two days after the duel at the age of 37.

Thus, Nabokov has created a kind of triangle of references and plot. The story of "That in Aleppo Once ..." seems like the plot of *Othello* and the biography of Pushkin, and those two seem like each other. Thus, for instance, Pushkin's killer Georges d'Anthes is like Shakespeare's Cassio, and both are like the man Nabokov's narrator is led to believe had an affair with his wife ... or maybe did not!

Nabokov's quite short story (it is only eight and a half pages in length) is filled with other tantalizing citations from *Othello*. After the narrator's wife confesses "I stayed for several nights in Montpellier with a brute of a man I met on the train" (560), the narrator responds with two quotations:

> *The time, the place, the torture. Her fan, her gloves her mask.* I spent that night and many others getting it out of her bit by bit, but not getting it all. (560)

The first of these lines is from the very end of *Othello*, when Iago has been captured, and Lodovico says of him:

> To you, lord governor,
> Remains the censure of this hellish villain,
> The time, the place the torture. O, enforce it! (5. 2. 366–8)

The next quotation comes when Othello is interrogating Emilia about Desdemona's relationship with Cassio:

> OTHELLO: What, did they never whisper?
> EMILIA: Never my lord.
> OTHELLO: Nor send you out o' th' way?
> EMILIA: Never.
> OTHELLO: To fetch her fan, her gloves, her mask, nor nothing?
> (4. 2. 6–9)

The narrator is invoking *Othello* in the first instance to describe his rage and thirst for revenge at his wife's possible infidelity; in the second case to describe his incessant probing of her for the details of that infidelity.

Another intriguing hint of the *Othello* motif comes when the narrator says that his disappeared wife has been spreading stories about him: that she had asked for a divorce, he refused, and "I had said I would rather shoot her and myself than sail to New York alone" (562–3). Does this perhaps suggest that one way to read "That in Aleppo Once ..." is to understand that the reason the narrator's wife disappears the second time is that he has killed her, and, moreover, he has subsequently killed himself, like the Moor of Venice, and is narrating the story from beyond the grave?

The final direct quotation from Shakespeare's drama comes in the last paragraph of Nabokov's short story:

> *Yet the pity of it.* Curse your art, I am hideously unhappy. She keeps on walking to and fro where the brown nets are spread to dry on the hot stone slabs and the dappled light of the water plays on the side of a moored fishing boat. Somewhere, somehow, I have made some fatal mistake. There are tiny pale bits of broken fish scales glistening here and there in the brown meshes. It may all end in *Aleppo* if I am not careful. Spare me, V.: you would load your dice with an unbearable implication if you took that for a title. (564—This is the entire final paragraph of the story.)

When Iago goads Othello to suspect Desdemona, Othello exclaims, "But yet the pity of it, Iago. O Iago, the pity of it, Iago" (4. 1. 195–6). Nabokov's story ends enigmatically. *Whom* do we pity and why? The narrator? His wife? Both? "V.?" What is the "unbearable implication" if V. names the story *Aleppo*—which, of course, he has? Is it that the narrator murdered his wife and/or killed himself? Is it that the whole fantastic tale is some sort of fiction which one writer is sharing with another? Is it that perhaps there is only one writer ("V.?") who has invented the narrator and his possibly unfaithful wife, and the entire mysterious and tangled plot? There is not a convincing answer to these questions. Sometimes, I believe, Nabokov constructs literary puzzles which have either multiple solutions, or none at all. "That in Aleppo Once ..." employs Shakespeare's *Othello* to create and deepen just such an engaging and insoluble maze.

## Eugene Onegin

To Vladimir Nabokov, Alexander Pushkin was "the greatest poet of his time (and perhaps of all time, excepting Shakespeare)" (*Nikolai Gogol*, 29). "Pushkin's blood" he comments elsewhere, "runs through the veins of modern Russian literature as inevitably as Shakespeare's through those of English literature" (*Strong Opinions*, 63). Given this admiration of the two poets, and the linking together of their greatness in Nabokov's estimation, it is worthwhile to look briefly at how Shakespeare appears in Nabokov's

Shakespeare & Onegin

monumental translation and commentary of Pushkin's novel in verse *Eugene*
*Onegin*.

Nabokov's version of the poem fills four volumes. The first contains an introduction and the actual translation; volumes 2 and 3 are copious notes on the poem; and the final book reproduces the 1837 definitive version. The translation is in doggedly literal prose, in which, purposefully, everything other than direct meaning falls by the wayside.

> In transposing *Eugene Onegin* from Pushkin's Russian into my English I have sacrificed to completeness of meaning every formal element save the iambic rhythm: its retention assisted rather than hindered fidelity ... In fact, to my ideal of literalism I sacrificed everything (elegance, euphony, clarity, good taste, modern usage, and even grammar) that the dainty mimic prizes higher than truth. Pushkin has likened translators to horses changed at the posthouses of civilization. The greatest reward I can think of is that students may use my work as a pony. (*Eugene Onegin* x)

To a number of critics and readers, most notably Edmund Wilson, Nabokov sacrificed too much of what was valuable in Pushkin's poem in order to preserve its literal meaning; others praised the purity with which he maintained the poem's sense.

If there might be any doubt about how seriously Nabokov takes the task of translating Pushkin, or how vehemently he takes exception to what he considers bad translations, his article in the *New York Review of Books* in 1964 discussing Walter Arndt's version makes clear both his seriousness and the scorn he heaps on those he considers to have botched the task. The first paragraph of the essay asserts:

> The author of a soon-to-be-published translation may find it awkward to criticize a just published translation of the same work, but in the present case I can, and should, master my embarrassment; for something must be done, some lone, hoarse voice must be raised, to defend both the helpless dead poet and the credulous college student from the kind of pitiless and irresponsible paraphrast whose product I am about to discuss. (*On Translating*)

Nabokov cites Shakespeare nearly thirty times throughout the four volumes of his translation and commentary. Over half the citations are general or biographical in nature. He also mentions five of the plays and the sonnets. Pushkin himself knew and occasionally cited Shakespeare, but he was familiar with the works only in the late eighteenth century French translation of Letourneur (which was itself a somewhat controversial translation).

Answers are elusive when we seek to discover how deeply Shakespeare influenced Nabokov in his version of *Eugene Onegin*, as opposed to Shakespeare's influence upon Pushkin, which Nabokov, as a conscientious annotator notes. Here, for example, is Stanza XXXVII of Chapter 2 (which is, as well, a good example of Nabokov's often awkward literal translation technique):

> Restored to his penates [*penates* = Roman household gods]
> Vladimir Lenski visited
> his neighbor's humble monument,
> and to the ashes consecrated
> a sigh, and long his heart was melancholy.
> "Poor Yorick!" mournfully he uttered, "he
> hath borne me in his arms."
> How oft I played in childhood
> with his Ochakov medal! [Naval medal commemorating the capture of Ochakov in 1788]
> He destined Olga to wed me;
> he used to say: "Shall I be there
> to see the day?" and full of sincere sadness,
> Vladimir there and then set down for him
> a gravestone madrigal. (Vol. I, 147)

In the "Translator's Introduction," in a discussion of "The Structure of *Eugene Onegin*," Nabokov in his thorough manner offers a brief précis of virtually every stanza of the poem. In this case, he says "Lenski quotes a footnote from the French version of *Hamlet*, and inscribes a "gravestone madrigal," which combination of terms renders perfectly the merging of this two themes: early death and fugitive poetry" (I. 31). Then, in Pushkin's Notes to this stanza, the author writes: "Poor Yorick!— Hamlet's exclamation over the skull of the fool (see Shakespeare and Sterne)" (I. 326).

In the Commentary on this stanza, Nabokov takes on another commentator on Pushkin:

> Poor Yorick:— Brodski (1950) referring to Pushkin's n. [note] 16, glosses: "By referring to Sterne ... Pushkin subtly discloses his ironic attitude to Lenski's applying the name of an English fool to Brigadier Larin."
>
>     Alas, poor Brodski. Pushkin's note comes straight from F. Guizot's and Amedee Pichot's revised edition of Letourneur's translation of *Hamlet*, in Pushkin's possession (*Oeuvres completes de Shakespeare*, vol. I, Paris, 1821), in which a note, pp. 386–7, reads: "Alas, poor Yorick.

Tout le monde se souvient et du chapitre de Sterne, ou il cite ce passage d'Hamlet, et comment dans le Voyage Sentimental [translated by J. P. Frenais, 1769], il s'est, a ce propos, donné à lui-même le nom d'Yorick."

...

The actual passage in Sterne's *Tristram Shandy* (vol. I, end of ch. 12) reads:

He [Parson Yorick] lies buried in the corner of his church-yard ... under a plain marble slab, which his friend Eugenius, by leave of his executors, laid upon his grave, with no more than these three words of inscription serving both for his epitaph and elegy: "Alas, poor Yorick!"

...

Pushkin's knowledge of Sterne was based on French versions such as *La Vie et les opinions de Tristram Shandy*, in 4 vols., the first two by Frenais, 1776, and the rest mainly by de Bonnay, 1785. (II, 304–5)

How much of this Kinbotian trail of *Hamlet* allusions should be attributed to Pushkin, how much to Nabokov? What is certainly clear is that Nabokov was relentlessly, one might even say compulsively, scholarly in tracking down and annotating *Eugene Onegin*!

*Hamlet* pops up a few more times in Nabokov's comments. For example, in another convoluted scholarly discussion of Pushkin's use of the color "purple," and purple flowers he notes:

Shakespeare's "long purples" (*Hamlet*, IV, vii, 170) become characteristically "fleurs rougeatres" with Letourneur, which, of course, makes nonsense of the comparison to the bluish fingers of dead men in the same passage. The bright-red variety of purple does crop up as a Europeanism in Shakespeare and other poets of his time, but its real ascendancy, of short duration happily, comes with the age of pseudo-classicism ... (II, 521)

A number of other plays are casually mentioned in Nabokov's comments, among them *Troilus and Cressida* (II, 118), *As You Like It* (II, 187), *Macbeth* (III. 82; II, 504), and *King Lear* (III, 463). There are also a number of quite casual references to Shakespeare, often as we have seen before, regarding his standing as one of the very few giants in the history of Western literature. Here are a few samples:

Goethe, whom he [Pushkin] placed above Voltaire and Byron, next to Shakespeare (Pierre Letourneur's Shakespeare, of course ...). (II, 236)

[The bucolic theme] there are echoes of it in the works of a number of great poets such as Shakespeare and La Fontaine. (II, 322)

a combination of "melancholy"... and of Renaissance vividness and vigor (e.g., Shakespeare). (III, 34)

Dostoevski the publicist is one of those megaphones of elephantine platitudes (still heard today), the roar of which so ridiculously demotes Shakespeare and Pushkin to the vague level of all the plaster idols of academic tradition, from Cervantes to George Eliot (not to speak of the crumbling Manns and Faulkners of our times). (III, 192)

Nabokov spends a considerable amount of his commentary discussing Pushkin's metrics, and he often uses Shakespearean comparisons in that discussion. Pushkin's stanzas are fourteen lines in length, and thus the same size as a Shakespearean sonnet, with, most commonly, its three quatrains and a couplet of iambic pentameter. They are, however, written in iambic tetrameter, with a rhyme scheme of AbAbCCddEffEgg (with capital letters representing masculine rhymes, lower case letters feminine ones). Thus, for example in Appendix Two, Nabokov reproduces Shakespeare's sonnet 145 ("Those lips that Love's own hands did make / Breathed forth the sound that said 'I hate'") with the comment:

In this elegant little sonnet (Shakespeare's only tetrametric one) the readers should note the comparatively high rate of scudding and, in the last line, the comparatively rare third-foot duplex tilt, here eased in by means of a concettic alliteration. (III, 500) ["concettic" here is, I believe, the adjectival form of "conceit."]

As this example illustrates, Nabokov evolved a rather idiosyncratic system of metrics to describe Pushkin's poem and its relation to English metrical analysis. Thus a "scud" is an unaccented stress word and a "duplex tilt" is a two syllable word accented normally on the first syllable. This system worked well for Nabokov's purposes in describing *Eugene Onegin*, but has never gained much currency elsewhere in the analysis of English poetry.

Elsewhere, Nabokov continues to use Shakespearean illustrations to explain Pushkin's verse:

a couplet resembling the code of an octave or that of a Shakespearean sonnet. (I, 10)

the form has been termed the Anacreontic sonnet ... Shakespeare handled it once (Sonnet CXLV) ... Shakespeare's tetrametric rarity has the sequence: bcbc dfdf ghgh jj: make-hate-sake-state, come-sweet-doom-greet, end-day-fiend-away, threw-you. (I, 12) if we regard the famous (perhaps accidentally fivefold, or, perhaps, meant as a prose interpolation) "never, never, never, never, never!" in *King Lear* (V. iii. 309) as a masculine line in iambic pentameter … (3. 463) [This line, as we have seen, is one of Nabokov's very favorites.]

*Eugene Onegin* is certainly not a work that either Shakespeare or Nabokov would have written. Its titular hero is a selfish St. Petersburg fop who kills, in an almost accidental duel, an idealistic young poet, Vladimir Lensky, over a flirtation with Olga, the sister of Tatyana Larina, who loves Onegin but is initially spurned by him. In subject matter, character, and in style, the novel in verse is unique to Pushkin. But to Nabokov, what links Pushkin and Shakespeare is poetic genius. The poem's very monolithic individuality ties it, in Nabokov's consciousness, to the equally solitary greatness of Shakespeare. And, it is unmistakable that to Nabokov that characteristic of one-of-a-kind literary brilliance is also what characterizes the writings of … Vladimir Nabokov!

## *Speak, Memory*

There are relatively few references to Shakespeare in Nabokov's autobiography, but those that there are are quite interesting.

Early in *Speak, Memory*, Nabokov discusses his efforts to plumb the past, and, in an aside, inserts one of his customary barbs at Freud and Freudians:

> I have ransacked my oldest dreams for keys and clues—and let me say at once that I reject completely the vulgar, shabby, fundamentally medieval world of Freud, with its crankish quest for sexual symbols (something like searching for Baconian acrostics in Shakespeare's works) and its bitter little embryos spying, from their natural nooks, upon the love life of their parents. (20)

This is, of course, an amusing little vignette (one can imagine those bitter little embryos and their natural nooks). But it is also revealing in terms of Nabokov's evolving thoughts concerning Shakespearean biography. As discussed above in the Introduction, the young Nabokov had anti-Stratfordian leanings. But his discovery, through Alfred Appel, of Samuel Schoenbaum's definitive *Shakespeare's Lives* appears to have reversed, or at least mitigated, his questioning of the authenticity of Shakespeare's authorship of the plays and poems. In this short passage, he equates those who believe Sir Francis Bacon was the true author of *Hamlet, King Lear, The Tempest*, and the sonnets with Freudian "cranks" who are "vulgar" and "shabby."[1] Since the Baconians are leading proponents of the anti-Strat-fordian cause, this seems clear evidence that Nabokov had come around to (or at least toward) the conviction that Shakespeare of Stratford was, in fact, the creator of Shakespeare's works.

In a touching passage later in *Speak, Memory* Nabokov describes his mother's life in Prague, after their exodus from Russia, the loss of the family fortune, and the assassination of his father:

> A soapbox covered with green cloth supported the dim little photo-graphs in crumbling frames she liked to have near her couch. She did not really need them, for nothing had been lost. As a company of traveling players carry with them everywhere, while they still remember their lines, a windy heath, a misty castle, an enchanted island, so she had with her all that her soul had stored. (49–50)

Clearly, this is as close as Nabokov comes to straightforward, unvarnished emotion, even sentiment. And at such a moment, it is revealing that he once again turns to Shakespeare.

For certainly, that company of traveling players are carrying with them Shakespearean plays. The "windy heath" is from *King Lear*, where much of Acts 3 and 4 take place on just such a heath. Lear begins 3, 2 exclaiming "Blow, winds, and crack your cheeks" (3. 2. 1). The "misty castle" could be that of Macbeth, where an army could be mistaken for a forest. More likely, it is Elsinore, where in the opening scene of Hamlet it is so dark on the ramparts of the castle that the guards cannot recognize each other:

> BARNARDO: Who's there?
> FRANCISCO: Nay, answer me. Stand and unfold yourself /
> BARNARDO: Long live the King.
> FRANCISCO: Barnardo?
> BARNARDO: He.

And the "enchanted island," which we have already encountered in *Lolita*, comes from *The Tempest*, where Prospero weaves his magic and lives among airy spirits. This section of the autobiography is a high point in Nabokov's effort to capture, recapture and hold the loves of his past. Just a few sentences later, he concludes:

> It is certainly not then—not in dreams—but when one is wide awake, at moments of robust joy and achievement, on the highest terrace of consciousness, that mortality has a chance to peer beyond its own limits, from the mast, from the past and its castle tower. And although nothing much can be seen through the mist, there is somehow the blissful feeling

that one is looking in the right direction. (50—Note the repetition of the "misty castle" motif.)

Thus, at such a moment of robust joy and achievement, at the highest level of consciousness, Nabokov turns once again to Shakespeare.

*King Lear* briefly returns later when Nabokov describes his grandfather Dmitri in his dotage:

> There is an extraordinary story, which I have not been able to piece together adequately, of his escaping from his attendants somewhere in Italy. There he wandered about, denouncing, with King-Lear like vehemence, his children to grinning strangers, until he was captured in a wild rocky place by some matter-of-fact *carabinieri*. (58)

Not only does Nabokov compare his mother's memories to the memorized repertory of a company of Shakespearean travelling players, he equates his senile grandfather to a Shakespearean tragic hero.

A final *Hamlet* allusion concerns another Nabokov relative, his uncle Ruka. Ruka is something of a tragic–comic figure in *Speak, Memory*. Obviously homosexual, his affectionate (and presumably innocent) fondling of young Vladimir embarrasses both Nabokov and his father. Nabokov mentions casually that when Uncle Ruka dies in 1916, "he left me what would amount nowadays to a couple of million dollars and his country estate, with its white-pillared mansion on a green, escarped hill and its two thousand acres of wildwood and peatbog" (72—the house still stands, and is functioning as a kind of Nabokov museum).

> He [Ruka] prided himself, however, on being an expert in decoding ciphered messages in any of the five languages he knew. We subjected him to a test one day, and in a twinkle he turned the sequence "5.13 24.11 13.16 9.13.5 5.13 24.11" into the opening words of a famous monologue in Shakespeare. (70)

The code, rather obviously, leads to Hamlet's "To be or not to be" speech. (Incidentally, it is telling that a kind of Eugene Onegin-like aristocratic dandy of pre-revolutionary Russia would know five languages.) We do not know the exact date of this little quiz, but it obviously precedes 1916 when Nabokov would have been 16 or 17. Since Vladimir was the oldest of the siblings, the "we" who subjected Ruka to this test probably includes his younger brother, Sergei (who worshipped Ruka and was generally ignored by him). It is worth noting that the young Vladimir Nabokov was composing cryptographic puzzles based on English quotations from Shakespeare at the age of 16, or younger, perhaps much younger.

The citations of Shakespeare in Nabokov's autobiography are not numerous, but those that we find there suggest that when he focuses upon some of his deepest and most dear family memories, Shakespeare is at least a small part of the picture.

## Reviews and notes

Shortly after his move to the United States, Nabokov found himself scrambling for means to support himself and his young family. Among other literary, quasi-literary, and non-literary occupations, he did some book reviewing for publication in periodicals, and some of his reviews and notes focused upon Shakespearean materials.

In a review published in *The New Republic* in May of 1941, Nabokov discusses *Mr. Shakespeare and the Globe* by Frayne Williams.[2] Nabokov's comments are somewhat caustic, but not without a bit of faint praise. He begins:

> "a book written with all the gusto of a modern popular biography" adds the blurb. Now frankly, I do not know what "modern popular" means except that it conveys the image of tremulous persuasion stretching a flattering hand towards that majestic and mythical monster: the "average reader." "Come, give it a try" persuasion seems to plead. "It is not the sort of school stuff you fear. It is snappy, colorful, human." The biographical art of the book will certainly not disappoint the imaginary not-too-bright giant for whom blurbs are fattened and human interest lavishly spread. (1)

Nabokov criticizes Frayne for the circularity of his biographical argument: the poet's environment influences his works, and we can deduce that environment from a careful reading his works. Thus,

> The method by which the author arrives at these happy conclusions is, as I have hinted, very simple: first he suggests that Shakespeare made Volumnia [*the mother of Coriolanus in the play of that name*] out of his [Shakespeare's] mother, then the process is reversed and Mary Arden is described as a Roman matron. No wonder it all fits so well. (1)

After noting this same circularity of argument in Frayne's discussion of Shakespeare's marriage, Nabokov sensibly concludes:

> It is also interesting to learn that "it takes two to make a conversation and the same number to make love"—which fact, together with the second-best

bed ("the most intimate monument of her life") is about all we and the voluble author really know concerning that particular marriage. (2)

Thus, Nabokov concludes that "the biographical chapters in this volume are just what the jacket promised" (2).

On the other hand, Nabokov notes that Frayne is much better when discussing the staging of Shakespeare's plays: "he turns out to be an intelligent critic" (3). In particular, Nabokov praises Frayne's

> account of the mutilation Shakespeare suffered and suffers still at the hands of actors and showmen: the powdered perversions of the eighteenth century and the purple violations of the nineteenth; the accumulation of dead theatrical traditions; and the horrors of our own time: stunt performances, the weird orgies of stage electricians, the step-step-step-and-platform complex, mystical backgrounds, open air foolery, the criminal cutting of the best bits, the re-shuffling of scenes and the platitudes of sociological suggestion. (3)

Although Nabokov did write a few plays, some of which he saw produced, he was primarily a novelist, and in particular a novelist who was especially concerned with his own control over his narrative. Clearly, he is bothered by ways in which a playwright loses that control: actors, directors, technicians kidnap the dramatist's words. They add to the written document, subtract from it, and distort it in countless ways. In some ways, Nabokov is a partisan of the closet drama. He sees Shakespeare as a towering genius and a splendid writer, but one whose works become subject to deformation the moment they are actually performed on stage, by actors. As we shall see, this is a recurrent theme.

The review of Frayne's book concludes with Nabokov's disappointment that its title does not actually suggest "a survey of his [Shakespeare's] influence in other countries" (3). Such a survey

> might afford perhaps more genuine fun and human interest than Shakespeare's filial affection or the hounding of masked W.H. and a disheveled brunette through the trimmed hedges of the Sonnets. (3)

The theme of theatrical staging as inevitably distorting dramas reappears in some unpublished, undated handwritten notes Nabokov made for himself after reading Brander Matthews' *Principles of Playmaking* (1919).[3] It is interesting to read Nabokov's unpolished observations as he reacts to the thoughts of another literary critic, e.g.:

> Advises the "novice" to begin by imitating the successful playwrights of your own times and your own country. (*My* advice would be: begin by avoiding their trivialities ~~their success~~ their ~~particular~~ successful plays.)

About one-third of the two-page note is taken up by a discussion of *Romeo and Juliet*, as follows (remembering that these are private, personal, unpublished jottings):

> We may [have?] enjoyed [*sic*] "Romeo and Juliet" under the unruffled smile of our reading lamp albeit Professor Matthews thinks that the student would enjoy it, oh, so much more if he had seen—or at least [heard?] about Adelaide Neilson[4] who was the first to cause Juliet on the balcony to pluck the flowers from her breast and to throw them down to Romeo. The unruffled reader may console himself by imagining some other actress who offered Romeo half of the fruit she was eating with a spontaneous childish gesture leaning down over the balcony. There is also this important point that even an actor of genius may now and then in his "addition" to the dramatist display a certain [illegible word, possibly "colourful"] vulgarity that is better appreciated by his fans than by the reader. The indefinite and infinite number of such possible gestures and dramatic effects "added" to the play is a very telling contrast with the constant of the immortal written dramas. Histrionic accretions cannot save a bad play from oblivion just as they cannot improve a good one. They change the play remains. (n.p.)

The contrast between the immortality of the written document, and the evanescent, random and arbitrary interpretations of stagecraft is, I believe, an important insight into Nabokov's attitude toward the theater, drama, and Shakespeare and the reception of his own art.

Another review of two books on Shakespeare was never published, but it can be found in the Vladimir Nabokov Papers archive in the Library of Congress. The review is in typescript, presumably from the hand of Vera Nabokov. The books discussed are *Shakespeare and Democracy* by Alvin Thaler and *Shakespeare's Audience* by Alfred Harbage. Both books were published in 1941, so it seems logical to assume the review dates from c. 1941–2.

Nabokov sees Thaler's work as a collection of essays. The first of these, which shares the title of the book as a whole Nabokov finds the "flimsiest." "The use of the word "democracy" "may be thought necessary in the present season [presumably during World War II] to justify the appearance of a scholarly work." Noting that he is one who "enjoys or studies a poet without bothering about his capacity to teach or convey a message," Nabokov distinguishes between those scholars who see Shakespeare as an advocate of modern democracy, and those who see his social and political thinking as belonging strictly to monarchial Tudor England. Thaler asks if Shakespeare was a Whig or a Tory, and compromises by suggesting that he is a conservative, with "good liberal instincts." Such political readings, Nabokov suggests, result in:

the interest of the reader is apt to shift from Shakespeare to the character of this or that commentator applying his own philosophy to more or less misread plays. (2)

The rest of the essays in the book are much more to Nabokov's taste. He likes that Thaler "brilliantly refutes the view held apparently by less keen-witted students, that no conscious art is perceptible in Shakespeare's works." He also enjoys Thaler's discussion of the gaps in the text of *Macbeth*. Nabokov is less taken with a discussion of the "original Malvolio." Such efforts to find the "real" person behind a literary character are "mere gossamers and gossip." Overall, the essays "are clearly and concisely written" and "afford some pleasant rambles along the footnote-bordered paths all around the 'Shakespear Tombe in Stretford.'"

Harbage's study of Shakespeare's audience presents the reader "with some interesting facts concerning the Elizabethan theatre." Nabokov agrees that it is probable that Shakespeare's audience was not characterized by "habitual riotousness" and was "on the whole … brighter than its critics."

But Nabokov is not convinced by Harbage's "inclination to idealise the groundlings." He does think that:

> it might be an invigorating experience for a modern dramatist to turn his back upon the unruffled rows and featureless faces of modern playgoers and suddenly find himself addressing the Globe seething with those unfortunatelt [*sic*] extinct spectators, enthusiastic tinkers, pewterers and fellmongers, bright-eyed button-makers, cropped-haired apprentices, red-faced bookbinders and … creatures such as ditchers, all spending the price of a quart of small beer—one Elizabethan penny or thirty-one Rooseveltan cents—to see Will Shakespeare stalk in as the Ghost. (5)

Harbage is less eager to discuss the merchants, lawyers, and lords in the more expensive seats. Nabokov faults Harbage for his rejection of the theory that Shakespeare wrote for two audiences—the "bulk of the audience" and the "humane minds" of the others. Harbage, he contends, is "all for the million, against the judicious few." Nabokov believes, on the contrary, that:

> By all means have a cake for the general, but cram [?] it with plums for the judicious—this seems to have been—whether Prof. Harbage likes it or not—Shakespeare's method. (7)

Happily, Nabokov does not subscribe to a rigid class breakdown of the audience. He refutes the notion that only those of the aristocratic or learned caste could bring a judicious understanding to the dramas:

the point is that not every grocer and not every lord could appreciate Hamlet at its worth, and naturally Shakespeare (as every honest writer) wrote with more pleasure for the more judicious of the lot.

Still, he is not above a certain consciousness of educational level (and perhaps social class) when it comes to allocating audience judiciousness:

> The question of the comparative percentage of perception among the groundlings and the nobles is hardly important but possibly it is not unreasonable to suppose that most of the students or inns-of-court men in the 2d seats might have been more likely to apprehend what most of the cordwainers in the 1d seats must have missed. (7)

These reviews and notes show Nabokov to have been a careful, scholarly, and opinionated reader of Shakespeare. His grounding in the plays is impressive and impeccable. At the same time, I believe this material reveals a persistent note of distrust of the theater, as opposed to a deep appreciation of the drama. At least at this point in his career as a reader and writer, Nabokov loved and grasped dramatic literature, but he was not much of a fan of putting that literature on the stage. Nabokov believed that authors are to be trusted; however, actors, directors, and audiences are not above suspicion.

# 11

# Concluding Thoughts

The overarching thesis of the preceding pages is that Vladimir Nabokov deeply admired and was profoundly influenced by the works of William Shakespeare. I hope, and have some confidence, that this survey of his novels, and the less extensive look at his stories, non-fiction, criticism, and poetry supports that general thesis conclusively. Huddled under the umbrella of this central premise are several linked conclusions.

Is it *necessary* to know Shakespeare reasonably well to read Nabokov with understanding? I think not. Nabokov cites so many literary sources, cultural traditions, and individuals that probably no reader can be expected to grasp them all. At the same time, it is a bit hard to imagine grasping some of his work without seeing the Shakespearean links: *Pale Fire*, which is no easy novel to comprehend under any circumstances, could be puzzling to one who knew nothing of *Timon of Athens* and even hopelessly confusing in parts to some. On the other hand, it is quite possible to read *Lolita* with enjoyment and understanding and miss entirely the network of allusions to *The Tempest*. What is clear is that the reader who brings Shakespeare to Nabokov will take away more of Nabokov than one who does not.

In contemplating the links between these two masters of the English language, it is almost easy to forget how much separates them. Obviously, they lived three centuries apart. One came from the heart of the English-speaking world, the other grew up surrounded by a Slavic culture. There are some less obvious differences worth pondering as well. Nabokov was a cosmopolitan: he lived in Russia, Germany, France, the United States, and Switzerland. His works were published in numerous countries, and translated into multiple languages. He himself was multi-lingual, writing in three tongues. Shakespeare, as far as we know, never ventured beyond the Stratford/London axis (although there have been unsubstantiated legends of his traveling to continental Europe, for example in Nabokov's poem *Shakespeare*). Although there is a bit of French in *Henry V*, there isn't much evidence Shakespeare knew non-English languages, other than Ben Jonson's "little Latin and less Greek."

The socio-cultural contexts in which the two writers matured were wildly different. Nabokov spent his early years in a wealthy, highly educated, aristocratic world. He had private tutors, nursemaids, a home in the city, and a country place; his father was an important and respected national figure. Then, with the Revolution, Nabokov spent about two decades living a relatively hand-to-mouth existence as an exile—he maintained an unremunerative career as a writer, but also worked as a language tutor and a tennis instructor. He came to the United States with a rather tenuous appointment as a temporary teacher (in an era when college teaching was considered a form of respectable poverty). But, with the international success of *Lolita*, Nabokov moved rapidly back into the world of affluence, spending his final years at the rather grand Montreux Palace hotel on the shore of Lake Geneva. Thus, Nabokov spent most of his life as a member of the upper socioeconomic class, with a hiatus in the middle as the breadwinner of a relatively poor family. Shakespeare, on the other hand, was born into and lived his entire life solidly in the middle class. His family in Stratford were apparently fairly successful merchants; he retired back to Stratford a successful man of affairs from London. He apparently received a grammar school education typical of the sons of the merchant class in a small city in rural Elizabethan England. Probably some of his early years in the theater paralleled Nabokov's decades in European exile, but we have little evidence of Shakespeare as anything other than a comfortably middle-class child, artist, theatrical businessman, and retiree. (Indeed, one of the apparent causes of disbelief that Shakespeare wrote his plays is the seemingly normal, even mundane, collection of facts that constitute his scant biography.) Given these vastly different cultural contexts, one might expect Nabokov to be drawn much more comfortably to, say, Tolstoy, like Nabokov—and unlike Shakespeare—a Russian of noble status.

There is, in my opinion, one more very important major difference between these two linked authors, which needs to be made clear. It is, to some extent, a consequence of the fact that Shakespeare is primarily a dramatist, Nabokov principally a novelist. It is the nature of the theater, and it is particularly the nature of Shakespeare's theater, that the author disappears behind the work. Nobody in Shakespeare's plays speaks for Shakespeare, not even Prospero. He is not Hamlet or Lear or Timon or Puck or Juliet. He is behind all his characters, but those characters each speak for herself or himself. Nabokov (and many other novelists, of course) is the opposite. He injects himself into his fiction. He never lets us forget Nabokov, just as Shakespeare does not ask us to remember that there is a Shakespeare. Nabokov reminds us that his characters *are* characters, that they do what he makes them do. He appears as a character himself in his fiction: at the end of *Bend Sinister* the author looks around his study, stretches, looks out the screen door, and concludes that it would be a good night to hunt moths. In *Pnin*, a group of Russian émigrés discuss whether or not the entomology of Vladimir Vladimirovich is "merely a pose" (127). Shakespeare disappears into his plays; sometimes Nabokov's novels disappear into Nabokov. This seems particularly relevant in Nabokov's final two English novels, *Transparent Things* and *Look at the Harlequins!*, both of which feature characters who are strikingly reminiscent of their creator himself.

And yet, as I hope the preceding pages have made very clear, the literary links between these two authors could not be stronger. In spite of linguistic, chronological, geographical, generic, and socio-economic gulfs between them, Shakespeare exerted a powerful and continuing influence on Nabokov.

Nabokov's admiration and debt to Shakespeare takes many forms. Sometimes his Shakespeareanisms seem casual and almost incidental— almost a kind of literary tic or a shared moment of literary recognition with the alert reader. Perhaps my favorite example of such an informal usage is Quilty's choice of Shakespearean birth and death dates for his license plates in *Lolita*, WS1564 and SH1616, cited earlier. At the other end of the spectrum, are the correspondences to *Timon of Athens* in *Pale Fire*, the extended *Hamlet* discussion, and references in *Bend Sinister*, and the structure and theme of the short story "That in Aleppo Once ..." These links to Shakespeare and his works seem central and essential to the fiction. Nabokov cites specific plays and characters and even Shakespearean locales ("windy heaths, misty castles, enchanted islands, Timonian caves"). He also invokes biographical facts of Shakespeare's life surprisingly often, including several references to their "shared" birthday. Many of these allusions to Shakespeare focus upon his status as a genius, and as the greatest English language writer of all time. Since Nabokov proclaimed "I think like a genius, I write like a distinguished author" (*Strong Opinions* 3) one can't help but wonder if he perceived himself linked to the Bard on the highest plane of English writers.

Nabokov often turns to Shakespeare at key moments in his narratives: we discover Charles Kinbote's unreliability as a narrator when he first refers to himself as Timon; in the autobiography *Speak, Memory*, Shakespeare seems to appear at junctures of particularly deep emotion. Nabokov saw Shakespeare as particularly gifted in the crafting of language which conveyed the most profound of feelings.

The quantitative scan of Nabokov's use of Shakespearean materials leads to a number of clear conclusions. Not surprisingly, the citations of the Bard increase sharply when Nabokov switches from his native Russian to English.[1] Nabokov surely recognized that his English-language readership would be less familiar with allusions to Russian literary traditions, but more at home with Shakespeare.

The plays which are cited most frequently are revealing. *Hamlet* tops the list, followed by *Othello*. Next is *The Tempest*, the drama most often associated with Shakespeare's own biography. Fourth on the list is another tragedy, *King Lear*, then *Timon of Athens*, probably not among the most familiar Shakespeare plays for most readers. The top half-dozen are completed by *A Midsummer Night's Dream*, which along with *Hamlet* features prominently a "play-within-a-play," a device obviously deeply akin to Nabokov's self-referential artifice within his fiction. Nabokov seems most interested in dramas which feature one predominant, flawed but fascinating protagonist and plays which might call some attention to the author who created them.

Indeed, Shakespeare's characters and Nabokov's often point to a kind of broad theme of common humanity. With very few exceptions, neither author created characters who were wholly evil or all virtuous. Iago and Humbert Humbert, for example, are surely both monsters, yet both can be wickedly clever, funny, fascinating to watch. Many of Nabokov's protagonists are deeply flawed—Charles Kinbote and Van Veen, for example. Likewise, Shakespeare's tragic heroes are often heroic in their virtue, but tragic in their failings: Macbeth murders for ambition; Lear foolishly divides his kingdom, and demands unreal and unrealistic love from his daughters; Hamlet rashly kills Polonius, then is responsible, albeit accidentally, for the death of both of Polonius's children. There is a profound humane truth to be learned from many of the most important characters of these two authors: "one touch of nature makes the whole world kin" says Ulysses in *Troilus and Cressida* (3. 3. 174). No good man or woman is ever all good, and no evil person is wholly bad. "The password is pity" says John Shade in *Pale Fire* (160): the deeper our understanding of our fellow humans, the less we can hold them in unreflective contempt. Pity replaces scorn. Great literature can help us see that touch of nature we all share, and teach us to pity even the least among us. Christians are sometimes wont to speak of "broken" humanity: the central characters of both these authors are often broken.

Least interesting to Nabokov, apparently, are Shakespeare's history plays, several of which are never cited by him, and none of which is cited often. This may well be a consequence of Nabokov's oft-pronounced disinterest in fiction which deals with political themes and issues of the "real" world.[2]

The other conclusion I draw from the quantitative profile is that Nabokov's greatest use of Shakespearean materials comes in his greatest works. The three novels with the highest number of citations to Shakespeare are *Ada*, *Pale Fire*, and *Lolita*, which surely are at the forefront of his finest fiction.

\*\*\*

*ghosts*

I am struck by the fact that Nabokov and Shakespeare both believed in—
or at least often wrote about—ghosts. The action of Nabokov's favorite
Shakespearean drama is initiated by the ghost of Old Hamlet, a part which
literary myth says was played by the Bard himself (although that is an
unproven theory). Nabokov was aware of that myth ("that Shakespeare—
Will—who played the Ghost in *Hamlet*" (*Shakespeare*, 11). Another
favorite Nabokov tragic drama, *Macbeth*, features ghosts prominently, as
do two of the less-favored plays, *Julius Caesar* and *Richard III*. As noted
above, Vera Nabokov proclaimed "the otherworld" the prime subject of her
late husband's writing, and ghosts and specters are scattered through his
works. Some of his fiction is narrated by ghosts (e.g., *Transparent Things*,
*The Vane Sisters*). In some, perhaps, ghosts influence the narration (*Pale
Fire*). Given Nabokov's curious insistence that he shared Shakespeare's
birthday, it is a temptation speculate with amusement that perhaps he felt
some sort of otherworldly kinship with Shakespeare. After entertaining
that temptation, though, it is almost certainly wisest to reject it. There is
certainly no evidence that Nabokov ever imagined a ghostly Shakespeare
guiding his pen or looking over his shoulder. The kinship is not spectral,
but literary.

"Oh, my Lolita, I have only words to play with" laments Humbert
Humbert (32). It is "words" and their magnificent and magical manipu-
lation which most link Vladimir Nabokov and William Shakespeare.
Shakespeare is surely the greatest wordsmith of our English language;
to many readers, myself included, Nabokov was the finest English prose
stylist of his era. It is abundantly clear that both authors delighted in their
mastery of language. But beyond stylistic delight lies an important shared
theme, that of art, literary art in particular, as the key to immortality.
"Lolita," both the novel by Nabokov and the character of Dolores Haze,
will "live in the minds of later generations," and that is the "only immortality" (309). In *Pale Fire*, John Shade proclaims "Dead is the mandible,
alive the song" (245). Nabokov is articulating exactly the same theme as
Shakespeare's Sonnet 18:

> But thy eternal summer shall not fade
> Nor lose possession of that fair thou ow'st
> Nor shall Death brag thou wand'rest in his shade,
> When in eternal lines to time thou grow'st.
> So long as men can breathe or eyes can see
> So long lives this, and this gives life to thee. (9–14)

This, surely, is the point: the point of reading, the point of writing. When
we read *Lolita*, from its first word ("Lolita") to its last ("Lolita"), Vladimir

Nabokov, who died in 1977, speaks to us: the song *is* alive, and thus the singer is immortal. And when the author of *Lolita* hears the voice of the writer of *Hamlet*, *Timon of Athens*, *The Tempest*, then that is an immortality we, Nabokov, and Shakespeare can share.

# Appendix

# Nabokov and Shakespeare:
# A Quantitative Approach

I have carefully examined all of Nabokov's fiction originally written in English or in authorized English translations and attempted to annotate every reference to Shakespeare and Shakespeare's works therein. This somewhat tedious exercise provides solid, verifiable evidence to support several decades of partial or impressionistic studies, including mine, about Nabokov's habitual dipping into the wellspring of the Bard. First, however, two quick caveats:

1. The late scholar of American and European modern drama, Ruby Cohn, used to observe "if you have to count it, it probably doesn't count." This sage comment should not be forgotten, although perhaps it can be at least temporarily put aside.
2. The veil of quantitative scientific objectivity may obscure the fact that not all citations are clear. I have surely missed some, and in other cases seen more than was actually in the text—pulled a rabbit out of a hat when, in fact, all that was in it was a hat band. So, while I doubt that these numbers are 100 per cent precise, I am confident that they are substantially—95 per cent—accurate.

To reiterate my central thesis: Nabokov's works and his consciousness are permeated by the art of the greatest writer produced by the English language tradition, and it is not possible to achieve a full and balanced understanding of Nabokov without grasping his debt to the author with which he almost shared his birthday. A careful and complete count of Nabokov's Shakespearean citations offers tangible substantiation of this assertion.

## A.

The works I have studied contain about 250 references to Shakespeare. I do not count multiple identical citations, multiple times—e.g., the several references to Voltemand (sent in *Hamlet* by Claudius as messenger to Norway in Act 1, scene 2) as Van's pseudonym as the author of *Letters from Terra* in *Ada* only count once. The greatest number of references is in *Ada*, which has 55 Shakespeareanisms from a total of 16 plays, and ranges down to a single citation to several works. *Laughter in the Dark* has but a single clear Shakespeare reference, the unfortunate "Othello" comment by Margot cited earlier (in the taxonomy of Nabokov's Shakespeareanisms in Chapter 1); *Mary* and *The Defense* have none. The chart below (Figure 1) shows the number of Shakespearean citations in each of Nabokov's novels.

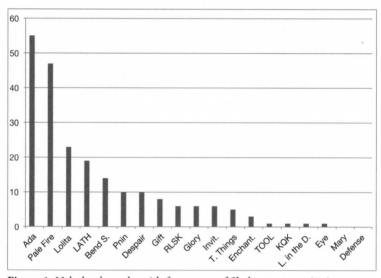

**Figure 1** Nabokov's works with frequency of Shakespearean citations

The first and most obvious and wholly unsurprising conclusion to be drawn from this configuration is that the English-language Nabokov was far more Shakespearean than his Russian-language shadow. This is true even of the works which were translated from Russian to English rather late in Nabokov's career. Thus, of the nineteen novels, the six with the greatest frequency of Shakespeare references were all written in English; the five with the fewest were in Russian. The English-language novels average about twenty references each; the Russian ones, three. Interestingly, in the collected stories there are twenty-two references to Shakespeare, of which five are in the *Othello*-titled "That in Aleppo Once ..."

Did Nabokov become more Shakespearean the more comfortable he grew with Shakespeare's native tongue, or did this development have to do with his growing powers as a mature artist? Below is a chronological listing showing the number of Shakespeare citations of Nabokov's Russian and English novels.

| *Title*, date | Number of citations |
|---|---|
| | **Russian Novels** |
| *Mary*, 1926 | 0 |
| *King, Queen, Knave*, 1928 | 1 |
| *The Defense*, 1930 | 0 |
| *The Eye*, 1930 | 1 |
| *Glory*, 1932 | 6 |
| *Laughter in the Dark*, 1932 | 1 |
| *Despair*, 1934 | 10 |
| *Invitation to a Beheading*, 1936 | 6 |
| *The Gift*, 1938 | 8 |
| *The Enchanter* (proto *Lolita*), 1939 | 3 |
| | **English Novels** |
| *The Real Life of Sebastian Knight*, 1941 | 6 |
| *Bend Sinister*, 1947 | 14 |
| *Lolita*, 1955 | 23 |
| *Pnin*, 1957 | 10 |
| *Pale Fire*, 1962 | 47 |
| *Ada*, 1969 | 55 |
| *Transparent Things*, 1972 | 5 |
| *Look at the Harlequins!*, 1974 | 19 |
| *The Original of Laura* (Posthumous, c. 1975) | 1 |

(Note: dates above are for completion of composition of the works, but the citation figures for the Russian novels refer to the authorized, later, English translations.)

Most Nabokov scholars see *Ada*, *Pale Fire*, and *Lolita* as Nabokov's greatest achievements. Is this a linguistic or a chronological phenomenon, or both? It is intriguing to note that his heaviest use of Shakespearean materials within the Russian novels is in *The Gift* (eight citations), his last, and generally judged to be his best in that category. *The Gift* was completed in 1938, *The Real Life of Sebastian Knight,* his first English-language novel, with two fewer (six) Shakespearean citations, was finished the next year, in 1939. *Bend Sinister*, the next English novel, with nearly double the Shakespeareanisms of any of the Russian novels was published in 1946. After *Ada*, *Transparent Things* and *Look at the Harlequins!* show a somewhat diminished use of

Shakespeare, with, respectively, just five and nineteen citations. I think a case can be made that Nabokov at his best is at his most Shakespearean.

## B.

We can also slice up this Nabokov/Shakespeare pie the other way: having looked at the frequency of citations in terms of Nabokov's works, let's now take a look at the frequency of references in terms of Shakespearean items.

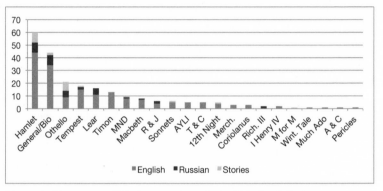

**Figure 2** Frequency of Shakespeare's works in Nabokov's fiction

This analysis produces somewhat less predictable results. Nabokov makes reference to some 20 of Shakespeare's 38 plays—that is, just over half. Additionally there are references to the Sonnets, and a great many general allusions to Shakespeare and his works. A surprise, at least for me, is that there are so many general citations of Shakespeare's life and literary achievements. This seems to suggest that Nabokov was interested in Shakespeare as more than just the author of *Hamlet*, or *A Midsummer Night's Dream*. He was interested in Shakespeare as a person and an artist. Who was Shakespeare? What is the alchemy of literary genius? It is significant that when Nabokov writes a poem about Shakespeare, it is a poem more about Shakespeare the man, less about the plays and poems he produced. "Amid grandees of times Elizabethan / you shimmered too, you followed / sumptuous custom; / the circle of ruff, the silv'ry satin that / encased your thigh, the wedgelike beard ..."

Secondly, a significant finding, is the predominance of *Hamlet* on this list. Of some 250 citations, 67 are to this play. Nabokov translated some passages of *Hamlet* into Russian, and toyed with a complete Russian version; he found Pasternak's translation unacceptable. It is obvious that Nabokov knew his

Shakespeare deeply and widely, but it is equally obvious that the drama of the melancholy Dane was the most fertile for his creative consciousness. Why, I wonder? Certainly there are no particular affinities between the life story of Nabokov and of the melancholy Dane. Like Hamlet's, Nabokov's father was murdered when the author was a young man, but the assassination was political, not familial/incestuous, as V. D. Nabokov was killed trying to protect politician and Kadet leader Pavel Miliukov. Nabokov lived a long and productive life, had a long and productive marriage, and never, so far as the record shows, was obsessed with revenge. Perhaps some explanation for this particular affinity may come from the fact that, of all of Shakespeare's articulate protagonists, Hamlet is the most masterful, and the most self-conscious, in his use of the English language. As noted above, the first three lines the young prince utters are clever puns. His ability to speak originally and memorably has enshrined a large volume of his dialog in the common culture of the English-speaking world. Perhaps it is Hamlet the poet, above all, to whom Nabokov is drawn.

Clearly, Shakespeare's tragedies are at the top of Nabokov's list: five of the six most commonly cited plays fall into this group, and the sixth is *The Tempest*, a comedy with a strong dark streak. Those 5 tragic dramas account for over 160 of the references I have found.

It is worthwhile to note which sorts of Shakespearean works Nabokov does *not* cite very often. The history plays are a striking omission. With  the exception of two works, very far down the list indeed, *I Henry IV* and *Richard II*, the histories are missing. In one sense, this is unexpected. The history plays, especially the best of them, exhibit a kind of mingling of light and darkness which should have been congruent with the tastes of the author of *Lolita*, *Pale Fire*, or *Pnin*. The mixture of pathos, pain, and laughter in Nabokov's best novels (if I may say so without sounding like Polonius and his "tragical–comical–historical–pastoral") seems very akin to the sensitivities of the author of the "Henry IV" plays, or of *Richard III*. My interpretation of this omission is that Nabokov's distaste for the topical, the political, or the relevant colored his reactions to Shakespeare's histories, which certainly do have an obvious relevance to the political realities of Elizabethan/Jacobean England. In *Lectures on Literature*, discussing Jane Austen, Nabokov remarks that "Crawford reads passages from *Henry VIII*, of course one of the poorest of Shakespeare's plays. But in 1808, it would be natural for the average reader to prefer Shakespeare's historical plays to the divine poetry of his fantastically great tragedies like *King Lear* or *Hamlet* (44).

Another noteworthy cluster of omissions on this list are the Roman  tragedies. Two of Shakespeare's tragic dramas Nabokov does not utilize at all, and both are set in classical Rome, *Julius Caesar* and *Titus Andronicus*. Two other Roman tragedies, *Anthony and Cleopatra* and *Coriolanus*, merit only one citation each in Nabokov's works. Here, again, some distaste for the politically relevant might color Nabokov's selection. One might speculate, as well, that there is something closer to the temper or mood of Slavic culture in the stories of medieval Scotland, England, or Denmark than in classical antiquity (although, certainly, *Timon of Athens* is a striking exception to this rule).

Finally, it is worth observing that while Nabokov's works often have romantic love as a central concern, he does not make much use of the Shakespearean works which share that theme. Of the plays and poems which focus upon romantic love, the most frequently cited is *A Midsummer Night's Dream* with seven references (and this is a play which makes much of "lunatics, lovers, and poets," a quintessential Nabokov theme), followed by *Twelfth Night*, the sonnets, *Romeo and Juliet*, and *As You Like It*. By my count, slightly over 14 per cent of Nabokov's Shakespeareanisms make reference to works in which romantic love is a central concern, a figure well below the occurrence of that theme in either author's works in themselves.

***

> The sun's a thief, and with his great attraction
> Robs the vast sea. The moon's an arrant thief,
> And her pale fire she snatches from the sun.
> The sea's a thief, whose liquid surge resolves
> The moon into salt tears / (4. 3. 437–41)

Shakespeare's "Timon of Athens" gave Nabokov the title "Pale Fire" for John Shade's poem, Charles Kinbote's narrative and the novel than includes them both. The meaning of this passage is that stellar objects illuminate and influence each other and our world. Surely some of the brilliant light which shines in Nabokov's magical works comes from the reflection there of the very brightest star in our literary heavens.

# Works Consulted

Alexandrov, Vladimir E. *The Garland Companion to Vladimir Nabokov*. New York: Garland, 1995.

—*Nabokov's Otherworld*. Princeton: Princeton University Press, 1991.

Alladaye, Rene. *The Darker Shades of Pale Fire: An Investigation into a Literary Mystery*. Paris: Michel Houdiard Editeur, 2013.

Alter, Robert. "*Invitation to a Beheading*: Nabokov and the Art of Politics." *Triquarterly* 17 (Winter 1970): 41–59.

Amis, Martin. "The Problem with Nabokov." *The Guardian* (November 14, 2009). http://www.guardian.co.uk/books/2009/nov/14/vladimir-nabokov-books-martin-amis.

—Review of Brian Boyd's *Stalking Nabokov*. *TLS* (December 23, 2011): 3–5.

—Interview in *Book Forum*. 20 August 2012. http://www.bookforum.com/interview/9965 [accessed 11 March 2014].

Appel, Alfred. *The Annotated Lolita*. New York: McGraw Hill, 1970.

—*Nabokov's Dark Cinema*. Oxford: Oxford University Press, 1974.

—"Ada: An Erotic Masterpiece that Explores the Nature of Time." *New York Times* (May 4, 1969). http://www.nytimes.com/books/97/03/02/lifetimes/nab-r-ada-appel.html [accessed 25 February 2014].

Bader, Julia. *Crystal Land: Artifice in Nabokov's English Novels*. Berkeley: University of California Press, 1974.

Barabtarlo, Gennady. "See Under Sebastian." *The Nabokovian* 24 (Spring 1990): 24–9.

—*Aerial View: Essays on Nabokov's Art and Metaphysics*. New York: Peter Lang, 1993.

Blackwell, Stephen. *The Quill and the Scalpel: Nabokov's Art and the World of Science*. Columbus: Ohio State University Press, 2009.

Boyd, Brian. AdaOnline. http://www.ada.auckland.ac.nz. [accessed 11 March 2014].

—*Vladimir Nabokov: The Russian Years*. Princeton: Princeton University Press, 1990.

—*Vladimir Nabokov: The American Years*. Princeton: Princeton University Press, 1991.

—*Nabokov's Pale Fire: The Magic of Artistic Discovery*. Princeton: Princeton University Press, 1999.

—*Nabokov's Ada: The Place of Consciousness*. Cybereditions Corporation: Christchurch NZ, 2009.

—*Stalking Nabokov*. New York: Columbia University Press, 2011.

—Personal e-mail regarding *Look at the Harlequins!* (3 September 2013).

Bozovic, Jarijeta. *From Onegin to Ada: Nabokov's Canon*. Evanston, IL: Northwestern University Press, 2014 scheduled.

Chabon, Michael. Cited in conversation with Giles Harvey, below.

Chamberlain, Leslie. "Nabokov's Early Tragedy." *Times Literary Supplement.* http://www.the-tls.co.uk/tls/public/article1093901.ece [accessed 11 March 2014].

Chiassen, Dan. Cited by Giles Harvey, below, in conversation.

Connolly, Julian, ed. *The Cambridge Companion to Nabokov.* Cambridge: Cambridge University Press, 2005.

Dembo, L. S., ed. *Nabokov: The Man and His Work.* Madison: University of Wisconsin Press, 1967.

Diment, Gayla. *Pniniad.* Seattle: University of Washington Press, 1997.

Field, Andrew. *Nabokov: His Life in Art.* Boston: Little, Brown, 1967.

Fogel, Ephim. "Recollection" in G. Gibian and S. J. Parker, eds. *The Achievements of Vladimir Nabokov.* Ithaca: Cornell University Press, 1984.

Frank, Mike. "Shakespeare's Existential Comedies," in R. C. Tobias and P. G. Zolbrod. *Shakespeare's Last Plays.* Athens, OH: Ohio State University Press, 1974, 142–65.

Gibian, George and Stephen Jan Parker, eds. *The Achievements of Vladimir Nabokov.* Ithaca: Cornell Center for International Studies, 1984. Includes Dmitri Nabokov's "Translating With Nabokov," 174–5.

Goodreads. www.goodreads.com.

Grabes, Herbert. "The Deconstruction of Autobiography: *Look at the Harlequins!*" *Cycnos* 10.1 (1993): 151–8.

Grayson, Jane. *Nabokov Translated: A Comparison of Nabokov's Russian and English Prose.* Oxford: Oxford University Press, 1977.

Harvey, Giles. "'Pale Fire,' The Poem: Does it Stand Alone as a Masterpiece?" *The New Yorker* (2 December 2011), www.NewYorker.com/online/blogs/culture/2011/12/pale-fire-the-poem.html [accessed 11 March 2014].

*The Holy Bible: Revised Standard Version.* New York: Thomas Nelson & Sons, 1952.

Hyde, G. M. *Vladimir Nabokov.* London: Marion Boyars, 1977.

Johnson, D. Barton. "The Ambidextrous Universe of Nabokov's *Look at the Harlequins!*" in Phyllis A. Roth, ed. *Critical Essays on Vladimir Nabokov.* Boston: G. K. Hall, 1984, 202–5.

—*Worlds in Regression: Some Novels of Vladimir Nabokov.* Ann Arbor, MI: Ardis, 1985.

—"The Labyrinth of Incest in Nabokov's *Ada.*" *Comparative Literature* 38.3 (Summer 1986): 224–55.

Johnson, Kurt and Steve Coates. *Nabokov's Blues: The Scientific Odyssey of a Literary Genius.* Cambridge, MA: Zoland Books, 1999.

Kakutani, Michiko. "Master's Blueprint, Born of Revolution." *New York Times* (March 24, 2013). http://wwwl.nytimes.com/2013/03/25/books [accessed 11 March 2014].

Kermode, Frank. "Introduction" to *The Arden Shakespeare* edition of *The Tempest.* Cambridge: Harvard University Press, 1954.

—Review of *Bend Sinister* in *Encounter* (June 1974), 81–6.

—Introduction to *Timon of Athens* in *The Riverside Shakespeare*. New York: Houghton Mifflin Co., 1981.

Kernan, Alvin. *The Imaginary Library: An Essay on Literature and Society*. Princeton: Princeton University Press, 1982.

Kuzmanovich, Zoran, ed. *Nabokov Studies*. Davidson, NC: Davidson College.

Leving, Yuri, ed. *Nabokov Online Journal*. Halifax, NS: Dalhousie University.

Lowell, James Russell. "Shakespeare Once More" in *Among My Books*. Boston: Houghton Mifflin, 1870.

Maar, Michael. *Speak, Nabokov*. Berlin: Verso, 2009.

Macdonald, Dwight. "Virtuosity Rewarded or Dr. Kinbote's Revenge." *Partisan Review* (Summer 1962): 437–42.

Manolescu-Oancea, Monica. "Humbert's Arctic Adventures: Some Intertextual Explorations." *Nabokov Studies* 11 (2007–2008): 1–23.

Mason, Bobbie Ann. *Nabokov's Garden: A Guide to Ada*. Ann Arbor, MI: Ardis, 1974.

McCarthy, Mary. "A Bolt from the Blue," *The New Republic* 146 (June 1962): 21–7.

Mello, Jansy. Post on Nabokov Listserv regarding *Look at the Harlequins!* (September 4, 2013).

Meyer, Priscilla. "Black and Violet Words: *Despair* and *The Real Life of Sebastian Knight* as Doubles." *Nabokov Studies* 4 (1997): 37–60.

—"Nabokov's Short Fiction." *The Cambridge Companion to Nabokov*. Julian Connolly, ed. Cambridge: Cambridge University Press, 2005, 119–34.

Mitchell, David. Interview in *The Paris Review*. "The Art of Fiction no. 204" (Summer 2010): 193. www.Theparisreview.org/interview/6034/theartoffiction-no-204-david-mitchell [accessed 11 March 2014].

Nabokov, Vera Slonim. "Introduction" to *Stikhi*. Ann Arbor, MI: Ardis, 1979.

Nabokov, Vladimir. "Translations from Shakespeare." *Rul* (October 19 and November 23, 1930); *Les Mois* 6 (June/July 1931): 143.

—Pouchkine ou le vrai et la vraisemble. *La Nouvelle Revue Francais* (March 1937): 362–78.

—"Mr. Williams' Shakespeare." *The New Republic* (May 19, 1941) http://www. newrepublic.com/article/books-and-arts/mr-williams-shakespeare [accessed February 24, 2014].

—"The Art of Translation." *New Republic* (August 4, 1941): 160–2.

—*The Real Life of Sebastian Knight*. Norfolk, CT: New Directions, 1941.

—*Nikolai Gogol*. New York: New Directions, 1944.

—*Bend Sinister*. New York: McGraw Hill, 1947. Reprinted with an Introduction by the author. New York: Time Magazine, 1981.

—*Invitation to a Beheading*. Tr. Dmitri Nabokov with Vladimir Nabokov. New York: G. P. Putnam, 1959.

—*The Gift*. New York: G. P. Putnam's Sons, 1963.

—*Eugene Onegin: A Novel in Verse. By Aleksandr Pushkin*. New York: Bolligen Foundation, 1964.

—"On Translating Pushkin Pounding the Clavicord." *New York Review of Books* (April 30, 1964): www.nybooks.com/articles/archives/1964/apr30/on-translating-Pushkin-pounding-the-clavicord/?pagination=false [accessed 11 March 2014].

—*Despair*. New York: Vintage International, 1966.

—Interview with Penelope Gilliatt. "Nabokov." *Vogue* (December 1966), 224–9, 279–81.

—*The Waltz Invention*. Translated by Dmitri and Vladimir Nabokov. New York: Phaedra Press, 1966.

—*Ada*. New York: McGraw Hill, 1969.

—*Glory*. Tr. Dmitri Nabokov with Vladimir Nabokov. New York: McGraw Hill, 1971.

—*Transparent Things*. New York: McGraw Hill, 1972.

—*Strong Opinions*. New York: McGraw-Hill, 1973.

—*Look at the Harlequins!* New York. Vintage Books, 1974.

—*Stikhi* (Ann Arbor, MI: Ardis, 1979). Includes a foreword by Vera Slonim Nabokov, which also appears in Gibian and Parker.

—*Lectures on Literature*. Fredson Bowers, ed. New York: Harcourt Brace Jovanovich, 1980.

—*Lectures on Russian Literature*. Fredson Bowers, ed. New York: Harcourt Brace Jovanovich, 1981.

—*Lectures on Don Quixote*. Fredson Bowers, ed. New York: Harcourt Brace Jovanovich, 1983.

—*The Enchanter*. New York: G. P. Putnam's Sons, 1986. Tr. by Dmitri Nabokov as "Pushkin or the True and the Probable," *New York Review of Book* (March 31, 1988).

—*Laughter in the Dark*. New York: Vintage International, 1989.

—*Pale Fire*. New York: G. P. Putnam's Sons, 1962, Vintage International Edition, New York: 1989.

—*Selected Letters*. Dmitri Nabokov and Matthew J. Bruccoli, eds. New York: Harcourt Brace Jovanovich/Bruccoli Clark Layman, 1989.

—*Speak, Memory: An Autobiography Revisited*. New York: Vintage International, 1989.

—"The Wood Sprite." Translated by Dmitri Nabokov. *The Stories of Vladimir Nabokov*. New York: Alfred A. Knopf, 1995.

—*Lolita*. New York: G. P. Putnam's Sons, 1958. Vintage International Edition, New York: 1997.

—*Pale Fire: A Poem in Four Cantos*. Edited with commentary, Brian Boyd and R. S. Gwynn. Berkeley: Ginko Press, 2011.

—*Selected Poems*. Thomas Karshan, ed. New York: Alfred A. Knopf, 2012.

—"Shakespeare." Translated by Dmitri Nabokov. *Vladimir Nabokov: Selected Poems*. Ed. Thomas Karshan. New York: Alfred A. Knopf, 2012.

—*The Tragedy of Mr. Morn*. Translated by Thomas Karshan and Anastasia Tolstoy. New York: Alfred A. Knopf, 2012.

—Draft. Review of Alvin Thaler, *Shakespeare and Democracy* and Alfred Harbage, *Shakespeare's Audience*. Vladimir Nabokov Papers, Box 10, Reel 8, The Library of Congress. http://lcweb2.loc.gov/service/mss/eadxmimss/eadpdfmss [accessed 11 March 2014].

—Notes on Brander Matthews, *Principles of Playmaking*. Nabokov archive, Montreux, Switzerland.

*Nabokv-L*. https://listserv.ucsb.edu/lsv-cgi-bin/wa?A0=NABOKV-L [accessed February 24, 2014].

Page, Norman. *Nabokov: The Critical Heritage*. London: Routledge & Kegan Paul, 1982.

Parker, Stephen Jan, ed. *The Nabokovian*. Lawrence, KS: The University of Kansas.

—*Understanding Nabokov*. Columbia: The University of South Carolina Press, 1987.

Peterson, Dale. "Knight's Move: Nabokov, Shklovsky and the Afterlife of Sirin." *Nabokov Studies* 11 (2007–8): 25–37.

Phillips, Arthur. Interview by Giles Harvey. *The New Yorker* (2 December 2011). www.newyorker.com/online/blogs/culture/2011/12/pale-fire-the-poem.html [accessed 11 March 2014].

—*The Tragedy of Arthur*. New York: Random House, 2011.

Pifer, Ellen. *Nabokov and the Novel*. Cambridge, MA: Harvard University Press, 1980.

Pitzer, Andrea. *The Secret History of Vladimir Nabokov*. New York: Pegasus Books, 2013.

Pyles, Thomas. "Ophelia's Nothing." *Modern Language Notes* 64.5 (1949): 322–3.

Quennell, Peter, ed. *Vladimir Nabokov: A Tribute*. London: Weidenfeld & Nicolson, 1979.

Rampton, David. *Vladimir Nabokov: A Critical Study of the Novels*. Cambridge: Cambridge University Press, 1974.

Richter, Anne. *Shakespeare and the Idea of the Play*. New York: Penguin, 1962.

Rivers, J. E. and Charles Nicol, eds. *Nabokov's Fifth Arc*. Austin: University of Texas Press, 1982.

Ronen, Omry. "Historical Modernism, Artistic Innovation, and Myth-Making in Vladimir Nabokov's System of Value Judgments." *Philologica* 7 (2001–2). http://www.rub.ru/philologica/07eng/07eng_ronen.htm [accessed 11 March 2014].

Roth, Phyllis, ed. *Critical Essays on Vladimir Nabokov*. Boston: G. K. Hall, 1984.

Rothman, Nathan L. Untitled review of *Bend Sinister*. *Saturday Review* (August 2, 1947).

Rowe, Eleanor. *Hamlet: A Window on Russia*. New York: New York University Press, 1976.

Rowe, W. W. *Nabokov's Deceptive World*. New York: New York University Press, 1971.

—*Nabokov's Spectal Dimension*. Ann Arbor, MI: Ardis, 1981.

Schiff, Stacy. *Vera (Mrs. Vladimir Nabokov)*. New York: Random House, 1999.

Schoenbaum, Samuel. *Shakespeare's Lives*. New York: Oxford University Press, 1970.

Schuman, Samuel. "'Despair and Die,' A note on Nabokov and Shakespeare's Tragedies." *Notes on Contemporary Literature* 121 (January, 1982): 11–12.

—"Nabokov and Shakespeare: The Russian Works." *The Garland Companion to Vladimir Nabokov*. Vladimir E. Alexandrov, ed. New York: Garland, 1995.

—"*Comment Dit-on 'Mourir' En Anglais?*": Translating Shakespeare in Nabokov's *Pale Fire*. In Ton Hoenselaars and Marius Buning, eds. *English Literature and the Other Languages*. Amsterdam: Rodopi, 1999.

—"Sprites." *ANQ* 14.1 (Winter 2001): 44–6.

—"Nabokov's God; God's Nabokov" (forthcoming).

Seidel, Michael. "Nabokov on Joyce, Shakespeare, Telemachus, and Hamlet." *James Joyce Quarterly* 20.3 (Spring 1983): 358–9.

Shakespeare, William. *The Complete Signet Classic Shakespeare*. General Editor Sylvan Barnet. New York: Harcourt Brace Jovanovich, 1972.

Sharpe, Tony. *Vladimir Nabokov*. Edward Arnold: London, 1991.

Shklovsky, Viktor. *The Knight's Move*. Translated by Richard Sheldon. Urbana-Champaign, IL: The Dalkey Archive Press, 1995 (orig. pub. 1923).

Stoppard, Tom. *Rosencrantz and Guildenstern Are Dead*. London: Faber & Faber, 1967.

Sweeney, Susan Elizabeth. "Playing Nabokov: Performances by Himself and Others." *Studies in Twentieth Century Literature* 22.2 (1977): 295–318.

Tammi, Pekka. *Problems of Nabokov's Poetics: A Narratological Analysis*. Helsinki: Academia Scientiarum Fennica, 1985.

Taylor, Benjamin. www.russianartandculture.com "The Tragedy of Mister Morn: Nabokov's first major work finally translated." *Russian Art and Culture* (August 28, 2012).

Toker, Leona. *Nabokov: The Mystery of Literary Structures*. Ithaca: Cornell University Press, 1989.

Updike, John. "Van Loves Ada, Ada Loves Van". *The New Yorker* (August 2, 1969): 67–75.

Van Doren, Mark. *Shakespeare*. New York: Holt, Rinehart, & Winston, 1939.

Vonnegut, Kurt, Jr. "Harrison Bergeron." First published in *The Magazine of Fantasy and Science Fiction* (1961); reprinted in *Welcome to the Monkey House*. New York: Dell, 1970: 7–13.

Wood, Michael. *The Magician's Doubts: Nabokov and the Risks of Fiction*. Princeton: Princeton University Press, 1995.

*Zembla*. http://www.libraries.psu.edu/nabokov/ [accessed February 24, 2014].

Zimmer, Dieter. *Nabokov's Berlin*. Berlin: Nicolai, 2001.

# Notes

## Foreword

1 *Strong Opinions*, 63.
2 Unpublished note from Russian survey lecture course, Vladimir Nabokov Archives, Henry W. and Albert A. Berg Collection, New York Public Library, cited in Boyd, *Vladimir Nabokov: The American Years*, 100.
3 See the end of Kinbote's note to line 71, and if the answer is still not clear, Boyd, *Nabokov's Pale Fire*, 176–9.
4 Cited in Boyd, *American Years*, 88.
5 Ibid., 316–17.
6 *Speak, Memory*, 221.
7 *Strong Opinions*, 89–90.
8 *Nikolay Gogol*, 54.
9 "Nabokov," *Vogue* (December 1966), p. 280.
10 *New Republic*, August 4, 1941.
11 Bozovic, *From* Onegin *to* Ada: *Nabokov's Canon*.
12 *Pnin*, 77.
13 *Pnin*, 78–9.
14 "Pouchkine ou le vrai et la vraisemblable," translated by Dmitri Nabokov as "Pushkin or the True and the Probable."
15 *Invitation to a Beheading*, 7.
16 *Strong Opinions*, 60. The citation of Shklovsky is from personal correspondence with Dr. Yuri Leving.

## Introduction

1 Brian Boyd on Nabokov Listserv, July 6, 2012. Online at https://listserv.ucsb.edu/lsv-cgi-bin/wa?A2=ind1207&L=nabokv-l&F=&S=&P=10391 [accessed February 24, 2014].

## Chapter 1

1 It is in the far southwest of the State, just outside today's Lordsburg, a few miles off I-10 which runs from Tucson to El Paso.
2 This material is nicely summarized in Chapters 2–4 of Pitzer's *The Secret History of Vladimir Nabokov*.

3  In the *English Review* of 1920. Boyd, *Vladimir Nabokov: The Russian Years*, 171.
4  For example, Sonnets XV, XIX, XXXII, XXXVIII, LIV, LV (So, till the judgment that yourself arise / You live in this, and dwell in lovers' eyes), LX, LXIII, LXV, LXXVI, LXXXI, C, CI, CVII, CXVI.

# Chapter 2

1  Some translate "Gospodina" as the abbreviated "Mr.," others as the complete "Mister."
2  Cervantes was in Italy from 1569 to 1575.
3  Pierre de Bourdeille, seigneur and abbé de Brantome (c. 1540–1614) wrote memoirs of the many renowned people he had met during his life.
4  I have a typed copy of an earlier, unpublished, translation by Dmitri Nabokov. It differs only in relatively small details. The poem is also to be found in Thomas Karshan's edition of Nabokov's *Selected Poems* (11–12).
5  As noted in the Introduction, in a curious Nabokovian coincidence, I actually worked for both Samuel Schoenbaum and Alfred Appel, Jr, the former as an editorial assistant, the latter as a graduate TA, when I was a Ph.D. student at Northwestern.
6  Nabokov very briefly cites Shakespeare in another poem, "The University Poem," written in Russian in 1926 and translated by Dmitri Nabokov. The work is a Pushkin-like narrative in verse of 63 stanzas, recounting the author's days at Cambridge, and his romance with a woman named "Violet," a name with some Shakespearean associations, as we have seen. In Stanza 19, Nabokov writes: "Violet turned up next to me / (the students were performing *Hamlet* / and heaven was out of joint for / the bard's illustrious shade)" (*Selected Poems*, 35).
7  I was able to review this material in the Swiss archives in 1990, thanks to funding from the NEH. I was, and am, grateful to the late Dmitri and Vera Nabokov for their cordiality and assistance during that visit.

# Chapter 3

1  Later (p. 210) discussing the characters in "The Waltz Invention" Field notes that "As in *The Real Life of Sebastian Knight* Viola Trance's name refers to Shakespeare's 'Twelfth Night.' She is described "a smart woman of 30 in black masculine dress Shakespearean-masquerade style." See Schuman, *Nabokov and Shakespeare*, 516.
2  It is just this sort of staging ambiguity that leaves Nabokov uncomfortable with actual productions of dramatic works.

3  I am grateful for the assistance of Professors Priscilla Meyer and D. Barton Johnson for, in the first case, pointing out this commentary in the Russian edition, and in the second for translating and summarizing it. There are a multitude of Violas in Nabokov's other works as well, some of which are clearly Shakespearean. As early as 1923, a year before his poem "Shakespeare," Nabokov's collection of early poems entitled "Grozd'" included a Russian poem with an English title, "Viola Tricolor." In "The University Poem," the narrator and Violet attend a performance of *Hamlet*. (See Yuri Leving's comments, p. 567, of the Symposium edition of Nabokov's *Works*, Vol. 2, St. Petersburg, 1999).

4  I am grateful to Dr. Yuri Leving for pointing out this connection to me. See also Peterson, "Knight's Move: Nabokov, Shklovsky and the Afterlife of Sirin."

# Chapter 4

1  *Time Magazine* has always been attentive to Nabokov. It reviewed *Bend Sinister* on June 16, 1947, one of only four American publications to offer a timely review. Perhaps the magazine has been attentive to the author's *Time*-like inventive and agile prose style and his (mid-twentieth-century) political conservativism?

2  This philosophy is remarkably similar to that depicted by Kurt Vonnegut Jr in his short story "Harrison Bergeron."

3  The recent novel *The Tragedy of Arthur* by Arthur Phillips, an enthusiastic reader of Nabokov (New York: Random House, 2011), imagines just such a forgery.

4  The satiric reference to the "Nordic" Fortinbras and the "Judeo-Latin Claudius" reminds us of Nabokov's life-long staunch stance opposing anti-Semitism.

5  In *Speak, Memory* the "to be or not to be" speech is "translated" into a simple numeric code, broken by the young Nabokov and his brother Sergei.

# Chapter 5

1  For some, *Lolita* is about America, even more than art or love.

2  Appel's note on the "Hotel Mirana" suggests several other word games: "a heat-shimmer blend of 'mirage,' '*se mirer*' (French: to look at oneself; admire oneself), 'Mirabella,' and 'Fata Morgana' (a kind of mirage most frequently seen in the strait of Messina …)." He does not suggest any possible connection to "Miranda" (336).

3  *The Enchanter*, as translated by Dmitri Nabokov, has only one reference to
   *The Tempest* as well as one to *King Lear* and another general biographical
   Shakespearean citation.

# Chapter 6

1  In *The Secret History of Vladimir Nabokov* Andrea Pitzer stresses the tragic
   connections between Pnin's life and the global political upheavals of the
   twentieth century.

# Chapter 7

1  It is interesting to speculate that the importance of the motifs of "shadow,"
   "cave," "shade," and "pale fire" in the novel might well remind the reader of
   Plato and the Allegory of the Cave. Plato, of course, suggests in his allegory
   that humans can be like prisoners in a cave, bound in such a way that they
   can see only the shadows on the wall in front of them. Those shadows or
   shades they come to mistake for reality. I am grateful to Daniel Schuman for
   pointing out this line of inquiry.
2  Note that in his Foreword Brian Boyd notes another, albeit less exact,
   potential Shakespearean reference from *Hamlet* 1. 5. (88–91) when the
   Ghost takes his leave of Hamlet:

> Fare thee well at once.
> The glowworm shows the matin to be near
> And 'gins to pale his uneffectual fire.
> Adieu, adieu, adieu. Remember me. *Exit.*

3  Some critics, such as Boyd, had noted the theme of the otherworld prior to
   Mrs. Nabokov's assertion, but few had seen it as a major theme in Nabokov's
   oeuvre.
4  In the Vintage edition of *Pale Fire* Kinbote's index citation of the
   conversation (312) with John Shade about education and Shakespeare is
   incorrectly listed as taking place on p. 172, but it is actually on p. 155.

# Chapter 8

1  *Pale Fire*, with 47 Shakespeareanisms in 301 pages, contains an allusion
   about every 6.5 pages; *Lolita*, with 23 Shakespeareanisms contains an
   allusion about every 14 pages. These are, of course, rough measures—for
   example, I count the 16 pages of Chapter 7 of *Bend Sinister* devoted to

*Hamlet* as one reference, although it covers several pages: it is surely of greater weight than, say, the allusion to "Gamlet, a hamlet" in *Ada*!

2   This is one of my personal very favorites of Nabokov's Shakespearean allusions. The parody of King Lear's lament at the end of Act 5 (5. 3. 309–10) is surely a high point of bilingual literary word play. Lear, of course, says "Thou'lt come no more, / Never, never, never, never, never." Ada first says that the garden will flower in winter "never" five times in French, then in a Franco-Anglo pun on "never" affirms another five times that it is "not green"—"n'est vert." Nabokov returns to this line multiple times in his works.

3   Hal's "I do, I will" is, for many including myself, the single most powerful line in all Shakespeare's history plays.

4   In an interestingly Shakespearean twist on "Demonia", at one point, describing the Italianate style of an apartment, Ada sees it "as a frame, as a form, something supporting and guarding life, otherwise unprovidenced on Desdemonia, where artists are the only gods" (521).

5   See the full discussion in Johnson, "The Labyrinth of Incest in Nabokov's *Ada*."

6   A contrary argument has been derived from Gertrude's comment a few lines later, "He's fat, and scant of breath. Here, Hamlet, take my napkin, rub thy brows" [289–290] and from Hamlet's soliloquy in Act 1 where he wishes that "this too too solid flesh would melt, / Thaw and resolve itself into a dew" (1. 2. 129–30). Most modern editors accept the reading "sullied" instead of "solid" and many interpret Gertrude's remarks to mean that Hamlet sweats.

7   Perhaps prefigured, Boyd notes, by Greg's observation that "Ruth and Grace were laid up with acute indigestion" (90).

# Chapter 9

1   *The Original of Laura* is extremely unfinished. Nabokov had requested that it be destroyed after his death, but after decades of indecision, Dmitri, his late son and literary executor, decided to bring the incomplete manuscript into the light of public scrutiny. Some commentators and critics praised this decision, for making public a significant document from an important writer. Others lambasted it for going against the author's wishes, and making public a work which was clearly in a relatively early stage of development. Generally critical reaction to what does exist of *The Original of Laura* has not found it to be of a quality equal to that of Nabokov's finished works.

2   Although I have not done a careful statistical check, it seems quite clear that references to other authors diminish in about the same proportion as citations of Shakespeare.

3   From a personal e-mail from Boyd of September 3, 2013. "Lines Written in Oregon" begins "Esmeralda! Now we rest / Here, in the bewitched and blest

/ Mountain forests of the West" and ends with the rather haunting triad "Where the woods get ever dimmer, / Where the Phantom Orchids glimmer —/ Esmeralda, *immer, immer* [always, always].

4  Cited by Jansy Mello on the Nabokov Listserv September 4, 2013. The Ronen citation is from "Historical Modernism, Artistic Innovation, and Myth-Making in Vladimir Nabokov's System of Value Judgments." *Philologica* 7 (2001–2) http://www.rub.ru/philologica/07eng/07eng_ronen. htm [accessed 11 March 2014].

## Chapter 10

1  Freud, as it happens, was an avid anti-Stratfordian.
2  I am using the typescript draft of this review, available in the Library of Congress Vladimir Nabokov Papers.
3  These notes appear in a spiral-bound notebook I perused in the Nabokov archives before they had been removed from the Montreux Palace Hotel in Switzerland.
4  An actress who lived from 1848–80, most famous for her portrayal of Juliet.

## Chapter 11

1  A useful study, for which my Russian language skills are inadequate, would be to compare the volume and nature of citations of Shakespeare in Nabokov's original Russian versions of his early novels, to those allusions in works he subsequently translated into English.
2  See Pitzer for a contrary view of the political content of Nabokov's works.

# Index